PLAYS BY
DENNIS J REARDON

BROADWAY PLAY PUBLISHING INC
56 E 81st St., NY NY 10028-0202
212 772-8334 fax: 212 772-8358
http://www.BroadwayPlayPubl.com

PLAYS BY DENNIS J REARDON
© Copyright 2001 by Dennis J Reardon

All rights reserved. This work is fully protected under the copyright laws of the United States of America.
No part of this publication may be photocopied, reproduced, stored in a retrieval system, or transmitted, in any form or by any means, electronic, mechanical, recording, or otherwise, without the prior permission of the publisher. Additional copies of this play are available from the publisher.

Written permission is required for live performance of any sort. This includes readings, cuttings, scenes, and excerpts. For amateur and stock performances, please contact Broadway Play Publishing Inc. For all other rights also please contact B P P I.

First printing: October 2001
I S B N: 0-88145-199-1

Special thanks: Angeline Larimer

Assistant to the Publisher: Michele Travis

Book design: Marie Donovan
Word processing: Microsoft Word for Windows
Typographic controls: Xerox Ventura Publisher 2.0 P E
Typeface: Palatino
Copy editing: Sue Gilad
Printed on recycled acid-free paper and bound in the U S A

CONTENTS

About the Author v
STEEPLE JACK 1
THE PEER PANEL 73
THE MISADVENTURES OF CYNTHIA M. 131

ABOUT THE AUTHOR

Dennis J Reardon was born in Massachusetts and grew up in California, Iowa, Louisiana, and Kansas. Ten days after getting out of the Army on New Year's Eve, 1969, Reardon moved to New York to begin rehearsals for his first play, THE HAPPINESS CAGE, produced by Joseph Papp's Public Theater.

Mr Papp subsequently produced Reardon's SIAMESE CONNECTIONS and—on Broadway at the Booth Theater—THE LEAF PEOPLE, the saga of an Amazonian Indian tribe. After living in various upstate New York locales during much of the 70s and 80s, Reardon settled in southern Indiana on the edge of the Hoosier National Forest.

Reardon's plays have received numerous honors throughout his career, most recently garnering national play awards from the Weissberger Foundation, the National Repertory Theater Foundation, and Theater Memphis for STEEPLE JACK and THE PEER PANEL. He is a recipient of a two-year National Endowment for the Arts Playwriting Fellowship and has served as playwright-in-residence at Hartwick College and the University of Michigan. Since 1987 he has headed the Playwriting Program at Indiana University.

For my parents

STEEPLE JACK

STEEPLE JACK premiered at the Bloomington Playwrights Project (Bloomington, IN) on 22 April 1988. The cast and creative contributors were:

JILL CADY	Isa-Jill Gordon
JAY CADY	John Frisco
GEORGE ANTIOCH	Christopher Reintz
MONICA WASHBURN	Maureen Ryan
GUS WASHBURN	Mark Simon
STEEPLE JACK	Ron Dye
Director	Doug Long
Set design	Jerry H Berebitsky
Costume design	Cathryn Bradshaw
Lighting design	Eric Arnold

Awards: 1985 **National Play Award** from the National Repertory Theater Foundation, final judges: John Houseman, Beatrice Straight, Dale Wasserman, Richard L Coe, Robert Ellis Miller, and Richard Wilson 1985 **Weissberger Foundation Award**, final judges: Mel Gussow, *New York Times*; Douglas Watt, *New York Daily News*; and Jack Kroll, *Time*

CHARACTERS & SETTING

JILL CADY, *just turning fifteen; thin*
JAY CADY, *her father; a contractor and a recent widower*
GEORGE ANTIOCH, *a nineteen year-old busboy*
MONICA WASHBURN, *mid-forties; a displaced easterner*
GUS WASHBURN, *her husband; a publisher and the acting jailer*
"STEEPLE JACK," *also known as* JOHN, *an unknown person; old but spry*

Four offstage C B voices; an Announcer's voice; Sheriff's voice

Bowie, Kansas (pronounced Boo-wee), the county seat of Clanford County in the southeastern part of the state.

Time: the present, mid-October

Sets: bulky representational sets should be avoided; props convey place. JAY's *living room features a large recliner, two smaller chairs, and a deer's head mounted stage right between the D R entryway and a door U R leading to* JAY's *bedroom. Another door far left with perhaps the suggestion of a kitchen behind it. D L and raised is* JILL's *area—a nook with an "invisible" door behind which is her bed. When she looks out her "window" she is facing front.*

This basic space must be fluid enough to permit the suggestion of a Sheriff's Office—one cage and a small desk separated by a sliding partition. Near the desk is a wallmap of Bowie and Clanford County. At one point in ACT TWO the set should suggest the Washburns' living room—three chairs, perhaps a small table. Finally, several scenes require a mock-up of the cab in a pick-up truck, and a couple moments call for a portion of a church steeple—probably best located far UR above the door to JAY's *bedroom.*

A note on lines enclosed by asterisks. *These "mufflers" are a typographical shorthand used to denote asides, parenthetical thoughts, stage whispers, remarks intended for one character but not for another—in brief, anything characterized by a sudden drop in volume.*

It could not be dangerous to be living
    in a town like this, of simple people,
who have a steeple-jack placing danger signs by the church
while he is gilding the solid-
    pointed star, which on a steeple
stands for hope.

Marianne Moore, *The Steeple-Jack*

from *The Complete Poems of Marianne Moore*, MacMillan Co/The Viking Press; NY, 1967

In memory of Jack Longhurst,
a wise and funny man.
Thanks for noticing, Jack.

ACT ONE
How They Came to the Party

Prologue

(Time and space in the Prologue is controlled by JILL. *Only she employs direct address. Initially, when the lights come up on* JILL *and* MONICA, *the two seem to be relaxing on a warm day—*MONICA *lounging in a lawn chair; drinking, snoozing.* JILL *is seated on a railing, swinging her legs and speculating aloud.)*

JILL: Have you ever noticed how when you say "History" real slow it comes out "His Story"? And when you say "My Story" real *fast*, it comes out "Mystery"? *(Pause; no response)* Makes you wonder, don't it?

MONICA: *(Reflexively)* Doesn't it.

(Pause)

JILL: You ever notice how hard it is sometimes to be "chipper"? *(Pause)* Huh, Monica?

MONICA: I can hardly summon up "chip."

JILL: I wonder who is "chippest"? Mirror mirror, on the wall, who's the chippest of them all? *(Pause)* No doubt some chippie somewhere. *(Pause)* Or a Chippewa squaw. *(Pause)* With a chip on her shoulder.

MONICA: Stop it, my God, will ya?

*(*JILL *looks over questioningly.)*

MONICA: You're turning into a word spastic!

JILL: Just trying to make a little light conversation.

MONICA: You wanna talk? Let's talk food.

JILL: Too heavy.

MONICA: You've turned into an anorexic little twit!

JILL: At least I'm not an alcoholic like everyone else around here.

MONICA: "Vampyra!" You like kids calling you "Vampyra"?

JILL: Stop!

(Lights out on MONICA. JILL *walks C S, composing herself. Her father* JAY CADY *pushes a La-Z-Boy recliner into position. Far U R* GEORGE ANTIOCH *begins slowly hitching his way across stage, carrying a sign that reads "Joplin.")*

JILL: That was not my mother. My mother was not a rude and vulgar person, whereas Monica prides herself upon those traits. My real mother was killed in a car wreck about eight months ago. *(Pause)* That's not what my story's about. I will never mention the subject again. *(Reconsiders)* Perhaps once more, just in passing.

(Lights up mid-stage on GUS *and* MONICA. *They are drinking and apparently hosting a party.* JAY *may or may not be present at it; he conveys an air of solitude as he broods in his big recliner. Sound: party noises)*

JILL: First, here are some common myths about Kansas, where this all happens. Kansas is too

JAY: Flat.

JILL: Too

GEORGE: Boring.

JILL: Too

GUS: Pious.

MONICA: And nothing good ever came from there.

JILL: *(Pauses judiciously)* These are serious charges.

MONICA: *(Regaling her guests)* Louise Brooks wrote that every state in the Union looks upon Kansas with disdain—except Nebraska!

JILL: Louise was a ravishingly beautiful star of the silent screen. She played a girl named Lulu in some German movie. But she was from Kansas. Cherryvale. So right there you see something good come out of the state.

JAY: General Dwight David Eisenhower. Abilene.

JILL: Several Miss Americas.

JAY: Great milers. Glen Cunningham, Jim Ryun—

JILL: A Wichita boy—

MONICA: And who can forget little Dorothy and the Yellow Brick Road?

GUS: And Toto her dog! *(Hoisting a glass)* By God, here's to Kansas, the other side of Oz!

*(*JAY *casts a sour look their way.)*

JILL: I should point out that Gus and Monica Washburn are not native to Bowie, Kansas. They moved across from us six years ago from some college town back in Massachusetts. Gus publishes a weekly paper. And Monica drinks.

JAY: There's only one thing wrong with Kansas: Outsider garbage.

JILL: Daddy is pioneer stock.

JAY: We're right in the middle of the goddam country. The oceans wash the garbage in toward us from both shores. Drifters. Failures. Sooner or later all that garbage passes over us, trying to escape to someplace else. Some of it sticks, like plaque on your teeth.

JILL: Daddy is of the opinion that everybody should go back where they came from. Starting with Gus and Monica.

GUS: Garcon! Another Tropical Dictator for the Little Lady!

MONICA: You elect them at midnight and by six in the morning there's a Revolution!

(She mimes vomiting in the general direction of JAY, *who cringes away.)*

JAY: Disgusting.

JILL: This is a story of the sacred and the profane. Monica plays the profane.

(Far U R the shutters of the steeple slowly crack, and STEEPLE JACK *cautiously peeps out.* JILL *stares up at him; none of the other characters sees him. When S J— as he will hereafter be known typographically—feels he is unobserved, he takes a deep breath, relaxes, and remarks reassuringly to himself:)*

S J: "A light shines in the darkness, and the darkness has not overcome it." *(He pulls the shutters closed again.)*

JILL: Steeple Jack. He plays the sacred.

GEORGE: Hey, what about me? I ain't here?

JILL: *(Smiling)* George.

GEORGE: Forget it, I'm just passing through.

*(*GEORGE *has now finished hitching his way across the stage and exits.* JILL *looks and sounds portentous.)*

JILL: Fate will have it otherwise. *(To the* WASHBURNS *and* JAY*)* Places.

*(*GUS *and* MONICA *exit amiably, drinks in hand.* JAY *exits, grabbing a jacket.* JILL *is now alone on stage. She crosses over and up to her bedroom nook D L, remarking as she goes:)*

JILL: Two days before my fifteenth birthday, all of these people were residing in or passing through Bowie in Clanford County, Kansas. Every last one of 'em ended up coming to my birthday party.

(End of Prologue)

(JILL *switches on a portable TV in her room. Sound of football game, featuring the Kansas City Chiefs.* JILL *takes up a position facing front on cushions beneath the sill of her imaginary window. From here she spies on the town with her binoculars. When she peers up through her "window", she is spying on the steeple of the nearby Lutheran church. When she peers down as she now does, she's spying on the townspeople. She addresses her remarks to her toy koala bear, which she calls B'ar.*)

JILL: There's Randy Blake talking to Susan Schmidt. That fluffbrain. This is fun, B'ar. Like eavesdropping with your eyeballs. When people don't know they're being watched, you can look right through them and out the other side. *(Pause)* Look how easy they talk to each other. How happy they are... *(She puts down the binocs and silently hugs her stuffed bear.)*

(Lights sharpen on the steeple's shutters. They open slowly on the lean, ancient face of STEEPLE JACK. *He surveys the town beneath him.* JILL *glimpses the steeple and immediately peers up with her binocs.)*

JILL: It's him, B'ar! Steeple Jack's back in Bowie! I *thought* that was you this morning, out there shopping in Mrs. Potter's garden. *She will be sooo mad.* Oh, he's cold, B'ar, see his breath. He don't look happy.

(S J *rolls a sloppy cigarette, all the while silently muttering intensely to himself.*)

JILL: Gonna have him a smoke. Bugler, same's Daddy. Oooo yuk, it's all hanging out both ends. Dang fool's striking matches up there, all that hay he sleeps in? Gonna set his butt on fire. Checking the moonrise. One night less of full, Mister Steeple Jack. Gonna be bright bright bright.

(S J *props himself on a railing of belfrey. He seems impatient, restless.*)

JILL: Would you look at those shoes? See his feet right through 'em.

(S J *also takes note of his shoes, suddenly grabbing them off his feet and throwing them over the side of the steeple.* JILL *recoils as though found out.*)

JILL: He heard me, B'ar! I swear he heard me! Gotta be more careful. *(She cautiously peeps out window again.)* Lookit that! Put that cigarette out twixt his thumb and finger and didn't even flinch.

(S J *scans Bowie one last time, then disappears down a trap in the belfrey.* JILL *solemnly confers with her bear.*)

JILL: Think about this, B'ar. The first last and onliest time this man passed through Bowie, my mother was buried. *(Pauses)* Something's getting set to happen to me.

(*Sound of door opening and closing offstage right. Lights up on Cady living room.* JILL *becomes a different person when she realizes her father's home. Where she was skinny, her posture now suggests emaciation and deep anxiety; she homes in on the TV game, knowing she'll be quizzed.* JAY *enters D R. Without stopping, he crosses quickly D S L and exits out the kitchen door, slinging his coat on the chair as he crosses. A door as well as a flight of stairs is presumed between* JAY *and* JILL, *yet she follows his movements as if she can see him. Offstage left, the sound of two beer cans popping.* JAY *re-enters with two beers, crosses to La-Z-Boy, turns on T V, and settles in to watch the remainder of the football game. Sound of the game increases; bluish-white light flickers over* JAY.)

JAY: What's the score, you gabby bastard? *(Pause, then shouts)* Jill, what's the score?

JILL: Nothin-nothin , Daddy!— Four minutes into second quarter. Chiefs' ball our forty-three.

JAY: Boring. *(He crosses back off-left where he inspects innards of refrigerator. He calls up to* JILL.) How come you didn't eat the potato salad I fixed? *(Silence)* There's plenty of fried chicken. Didn't touch that neither.

(JAY *crosses back to T V, doing a slow burn. Tries to watch game but can't focus on it. He jumps up, starts to storm* JILL's *room, then stops, gets himself under control. He knocks on the frame that represents her door.* JILL *is rigid.)*

JAY: I got to talk through this door, Ji'Lady? *(Silence)* I'm taking that lock out tomorrow. How you like that?

JILL: Daddy, that ain't fair.

JAY: What's that? Fair? I told you about fair, didn't I? *(Pause)* Didn't I, girl?

JILL: Yes, Daddy.

JAY: What'd I say?

JILL: Ain't no such thing.

JAY: Ain't no such thing! You got that, Baby Girl. *(Pause)* Darlin, you on a hunger strike in there? *(Silence)* I got three days and counting since you ate solid food. What am I supposed to make of that fact? *(Silence)* You know what I'm gonna do, Baby Girl? Tomorrow after I remove your lock? I'm gonna drive you in to Wichita, and I'm gonna take you into Saint Boniface, and the nuns in there? The women all in black? I'm gonna hand you over to them, and they're gonna take you and hook you up to a bottle, you hear what I say? They'll stick a big needle in one of your arm veins and hook you up to a hose and plug you into a bottle filled with salt and sugar, and they'll pump it right into ya, and they'll call it Food and they'll say, "There now, the sweet l'il thing's been fed," and you'll go "Mmm-mmm good," won't you, Baby Girl? *(Silence)* I won't put up with this, Jill.

JILL: Daddy, I can't keep it down.

JAY: Well ya see? That's why we gotta get ya into Boniface. You're sick, Ji'Lady. *(Attempting a joke)* Either that, or you're in love. And ya can't be in love cause you're too damn *scrawny*!

JILL: LEAVE ME ALONE!

JAY: I was just foolin, Baby Girl. You're the best-lookin thing in Clanford County. Soon as you flesh out a bit.

JILL: You don't know *nothin* about *nothin*!

JAY: You got that right. Anytime you feelin' smarter, why you just set me down and tell me what it's all about. O K honey? Whatever's on your pretty little mind. *(He crosses back to his chair, tries to become involved in the newspaper. Everything in it irritates him further.)* Unions! Every yo-yo in a garbage truck's got a god-given right to earn ten grand a year more than me!

(Sound: Interrupt drone of football game with ANNOUNCER *of News Bulletin)*

ANNOUNCER'S VOICE: The body of an eleven year-old Cherokee County boy was found beaten and stabbed to death around seven o'clock this evening. Identity of the child is being withheld pending further investigation. Details on the eleven o'clock news. Now, back to football.

*(*JAY *and* JILL *both turn off their T Vs. Sound: kill loop of football game.)*

JAY: You hear that, Jill?

JILL: *(Calling down)* Yes, Daddy.

*(*JAY *momentarily exits to his bedroom U R; soon returns carrying a deer rifle, such as a thirty-five caliber Marlin.)*

JAY: I'm gonna help Baker catch this child-killing bastard. I'm locking all the doors. If you get nervous, call up one of your friends. *(Under his breath as he heads for door)* *If you still got any.* You be O K, Ji'Lady?

JILL: I'm fine.

*(*JAY *exits. Sound of door closing. Sound of pick-up truck starting and driving off. Only when the sound fades does* JILL *seem to relax. She crosses down to a point near the kitchen exit. A C B sits on a table. She switches it on. Sound of* C B VOICES. *All try to sound like airplane pilots.)*

RED DUST: Charley-one, you got Red Dust here outta Barnerville to'rd Baxter on one-seventeen, position?

CHARLEY-ONE: Hey, Dust, comin at ya off Sluicemill Road, you got Charley-one.

JILL: *(To audience)* The Clanford County Sheriff's Department consists of Sheriff Darryl Baker, two Deputies, and—during manhunts—twenty thousand armed auxiliaries in pick-up trucks.

RED DUST: We got us an abandoned car out here, looks to be anyways.

CHARLEY-ONE: Copy.

JILL: The only thing the boys enjoy more than a Dragnet is chasing after tornadoes, seeing who can come closest. Sometimes the rain comes down so hard all around you that you lose sight of the funnel. You're down there in your car, like you're under a river, an it's all dark and constant roaring an you know at any second that evil black funnel can zig-zag over and hop right down on you like a panther, and it's a quick trip to the Land of Oz.

CHARLEY-ONE: Hey, Red Dust! Charley-one here wants the scam on that abandoned car? *(Some laughter on the channel)*

RED DUST: T'weren't abandoned, Charley-one. *(Suppressed mirth)* Well, mebbe she was.

JILL: Dirty old men.

LITTLE RED ROOSTER: Hey, this is Little Red Rooster. Anybody down near Floodriver Farm?

(Pause, then a different voice, whispering intensely)

ROOSTER'S RIDER: There! Over by that tool shed, see him?

LITTLE RED ROOSTER: This is Little Red Rooster and we got Bigfoot or somethin' scurryin' across Floodriver Farm. Intercept southbound 42 at County Double E, over.

MATTERHORN: Roger, Rooster, Matterhorn at West Forks and closing on Double E.

JILL: Matterhorn. That's Daddy.

LITTLE RED ROOSTER: Hey Matterhorn, deer season come early this year!

JILL: *(Turns off the C B)* This, of all nights, was the night George picked to hitchhike through Clanford County.

(Lights out on JILL. Sound: Muted "nature" noises—chirps of redwings and meadowlarks, rhythmic drone of crickets. It is end of dusk on a minor Kansas highway. A full moon is on the rise. We hear GEORGE before we see him.)

GEORGE: *(Singing from off-stage)* "Way down yonder in the Indian nation ride my pony on the reservation..."

(Enter GEORGE with his "Joplin" sign. Sound of approaching semi-truck)

GEORGE: "...Oklahoma hills where I was born..."

(GEORGE halts and gives the oncoming trucker his best hitch. Lights glare. Sound of truck roaring by. A forceful gust of air sweeps over George. For good measure the trucker blasts his horn as he passes. Abruptly, the violence of the moment is past. Again, sounds of crickets and birds. GEORGE stares pensively after the truck. Having given the incident enough thought, GEORGE continues his journey, trooping toward center-stage, absently singing:)

GEORGE: "Way down yonder in the Indian nation
ride my pony on the reservation
Oklahoma hills where I was born...." *(Pause)* Wish I knew the rest of that song. *(Observing the Moonrise)*

"Shine on, shine on harvest moon,
up in the sky,
I ain't had no lovin' since—"
(Throws in a little dance step) "January, February, June or July!" Yeah!
(He smiles warmly, bows smoothly to the evening air all around him.) Thank you, thank you, you're beautiful, love ya. *(Blows a kiss to his audience. It is now almost dark. He wears only a cheap silver and black "Korea" windbreaker over his busboy uniform of black slacks, black shoes and socks, and white shirt. The last evening breeze chills him through, and he hugs himself ruefully.)* This ain't gettin me ta Miami. *Not even Joplin.* *(Looks around for a suitable place to lay his sleeping bag, singing:)*
"Carolina Moon, keep shining,
shining on the one who waits for me."
(Having settled D S C, he tries to sleep but can't; sits up, snaps at the moon:) Now how my sposed to sleep wit *you* in my eyes all night? *(Pulls out a miniature tape recorder, composes a "letter" to his mother)* Dear Mom. Still Tuesday, and I'm still in Kansas, but I think it's coming to an end. They sure waste a lot of space in this state. No motels, no trees, no nuttin when you need it. *(Not recording, to himself)* It's cold here, Ma. *(Recording again)* I think I'm getting close to Joplin. I plan to call on Cousin Simona. *(Not recording)* Maybe she'll stake me to a bus ticket partway to Miami. Hey, at least a warm bed and a shower for Aunt Emma's Georgie Porgie, right? *(Recording again)* There's an enormous, humongous moon up tonight, Ma, like it's gonna explode all over the sky. If it was sixty degrees warmer and if that was an ocean out there, this place would remind me of Florida. But it ain't, and it don't. *(Pause)* Ma, sometimes I think where I'll be just this time exactly ten years from now. Usually I'm a great chef in a famous restaurant. Sometimes I'm a singer in a Las Vegas lounge. Once in a while I'm begging change in the street. I see myself holding a kid, a baby boy. But you know what, Ma? No matter where I am or what I'm doing, I see myself *happy*. Night, Ma. Write more when I'm not so cold. Your loving son, Georgie. *(He places his black shoes by the foot of his bag. His day pack disappears inside the sleeping bag. And his windbreaker, scrunched up, becomes his pillow. He goes to sleep.)*

(Brief blackout. Subdued sounds of low wind, night insects. Then, bluish-white moonlight on GEORGE. *From deep U C, back-lit by blue source, a crouching figure approaches George. He is barefoot. It takes a moment to realize this is S J. He crouches low over* GEORGE, *carefully inspecting him and the area around him. He discovers the shoes. Without making a sound, he pulls them on and ties them. Then he slowly kneels down and slips his hand under* GEORGE's *head. Gently he removes the windbreaker.* GEORGE *partially awakens.)*

GEORGE: Uuh...ah—what time izzit?

S J: Too late. Go back to sleep.

(GEORGE *tries to do just that.* S J *quickly and silently creeps off-stage. After about a five-count,* GEORGE *sits bolt upright in the bag.*)

GEORGE: What was that? What happened? *(Jumps to his feet and looks around. Calms somewhat; glares at the Moon.)* Stupid Moon. Giving me bad dreams. Gawd it's cold! *(Throws himself back inside his sleeping bag)* Where's my pillow? *(Thrashes around for his jacket)* Stupid slippery jacket—my God, it's gone. And my shoes! He took my shoes! *(Furious, screaming into the night)* Gimme my shoes! You want me to *freeze*? *(Silence. It scares him. When he next speaks, he does so softly.)* Forget the shoes. *(He quickly gathers up the remainder of his belongings, nervously muttering:)* I'm just passing through. Got nothing against you or nobody else. Don't even know where I am, and I sure ain't coming back, so we got no reason to get to know each other better.

(*He gets the bag and day pack arranged on his back, takes two steps toward the wings, and nearly bumps into* JAY's *.35 Marlin.* GEORGE *takes a shocked step backwards, loses his balance, and falls down.* JAY *speaks calmly and slowly.*)

JAY: I want you to roll over on your stomach, slowly, and put your hands behind your back.

(GEORGE *does as instructed.* JAY *drops a small noose of cord around* GEORGE's *wrists, secures it.*)

GEORGE: I got six bucks. Don't do nuttin for six bucks.

(JAY *pulls him to his feet and shoves him S R, where they exit. Blackout. Sound of portable radio, low*)

ANNOUNCER'S VOICE: The murdered youth has now been identified as Keith Frantz of Somerville. His mother is reported under sedation in the care of her physician. The Cherokee County Sheriff says no accurate description of the suspect can be given until Mrs Frantz is well enough to be interrogated. In the meantime anyone observing anything unusual is asked to call 555-3960.

(*Sound: doorbell ringing.* JILL *turns off radio. When the doorbell rings again,* JILL, *who has been sleeping on her cushions beneath her window, leaps up and grabs her .22 rifle.* MONICA *yells from O S R.*)

MONICA: *(Offstage)* Hey Jilly Pill! Want some company?

(JILL *relaxes, puts away the .22, and runs down to let* MONICA *in.*)

MONICA: Hi Toots!

JILL: You scared the wits out of me!

MONICA: You're alone, right? Jay sniffed the blood lust and ran off howling, am I right?

JILL: Where's Gus?

MONICA: Oh, *him*! He's been drafted as Chief Jailer while the Sheriff chases the Bad Guy. *(Fixing herself a drink)* He's having a ball, sitting down there taking telephone calls, pretending he's Wyatt Earp.

JILL: Exciting, isn't it?

MONICA: What, a nut on the loose? Honey, where I come from, that's a way of life. *(Eyeing* JAY's *La-Z-Boy)* I've always wanted to try this thing.

JILL: Daddy won't let no one near that.

(MONICA *sits in it, smiles)*

MONICA: You won't tell on me, will you? *(She takes the chair through its various inclinations, finding it a bit of a struggle.)* This stupid thing's bigger than Cleopatra's Barge. *(Finally settles on a half-reclined position; still, she's disappointed.)* I don't know what Jay sees in this. Maybe if I had a pipe or a dog at my feet?

JILL: You got tornadoes?

MONICA: Huh?

JILL: Back in Massachusetts.

MONICA: Damn right! A nasty one back in '53.

JILL: You got everything back there.

MONICA: Only compared to here.

JILL: We got tornadoes and psycho killers. Not much else to get worked up about.

MONICA: Don't be bored! Not at your age. Not ever, dammit!

(JILL *is abashed;* MONICA *softens.)*

MONICA: Only people who have stopped hoping and thinking are bored.

(JILL *says nothing.)*

MONICA: Look Sweetie, Monica's been partying all night at the Best Western, so maybe you better run along to bed before I become disgusting.

JILL: You know I wasn't always like this.

MONICA: I know.

JILL: I was never bored living here. The same things happened at the same time, over and over, year after year. I loved it, Monica.

MONICA: Yes, Sweet.

JILL: No change. No fear. My life was seamless. And then one night last February, with no one to warn me, my life got all ripped up, and I aged about thirty-seven years.

MONICA: Jilly Pill, you got to stop picking at that scab.

JILL: That's it, shush me up like everyone else.

MONICA: No, no...

JILL: A girl can get ripped open from belly to brains and if she so much as groans out loud just once, people tell her to shut up, she's wallowing in self-pity!

MONICA: Honey Baby, the saddest thing about life is that it ends. But it does, for everyone. People die all the time.

JILL: My mother only died once! *(More ferocious than weepy)* It still hurts. And you can't make it stop by shaming me. Only she can make it stop. She will send me a sign to say, "That's enough. You can live now."

(MONICA *is exhausted. Her eyes are closed and she hardly hears* JILL.)

MONICA: Good night, Jill.

(JILL *kisses* MONICA's *forehead.*)

JILL: Good night, Monica. Thank you for looking after me.

MONICA: *(Slurred)* Don't worry bout a thing...anyone come round here, I'll breathe on 'em.

(MONICA *falls asleep.* JILL *arranges a blanket and pillow for her, then sits where she can study* MONICA *to her full satisfaction. After a few moments, she murmurs:*)

JILL: Wherever you're from, Monica, I want to go.

(Lights out on JILL *and* MONICA. *In blackout sound of* C B VOICES*)*

LITTLE RED ROOSTER: This is Little Red Rooster southbound on 42. We've lost sight of suspect. Matterhorn! Where *were* ya'll, over?

MATTERHORN: This is Matterhorn! Go get ya some sleep, Rooster, I bagged your Bigfoot.

LITTLE RED ROOSTER: Say again, Matterhorn?

MATTERHORN: Suspect has been apprehended, over.

(Lights up on GUS WASHBURN *in office area of Clanford County Jail. He is sticking another pin in a detailed area map of Bowie and environs when...sound: The phone rings.)*

GUS: Clanford County Sheriff. Yes, Mrs Keltner. Um-hmm. Something knocked over your garbage pail...and then you heard unearthly screeching. *(He stops taking notes.)* I'm sorry, I'm afraid we can't spare an officer. *(He winces, holds the phone at arm's length and shouts.)* Mrs Keltner! Haven't you ever heard cats fornicating? *(He hangs up.)* I'll pay for that.

(Sound of pick-up pulling to a stop)

JAY: *(Offstage)* Slide down!

(The Sheriff's door flies open, and JAY, *excited and proud, shoves* GEORGE *through it.* GUS *looks over with mild interest.)*

JAY: Bagged him!

GUS: Him?

JAY: The killer, you jackass! Down the steps!

GEORGE: Whadaya saying "killer"? I'm George Antioch, Mister. You got me confused—

*(*JAY *grabs the keys off the desk and roughly shoves* GEORGE *down into the cell, then steps in with him threateningly.)*

JAY: You're a murderin piece of outsider garbage, and you stabbed and raped and killed an eleven year-old boy one county over—

GEORGE: HOLY JESUS NO!

JAY: We're gonna hang your nuts out to dry!

*(*JAY *slaps* GEORGE.*)*

GUS: JAY!

*(*GUS *tries to restrain* JAY.*)*

JAY: Hands off!

*(*JAY *easily throws* GUS *halfway across the room.)*

GUS: You drunken pig!

*(*JAY *realizes he's exceeded himself and that the Sheriff will hear of it. He goes to* GUS' *aid.)*

JAY: You O K?

GUS: *(Shoves him away)* Get out of here.

*(*JAY *backs off to the sliding partition separating the cell area from office.* GUS *composes himself, begins interrogation.)*

GUS: Your name is George?

GEORGE: Yeah, and I'm innocent of everything and I can prove it!

GUS: I'm sure you can, and will.

GEORGE: I never done nuttin ta nobody! I been robbed! Somebody stole my shoes and jacket and I thought it was that guy— *(Pointing at* JAY*)* —and now *he's* fingerin *me*! That ain't Justice! I wanna call my cousin in Joplin—Simona Jones! She'll tell ya, I'm clean as a bone!

GUS: You from Joplin?

GEORGE: No, Miami.

GUS: Ah, a Florida boy. That why you run around barefoot?

(GEORGE *is actually wearing black socks.*)

GEORGE: *He stole em!*

GUS: Who?

GEORGE: *(Looking at* JAY *dubiously)* Him?

GUS: No, say what you will about Jay Cady, he buys all his own shoes. *(Pouring a cup)* You drink coffee?

(GEORGE *gratefully accepts it.*)

GUS: How old are you, George?

GEORGE: Nineteen.

GUS: Mmph. I used to be nineteen.

(GEORGE *smiles uncertainly.*)

GUS: Tell me what happened to you, George.

GEORGE: I'm hitching through, just camping out, couldn't get no ride, I ain't *never* gettin outta this state!

GUS: Calm down.

GEORGE: It was a full moon, see, and it was giving me bad dreams. I kept dreaming about lost things. Destroyed things. My car. Totalled my '41 Ford last week. Asshole drove me over a bank into the Big Thompson River.

GUS: In Colorado?

GEORGE: Yeah, that's the one, a killer creek! Terrible! I'm lucky to be alive.

GUS: The guy that robbed you, can you describe him?

GEORGE: Naw, I was sleepin.

JAY: Like hell. He was screamin like a Banshee.

GEORGE: That was after!

GUS: Was he armed? Did he pull a knife on you?

GEORGE: I couldn't tell, I thought I felt somethin, but...he was like a ghost.

JAY: What a crock! This punk's lying through his teeth!

GEORGE: I ain't lying! Lemme call Simona! Or Mr Tony, he'll vouch for me.

GUS: Mr Tony?

GEORGE: Yeah! Floor Captain of the Dining Crew at the Fontainebleu! He's holding a job for me, but I gotta be there *fast*!

GUS: You a busboy?

GEORGE: How'd you know?

GUS: Not many people dress the way you do voluntarily.

GEORGE: Oh. My uniform. Lost all my other clothes in the Big Thompson.

GUS: I'll tell you, George. That story won't float. I'm tempted to let this drunken redneck— *(Indicating* JAY*)* —beat on you for a while, see if you can't recall better what you were doing wandering around at night twenty miles down the road from that stabbed boy.

GEORGE: Gimme a lie detector! Get a hypnotist! I ain't hiding *nothing*!

GUS: I'm gonna keep you locked up for your own personal safety. Farmers around here been known to use pitchforks on your kind.

GEORGE: Am I still dreaming?

GUS: Well if you are, maybe you'll wake up remembering more about the man you claim was with you out in that field tonight.

(GUS *closes sliding partition.* JAY *is grinning conspiratorially.*)

JAY: That was good, about the farmers and their pitchforks.

GUS: Just where did you dig up this bedraggled specimen?

JAY: Floodriver Farm off Double E.

GUS: *(Studying his map)* Around eleven-thirty?

JAY: Sounds about right.

(GUS *puts another pin in his wall map,* JAY *commandeers the office C B.*)

JAY: Clanford One, do you copy?

GUS: Get off that thing!

SHERIFF'S VOICE: Acknowledge.

JAY: Jay Cady here, Sheriff.

SHERIFF'S VOICE: What're you doing there? Where's Gus?

JAY: He's been interrogating the suspect I apprehended, Darryl.

(GUS *takes transmitter from* JAY.)

GUS: Gus here, Darryl. We got a live one. Come on home and dress him out.

SHERIFF'S VOICE: Might as well. Bout outta gas. Over.

JAY: Gas! That's why they're falling all over each other out there! Too lazy to get their fat butts out from under their steering wheels. I caught mine on *foot*, like an Indian!

GUS: *(Studying his wall map)* You're wonderful, Jay. *(Turning to him)* Not only did you bag the wrong man, you could have got the right one, and you didn't. *(He smiles.)*

JAY: That kid's the killer!

GUS: You bagged a hitch-hiker, Jay.

JAY: An itinerant! A bum!

GUS: A nineteen year-old busboy. A baby.

JAY: You don't think they got nineteen year-old killers in Florida? The place is *crawling* with em! They can't fry em fast enough!

GUS: The probable killer is the man who stole that boy's shoes. *(Indicating map)* Eleven different C B sightings of something running around, with their times. Last sighting puts him in your vicinity about the time you collared this busboy.

(GEORGE makes a sudden racket.)

GEORGE: Somebody call Simona Jones! Area code eight oh seven, two two six eighty-one twenty-two! Just call her, she'll tell you!

(JAY and GUS exchange a look, and JAY entertains a moment of doubt.)

GUS: If I was you, Jay, I'd get a lawyer.

JAY: That's the trouble with this country in a nutshell! I risk my life seizing a murderer, burn up over half a tank of gas just gettin here, you tell me get a lawyer you're being sued and the killer be out right after lunch tomorrow, you watch. Shit!

GUS: The killer is out right now. He zigs and zags a bit, but he appears to be heading right toward our bucolic little town. *(Pause)* Don't you think you should be home protecting that remarkable daughter of yours?

JAY: Don't you lecture me on my responsibilities! I ain't her mother! Her mother's *dead*, and the faster she gets that through her head, the stronger she'll be! *(Pauses, suffused with rage)* You pompous little prick. You bring me down so hard. So fast. The day's coming when I'll smash your ugly face in.

(The two men stare at each other—GUS with a calm, sardonic smile; JAY with absolute detestation. Sound of C B traffic on Office C B)

RED DUST: Hey, anybody out there know when Star-Vu Drive-in opens? This boy's ready for some chicken fried steaks, over? *(Crackling noises, static, then:)*

CHARLEY-ONE: *(Singing)* "Turn out the lights, the party's over...."

(Lights on Sheriff's office go to blackout. Lights up dim on Cady living room. Pre-dawn. JILL is curled up on the floor beneath a blanket near the La-Z-Boy. MONICA, also covered, sleeps with hungover discomfort on the recliner. Sound of

front door slamming. JILL *sits bolt upright.* MONICA *stirs and moans softly.* JAY *flips on the entryway light, stands framed by backlighting, his face obscured. He lurches toward the two of them.* JILL *tries to run but he grabs her, and she screams as he tries to hug and kiss her.* MONICA *tries to separate sleep from drunkeness and is of little help.*)

JAY: Ji'Lady... Baby Girl...

JILL: NO! *Get away!*

MONICA: Gus? What is it, Gus?

(JILL *breaks free as* JAY *is momentarily distracted by* MONICA. JILL *races to her room, locks herself in, grabs her .22, and aims it at her door.* JAY *lumbers clumsily after her.*)

JAY: It's me, Baby Girl, it's your poppa. Don't be scared, Ji'Lady, your poppa loves you....

JILL: MONICA! Help me!

MONICA: *Oh my god*

JAY: *Get out of my house, Monica! (Screaming at* JILL's *door)* Open that door, god damn it! This is your father talking!

MONICA: Jay, *please* leave her be.

(JAY *storms toward the recliner;* MONICA *has been unable to get it upright.*)

JAY: Outta my chair!

(*He jerks the chair to full upright position and effortlessly hurls* MONICA *onto the floor. Jay flips living room lights on bright.* MONICA *is on her hands and knees, close to being sick.* JAY *stares down at her with unadulterated hatred.*)

JAY: You drunken old whore.

MONICA: What...did you call me?

JAY: Nothing the whole town don't.

(MONICA *half crawls, half staggers offstage toward toilet. She can be heard gagging softly under* JAY's *harangue.*)

JAY: You're an object of disgust, Monica, you didn't know that? You can't hold your booze. *(Weaves a bit as he lights a cig)* I WANT YOU TO STAY AWAY FROM MY DAUGHTER! Don't want you corrupting my Ji'Lady! And keep your ASSHOLE HUSBAND out of my sight, too! You hear me, Monica?

(MONICA *reappears, upright but leaning on a door frame, holding her head.*)

MONICA: It's like you to attack me when I'm sick. For what, Jay? For looking after your daughter?

JAY: Making her queer for you.

MONICA: What evil sickness is in you, Jay?

(JAY *points to the door.* MONICA *grabs her things and exits.* JAY *falls onto his recliner. He rests.* JILL *finally calms enough to lay aside her rifle; she stretches out on her cushions, tries to sleep. Blackout. Then, dawn light revealing* JAY *and* JILL *in same positions. Light focuses on the belfry of the steeple. The shutters of the belfry slowly open.* S J *appears, cautiously assessing the terrain below. He is wearing* GEORGE's *"Korea" jacket.* JILL *stirs in her room, then becomes fully alert, grabs her binocs, and focuses in on* S J. *He relaxes, props himself up on belfry railing, and rolls a cigarette. He is now wearing* GEORGE's *shoes, and he seems content.*)

JILL: Steeple Jack got him some shoes, B'ar. The man's a thief. *(Pause)* And maybe worse. Maybe much worse. *(Irritated)* How'd he get away last night, B'ar? Twenty thousand drunken farm boys couldn't catch that poor old crazy man. Now it's down to me, B'ar. I gotta go tell the Sheriff, don't I? *(Staring at* S J*)* He looks mean, B'ar, there's no denying it. But he came to my mother's funeral, and I saw him crying for her. That day he looked gentle as an angel. A poor crazy angel. *(Thinking it through)* Of course, that was eight months ago. And I don't know what time the boy was killed yesterday, nor where you were then, Mister Steeple Jack, do I?

(*At this moment* S J *directs a sharp stare to some object below him. In her room* JILL *perceives it as* S J *suddenly looking straight into her eyes. She recoils, clutching her bear.*)

JILL: He saw me, B'ar! No two ways about it, he looked right through me. He'll be coming after me! I'm not safe, not even here.

(*She sneaks out of her room. Lights out on* S J *in steeple and on* JILL's *room.* JILL *tries to sneak past her dozing father, but* JAY *senses her and asks softly:*)

JAY: Where you going, Ji'Lady?

JILL: *(Freezing)* To church, Daddy.

JAY: You want a ride?

JILL: No, I feel like walking.

JAY: You know your Daddy caught the child killer last night?

JILL: *(Surprised, hopeful)* You did?

JAY: Sure nuff.

JILL: He confessed?

JAY: Probly by now. That's why I, uh, celebrated, Jill. I hope I didn't, uh...

JILL: I'm late, Daddy.

(*She exits.* JAY *stares after her, full of regret, conscious of the abyss between them. He reflexively turns on the TV. Sound: Inter-channel static continuous as* JAY *flips the selector. Nothing on. He turns set off. Kill sound of static.* JAY *blearily rubs his eyes, sighs, and quietly recites an encyclopedia passage as if it were his mantra:)*

JAY: "The Matterhorn—14,691 feet—is one of the best-known mountains in the world. It straddles the frontier between Switzerland and Italy. The Swiss slope is not nearly so steep or difficult to climb as the grand terraced walls of the Italian slope."

(Blackout on JAY. *Lights up on cell area of jail.* GEORGE *is snoozing on his cot.* JILL *studies him from a chair placed outside his cell. After a few moments he rolls over and spots her.)*

GEORGE: Who're you?

*(*JILL *just stares evenly at him.)*

GEORGE: Get outta here, will ya? Hey Gus! What is this, a zoo?

JILL: My daddy caught you.

GEORGE: Yeah? You Jay Cady's kid?

JILL: My grandfather built this jail. Daddy helped.

GEORGE: *(Looking around)* Nice. Solid, you know?

JILL: No one's ever escaped from here.

GEORGE: *(Depressed)* Shouldn't you be in school or somewhere?

JILL: What could be more educational than talking with a murderer?

GEORGE: I ain't no murderer! Gus!

(A bleary-eyed GUS *appears.)*

GEORGE: Where is it written she can grill me?

GUS: Be polite. She's got influence.

JILL: The Sheriff is my godfather.

GEORGE: You so hot, make em give me my phone call.

JILL: *(To* GUS*)* Isn't he entitled?

GEORGE: It's guaranteed! I seen it in hundreds of movies.

*(*GUS *unlocks him, taking care to keep him well away from* JILL.*)*

GUS: O K George, whoever you're gonna upset should be awake by now.

GEORGE: *(As he's led to office phone)* All right! Hey, I owe you one! *(Dialing)* Now we'll finally get this all straightened out. It's ringing. Hello, Simona? It's me, George Antioch! Now you shouldn't be nervous, but I'm calling from a jail in Kansas—

JILL: The Clanford County Jail! In Bowie!

GEORGE: What? *George! ANTIOCH!* Cousin Georgie from Miami! Now listen, they're looking for a killer, and they think I'm it, so listen— hello? Simona? *(To* GUS, *dismayed)* She hung up!

GUS: *(Leading him back to cell)* They do that sometimes.

GEORGE: So that was it? That was my phone call?

(GUS *locks cell door on him.)*

GEORGE: I keep getting robbed.

(GEORGE *sits disconsolately on his cot as* GUS *exits;* JILL *stares at him.)*

JILL: Are you on drugs?

GEORGE: What's *wit* you? I'm a healthy clean-living person! I'm more innocent than the day you was born! It's a set-up! Here I am, hitching my way to Miami from Colorado. Fell asleep off by the road. Got robbed! Stole my shoes and jacket! Boom! I'm doing twenty to life! What kind of world is this?

JILL: An unfair one.

GEORGE: Yeah?

(JILL *nods solemnly.)*

JILL: How come you dress so weird?

GEORGE: What's weird? It's my uniform.

JILL: What do you play?

GEORGE: Play? Whadaya talkin, play? I'm a busboy!

JILL: You fix buses?

GEORGE: Buses? *(Looking around, disoriented)* Am I still in America? What language we speaking? *"Busboy."* You never been to a restaurant?

JILL: No.

GEORGE: *No?*

JILL: A & W. The Bowie Burger.

GEORGE: *Restaurants!* Maitre Ds and entrees! Tablecloths!

(She stares at him blankly. He sizes her up anew and feels some pity mingle with his annoyance.)

GEORGE: Jeez, no wonder you're so scrawny.

(She glares at him.)

GEORGE: Thin?

JILL: *(Crossing to office)* From what I hear, it'll be about thirty-five years before *you* see another restaurant.

(She closes the partition on him; she and GUS *stare at each other.)*

JILL: *That's* the *murderer*?

GUS: Best we could do on short notice.

JILL: That boy couldn't bring himself to gig a frog. *(She uneasily wrestles with a decision; then:)* The man who stole his shoes and jacket is holed up in the steeple of the Lutheran church.

GUS: Is that a fact?

JILL: I don't think he's dangerous. He didn't hurt the busboy.

*(*GUS *is on the phone.)*

JILL: You'll take him safe?

GUS: We'll sure try, Jill. Hello, Sheriff? We got a development here.

(Blackout. Then lights up on the steeple. S J is lying on a plank mounted in front of the belfry blacking. The effect is as if we were viewing S J from within the louvered shutters of the belfry. He seems to be floating in space, lit only by the strips of light filtering through the closed shutters. Sound of SHERIFF'S VOICE *through bullhorn. It sounds spectral, menacing.)*

SHERIFF'S VOICE: This is the County Sheriff.

(S J bolts awake.)

SHERIFF'S VOICE: You will descend from that belfry at once. If you have weapons, open the shutters and throw them down.

(S J edges to his feet and seems to peer down through the louvers, assessing his chances. His posture and movements suggest a trapped and desperate woods creature. Suddenly he drops to his knees and begins to pray.)

SHERIFF'S VOICE: If you come down, I will be pleased. If I have to come up, I will be angry.

(S J slowly stands, then mimes hurling open D S shutters. Full light on S J, as if framed by belfry. He looks ferocious, and his voice is resonant and powerful.)

S J: "The hour is coming, indeed it has come, when you will be *scattered*! Every man to his home! And will *leave me alone*!"

(He pulls the shutters closed. Blackout. Lights up on JILL *D L, seated on a stool, talking softly to audience.)*

JILL: The way the boys tell it, Steeple Jack slipped while trying to escape and hit his head. This may be so. What's more likely is that one of them couldn't pass up a cheap shot. *They get excited that way.* In any event, Jack arrived via stretcher, was examined by Doc Metcalf, and was pronounced healthy enough to be jailed.

(Lights up on cell area. GEORGE *is staring at his new cellmate, who is still wearing* GEORGE's *jacket and shoes.* S J *is prostrate and semi-conscious.)*

JILL: Since this was my first experience as an informer, I was astonished to be treated like a hero. Gus told me this could be a big story if we'd caught the child killer. He was gonna put it on the wire, he said. Go national with it. *(She begins slow cross U S.)* I have since thought of a couple good things I should have said. Here's one: "My dear Mr Washburn, I intend to attain a less fleeting and more literary variety of fame." *He would have known that referred to my nearly secret dream of being a novelist.* Or I could have slipped into my wispy and sensitive Emily Dickinson voice: "My dear Gus, I am scarcely prepared to Go Local, much less National." *This an allusion to the problem I was then having in forcing myself to leave my bedroom.* As it is, the best I could come up with was... *(Turning to stare at S J, her voice filled with remorse and pain:)* Oh Gus, I've made a terrible mistake, and I feel so ashamed!

(She ends with her back to audience, leaning on the partition between cell and office. GUS *emerges from the office area to comfort her. In the cell,* S J *stirs and sits up. He sees* GEORGE *glaring at him and recoils slightly, trying to orient himself.)*

GEORGE: I like your jacket. It's just like one I used to have.

(S J wordlessly takes it off and hands it to GEORGE, *who adds:)*

GEORGE: And my shoes?

(S J is more reluctant to surrender the shoes, but does.)

GEORGE: You oughta be ashamed.

S J: Cold feet impair my judgment. *(He notices his "emblem" is gone.)* My emblem. They've taken my emblem. Jailer!

(His head throbs, forcing him back to his cot. GUS *enters with the package.)*

GUS: How you feeling?

S J: Please...my emblem.

(He reaches hesitantly for the package but GUS *retains it.)*

GUS: What is this?

S J: Nothing of harm, nor worth, save to me.

GUS: Well, we'll just safeguard it for you, then.

S J: The last man to abscond with my emblem died a violent and terrifying death.

*(*GEORGE *exchanges a nervous glance with* GUS *and* JILL.*)*

GUS: By your hands?

S J: By God's. *(With sudden power in a tone full of foreboding:)* "Behold, I am coming soon, bringing my recompense, to repay every one for what he has done!"

(S J stares magisterially at the others, who are dumbfounded, then concludes in a voice filled with menace:)

S J: "I am the Alpha and the Omega, the first and the last, the beginning and the end."

(At that, S J drops to his knees, head bowed in abject submission. GUS studies him for a moment, then crosses to office phone as GEORGE calls after:)

GEORGE: Is this the only cell you got in this jail?

(JILL draws nearer, staring at S J with unadorned wonder.)

GUS: Hello, Sheriff. That steeple suspect has revived. Looks like we've got a religious fanatic here...

(Lights dim on GUS. Despite his ongoing muted phone conversation the focus shifts clearly to the cell area where S J continues to pray silently. GEORGE keeps as much distance as possible between them. And JILL seems entranced.)

GUS: What about the kid? You think Cady could transfer him? Maybe take em both over at the same time? O K, whatever. I'll see what I can get out of him. Yeah, I'm real beat, good for about another hour, then I put out the NO VACANCY sign and go home to Monica. Right. 'So long.

(GUS hangs up and immediately phones JAY. No answer. In the cell area S J meets JILL's gaze.)

JILL: It's my fault they caught you. *(Silence)* They think you killed a little boy over in Cherokee County.

S J: I am cursed. Wherever I go, Abaddon the Destroyer follows. I am too much for him, so he slaughters the innocent. He knows this brings me great pain.

JILL: What's your name?

S J: John.

GEORGE: That's a relief. I was afraid he was gonna say Jesus.

(GEORGE laughs but S J is outraged and struggles to his feet to get at GEORGE, all the while shouting:)

S J: Blasphemer! Blasphemer!

(GUS rushes in to intercede.)

GEORGE: Murderer! Pervert!

GUS: Back off, *back off*, you two!

(In the midst of this outburst, JAY *saunters in. He is pleased to view the uproar as* GUS' *incompetence.)*

GEORGE: Child raper!

JILL: Don't call him that!

GUS: Enough!

(S J backs off.)

S J: No! I will not be unsettled by *imbeciles*! The world needs its clowns.

GEORGE: Clown? Clown, huh? O K, better a clown than a crackpot! Who needs crackpots?

GUS: Children, children! This is a *jail*! A place for quiet reflection upon the sins that brought you to this pass. *(He notices* JAY.*)* I just called you, Cady. Sheriff wants to know if you'll transfer George to Cherokee County. Slade wants a look at him over there.

GEORGE: I'm getting outta here?

JAY: Office pay for my gas?

GEORGE: I'm getting away from this fruitcake?

GUS: If Sheriff Slade wants you, he keeps you. If he doesn't, you're gone.

GEORGE: Hey hey *hey*, it's eighty-three in Mi-a-*mee*!

JAY: Don't break out your sun tan lotion just yet, boy. Cherokee County ain't slack like here. Slade don't like your story, he'll beat another one out of you.

(This sombers GEORGE *somewhat.* JAY *strolls over to inspect* S J, *who glares at him.)*

JAY: What's the story on *this* ole bird?

S J: "And this is the judgment, that the light has come into the world, and men loved darkness rather than light because their deeds were EVIL!"

JAY: *(To* GUS*)* Preacher? Or Looney Tunes?

*(*GUS *shrugs.)*

JAY: C'mon Jill, you riding with me.

GUS: No. Baker wants to ask her about this guy. *(Indicates* S J*)*

JAY: Him? What could she know about him?

GUS: Oh, you'd be surprised how much Jill knows about things, Jay. She knows what went on in your house last night, just for an instance. Don't you, Jill?

(Silence; JILL *is nervous and embarrassed.)*

GUS: Monica wouldn't go into details over the phone, but I gather it wasn't pretty.

JAY: No big deal. I come home, find your wife drunk passed out in my chair, and I send her home. Ain't that right, Jill?

JILL: Yes, Daddy.

JAY: Ya see? Anything else is just Monica's hot-blooded imagination. *(Shoving GEORGE toward door)* C'mon, you.

GUS: Jay, you're a bully.

JAY: How do you know what I am? Can you see inside my head? Keep your wife at home, Gus. She can't get into trouble there.

GEORGE: Bye Jill! Ya ever in Florida, look me up!

(JAY and GEORGE exit. GUS phones MONICA.)

GUS: Did I wake you, Monica? How ya feel? Can you stop by? This dragnet hauled in a pretty weird fish. Want your opinion. Good. Bye.

(GUS hangs up. S J, after staring at JILL, motions her closer; she moves near enough for him to reach through the bars and touch her face.)

S J: "Your mother was like a vine in your blood, transplanted by the water. But the vine was plucked up in a fury, cast down to the ground. Its fruit was stripped off, its strong stem was withered; the fire consumed it. Now it is transplanted in the wilderness, in a dry and thirsty land."

(After a moment JILL covers her face and weeps softly. GUS moves to comfort her: They assume identical position to start of this scene.)

JILL: Oh Gus, I've made a terrible mistake, and I feel so ashamed!

(Blackout. Sound of pick-up truck cruising and country music on radio. Lights up on mock-up of pick-up truck cab. JAY mimes driving while GEORGE, chewing gum happily, sits handcuffed next to him. They must shout a bit to make themselves heard.)

GEORGE: You got the slickest pick-up I ever seen!

(JAY does not react.)

GEORGE: FuzzBuster, power windows, stereo tape, C B—what's your handle?

JAY: Matterhorn. *(Glancing warily at GEORGE)* It's a mountain in Switzerland. The most beautiful mountain on earth.

GEORGE: You been there?

JAY: Not yet. But I'm going someday. *(Resentfully)* Those people over there got it all whipped.

(GEORGE *glances up and over his shoulder at two mounted rifles.*)

GEORGE: I like your rifles. What kind are they?

JAY: Thirty-five caliber Marlin and a Winchester 30-30.

(GEORGE, *who knows nothing about rifles, thinks it over and asks:*)

GEORGE: Which one ja catch me with?

JAY: *(Detached, mechanical throughout)* The Marlin.

GEORGE: Nice. I like your daughter.

JAY: You what?

GEORGE: You got a nice little girl. Skinny.

JAY: Yeah. Starvin.

GEORGE: What's the matter with her?

JAY: She turned into a teenager. Says she's too fat, can't keep it down, not hungry, tastes bad. Kid's as screwed up as her Ma was.

GEORGE: You divorced?

JAY: You're a nosey son of a bitch, aren't you?

GEORGE: Sorry.

JAY: I'm a widower, you know what that means?

GEORGE: Yes sir, Mr Cady.

JAY: My wife was a boozer. Last February, coming back from her favorite bar, she smacked into a bridge abutment at about eighty miles per.

(*There is silence. At last, just to say something,* GEORGE *ventures:*)

GEORGE: Maybe she's happier where she is now.

JAY: *(Stares at him a moment)* Horse shit. *(Drives some more, then)* I was you, Kid, I'd start working on my alibi. This Cherokee County Sheriff goes about two-fifty and he don't play pattycake. He's gonna wanna know where you were yesterday.

GEORGE: I was hitching, just heading east. The people I met are all gone.

JAY: You're gonna have to do better than that, boy.

GEORGE: Just tell me somepin: Kansas is the same as the rest of the Free World, ain't it? A man is innocent until proven guilty?

JAY: *(Smiling)* So they say.

GEORGE: Then prove I ain't innocent! Ya can't, can ya?

JAY: Now calm down...

GEORGE: I'm calm, I'm calm!

JAY: I tell ya, George, about the only thing you got going for you is that bum ya shared your cell with.

GEORGE: Exactly!

JAY: I think Slade will take one look at that creep, and—*(Snaps his fingers)*—Case closed.

GEORGE: Oh, he done it, he done it, no question.

JAY: *Outsider garbage.*

GEORGE: I got a job waiting for me, I got a mother, my whole *life* is out there, and what's *he* got? An *emblem*, whatever that is. He's old, too. He could be dead tomorrow.

JAY: Ain't none of us immune to that. *(Turns, smiles mirthlessly)* I could turn to smile at you like this, take my eyes off the road a split second too long. I could lose control of this big ole truck.

GEORGE: Could you please watch the road, Mr Cady?

JAY: *(Still smiling at GEORGE)* We could slam smack into a telephone pole.

GEORGE: Please, Mr Cady!

JAY: They'd have to wash you out of the glove compartment!

GEORGE: STOP IT!

(JAY turns back to road.)

JAY: Makes you think, don't it?

GEORGE: *Crazy. Everybody's crazy here.* *(Shouting, furious at JAY)* You people all spinning in quicksand! I still got a future!

JAY: Yeah? You gonna break the bank in Monte Carlo?

GEORGE: I got a chance to be Assistant Salad Chef at the Fontainbleu!

(JAY considers this a moment, then bursts into derisive laughter.)

GEORGE: You got a noive! You got no respect for people!

(JAY glances over.)

GEORGE: Somebody trying to bring hisself up, what's funny about that?

JAY: Nothing, George.

GEORGE: I been a busboy seven years, ever since I was twelve. Seven summers in Colorado, seven winters in Florida. I get out. I meet people. I got a good life and it's gonna get a whole lot better!

JAY: It struck me funny. Your job. Very few things strike me funny.

GEORGE: Only reason they won't make me a waiter is because I can't read.

JAY: You can't read?

GEORGE: That don't mean I'm stupid. I got a learning disability, that's all. *(Pause)* Besides, it don't matter in the kitchen, not if you keep your eyes and ears open. To hell with waiters! They should wear skirts! Starting this winter I'm in the Kitchen with the Maestro! That's if Mister Tony hasn't got tired of waiting for me and hired someone else. *(Considers that nightmare a moment)* Nah! He wouldn't do that. He tole me in Colorado, "George, I got good things in store for you." That's what he tole me, just two weeks ago. *(Flourishing his handcuffs)* Now look at me!

JAY: You saying you can cook?

GEORGE: Cook? Mister Cady, I got it in me to be a Master Chef. I'm saying I could be Number *One*! Me, George Antioch!

(He slumps back in his seat, awed by the splendor of his vision. JAY *drives in thoughtful silence; then:)*

JAY: You can cook, huh?

(Brief hold, then blackout. Lights up on Sheriff's office. MONICA *is present now and she listens intently along with* GUS *and* JILL *as* S J, *lost in ecstatic recall, booms out one of his visions.)*

S J: "Then I saw an angel standing in the sun, and with a loud voice he called to all the birds that fly in midheaven, 'Come, gather for the great supper of God, to eat the flesh of kings, the flesh of captains, the flesh of mighty men, the flesh of horses and their riders, and the flesh of *all* men, both free and slave, both small and great." *(Softer, more intimate)* "And I saw the Beast and the kings of the earth with their armies gathered to make war against him who sits upon the horse and against *his* army." *(He nods knowingly to his auditors, as if sharing a sordid joke, then stretches out on his cot and rests.)*

MONICA: Revelations?

*(*GUS *nods;* S J *looks over at* MONICA.*)*

S J: You know the Book?

MONICA: Parts of it.

S J: I *wrote* the Book. *(A self-deprecating gesture)* Parts of it.

GUS: John, if we may be serious for a moment? Get back to basics? I don't understand you when you say your last name. *(Handing him pen and paper)* Please write it out.

S J: *(Willingly but humbly)* I speak better than I write. *(Scrawls, hands it back)*

GUS: "Zebedee." Odd name, John. Where you from?

S J: Originally? Galilee.

GUS: Galilee. The one in Israel?

S J: There's another?

GUS: Where you living now, John? When you're not holed up in our church steeple?

S J: "I am like a vulture of the wilderness, like an owl of the waste places. I lie awake. I am like a lonely bird on the housetop."

(GUS *is rather moved, but he's also increasingly frustrated.*)

GUS: Brothers or sisters living?

S J: Long dead and forgiven.

GUS: Sons? Daughters?

S J: Dead, all dead.

GUS: You have no next of kin?

(S J *looks at* JILL *and smiles.*)

S J: Her. (*He laughs at her expression.*) "He came to his own home, and his own people received him not."

GUS: You're not being very responsive, John. I ask again: Who are you?

S J: And I tell you once more: "John, the brother of James, whom He called the Sons of Thunder." And who are you? And why should I care?

GUS: Because half this county would lynch you for a murderer if not for me. You understand? We think you killed a child.

S J: Abaddon killed that boy! Must I summon him forth to boast of the deed? And hearken well to this: He may strike again before I am gone. *That evil which falls not on me, falls randomly.*

MONICA: How old are you?

S J: (*Sizing her up, smiling*) "Behold, an Israelite indeed, in whom is no guile!" I am old, my daughter.

MONICA: If you're who you claim to be, you're nearly two thousand years old.

S J: (*Shrugs*) So be it.

(MONICA, GUS, *and* JILL *huddle away from* S J's *cell.*)

MONICA: *This creature thinks he's one of the Apostles. St. John the Evangelist, to be precise.*

GUS: *I was afraid that's what he was getting at.* (*Calling over*) Am I to understand that you are the author of the Gospel according to John?

S J: *(Nods solemnly, adding)* And the Book of Revelations.

GUS: That too? Well done. *(Back to MONICA)* *Now what?*

MONICA: *The man needs protection.*

JILL: *Could be he wandered away from the Crossroads.*

GUS: *The Rest Home. Yes, worth checking out.*

MONICA: *Jill, he called you his next of kin.*

JILL: *I never saw him in my life, not till he showed at the funeral.* *(Pause)* *But I *do* feel kin to him somehow.*

S J: *(Calling over, laughing)* "I know whence I have come and whither I am going, but you do not know whence I come or whither I go."

GUS: That about says it, John. And until you want to share your little secret with me, you're staying in this jail.

S J: *(Glancing round approvingly)* Clean, dry, and warm—an improvement upon my previous accommodations.

(Sound: the phone rings.)

JILL: Clanford County Sheriff's Office, Deputy Jill Cady speaking. *(She beams.)* Hi George, you O K?

(Lights up on GEORGE at a pay phone)

GEORGE: Yeah, I'm fine, listen—

JILL: *(To GUS)* *It's George, he's fine.*

GEORGE: You see my pack around there?

JILL: Yeah, it's still in Property.

GEORGE: Good. Bring it to your home.

JILL: You coming to my house? You're free?

GEORGE: Of course I'm free! This is America, ain't it?

JILL: What did you tell them?

GEORGE: Nothing. They got a confession half an hour before I showed. The kid's mother did it.

JILL: The boy's *mother*? That's horrible.

GEORGE: Well yeah, people go berserk, that's life.

JILL: But his *mother*!

GUS: What about her?

JILL: She's the killer. She confessed.

S J: She was no match for Abaddon, poor woman.

GEORGE: O K lissen, I gotta run. Don't forget my cassette recorder.

JILL: I won't.

GEORGE: Hey Jill, you know your father's crazy as a loon? See ya soon.

(Lights out on GEORGE as he hangs up.)

(JILL hangs up; All turn to stare at S J.)

S J: Does this mean I have to leave?

(GUS and MONICA seem perplexed. JILL breaks the freeze and crosses D L. Lights crossfade to JILL's room.)

JILL: The Pastor of the church declined to press charges and later that day, there being no grounds to hold him, Steeple Jack was released. Gus and Monica invited him to stay a while with them and he accepted.

(JILL, now in her room, presses a button on cassette recorder: sound of GEORGE's voice.)

GEORGE'S VOICE: Dear Ma. Here is some history of Kansas, as tole to me by my last ride. *He was older than Adam, so he must know.* Seventy million years ago this whole state was covered with water, and twenty foot long water dinosaurs used to swim over these fields. This old man had some bones, or so he said.

JILL: Tylosaurus fossils, B'ar, like in Lawrence.

GEORGE'S VOICE: I hear things like that, Ma, and I wanna *see* it, I wanna *be* there, I wanna be invisible and just float through time!

JILL: Yeah!

GEORGE'S VOICE: Ah, Ma! I love you so much! Please don't ever die!

(JILL punches the tape off and jumps away from it like it's a rattlesnake.)

JILL: Why'd he say that? He had no call to say that, B'ar! *(Shouting at tape)* You're a stupid boy! Of course your mother will die, and so will you, and so will I!

(Sound of a truck pulling up. JILL glances out her window.)

JILL: He's here! *(She begins a losing battle to regain her composure. She grabs a hand mirror and addresses it.)* I am Jill Cady. Everybody says I'm messed up because of my tragedy, but that's just on the outside where everybody can see. Inside, where I'm invisible, I am really a very together person. *(She stares at herself a moment longer, then screams:)* LIES!

(Enter GEORGE and JAY, who are trying to make a deal. JILL frantically tries to transform herself into an attractive young lady, resorting even to the Kleenex-in-the-bra ploy.)

JAY: At the rate you're going, how long before you hit Miami?

GEORGE: At *this* rate? Never!

JAY: I'll buy your bus ticket. You could be there in a day.

GEORGE: I like the bait. Where's the hook?

JAY: Cook for us three days. Make stuff my daughter can't keep from eating.

GEORGE: Three days, huh?

JAY: Hey Ji'Lady! I'm home and we got company! C'mon down!

JILL: *Oh my god, how did I get so ugly?*

GEORGE: You got a beautiful place here, Mr Cady.

JAY: Built it myself. C'mere and look at my kitchen. Gloria always insisted on the best from freezers to copper pans.

(If set can accommodate space for the suggestion of a kitchen far left, they cross to that spot. Otherwise they exit and their dialogue continues from offstage. JILL creeps from her room and silently stations herself next to the big reclining chair.)

GEORGE: *(O S)* Jeez, look at the counter space—and all that butcher block!

JAY: *(O S)* Deep fat fryer, eight-speed blender, crockpot, slo-cooker, wok—

GEORGE: *(O S)* And you don't know what to do with any of it, do you, Mr Cady?

JAY: *(O S)* A man's only got time to learn a few things in life, George, and cooking wasn't meant to be one of 'em.

GEORGE: *(O S)* Woman's work, huh?

JAY: *(O S)* The man kills it, the woman cooks it. Been that way since we were cavemen.

(JILL suddenly gets a terrified look and impulsively ducks out of sight behind the recliner. An instant later an angry GEORGE storms into the living room, grabbing for his Korea coat. JAY follows placatingly.)

JAY: Hey, you taking this personal?

GEORGE: Just tell me somepin: Where would you be without the chefs of this world? Huh? You'd still be up in a tree, sucking on a berry and dodging bird shit!

JAY: Will you calm down?

GEORGE: I'm calm, I'm calm!

JAY: Look, I'm not asking you to do this for me. It's strictly for my little girl. She's been totally whacked out since the accident, and I'm grasping at straws, ya understand?

(GEORGE *nods.*)

JAY: There's the phone. Why not call your boss and tell him you'll be there in four days? Hey Jill! Where in hell is she? (*Crosses to her landing, knocks at her "door"*) Jill? You sleeping? Or just hiding? (*He mimes opening her door, peers around, "shuts" it.*) When she ain't cooped up in here, she's hanging around the Sheriff's office. (*Crosses back to living room*) I got a strange little girl, George.

GEORGE: I like her fine.

JAY: Ya ever have an accident, George? Jill was my accident.

GEORGE: Uh. Mr Cady—

JAY: I was a Navy man. What a great time that was. Drunk three times a week and all the pussy I could handle.

GEORGE: If I'm gonna do this, I oughta call now.

JAY: It'll keep. Siddown, relax. I met her mother on leave when I was stationed in Newport News. You know the story: Two weeks of bliss, a lifetime of regret. (*Pontifical*) Keep it circulating, George. It's the key to a happy man.

GEORGE: Uh, what sort of things did Jill like to eat before she quit?

JAY: Same shit her mother ate. Anything you couldn't get at the A & P. Snails. Seafood. Pretentious innards. (*Pauses, then explodes*) God *damn* that woman and the life she left me!

(JILL *stands up from her hiding place and stares silently at* JAY. GEORGE *is startled, then appalled.* JAY *returns her stare, then:*)

JAY: The punishment for eavesdropping is to hear the truth.

JILL: I didn't hear nothing I didn't know.

JAY: Yeah, you think you know it all, don't you? Believe me, I've spared you the worst of me and your mother.

JILL: You turned her into an alcoholic.

JAY: Wise up, will you? She could drink me under the table from Day One.

GEORGE: I don't want nothing to do with any of this!

(JAY *hands* GEORGE *some money.*)

JAY: Go buy some groceries, George. Whatever strikes your fancy. (*To* JILL) Show him to the A & P.

(GEORGE *and* JILL *exit.* JAY *sits in his big chair. He stares unblinkingly. It is doom that he feels. Sound of truck starting up, pulling away. Lights dim to blackout. The sound of cruising truck is muted but continuous through the following scene.*)

Lights up on JILL *and* GEORGE *in cab of pick-up. She is thoughtful and withdrawn.* GEORGE *tries to cheer her up as he drives.)*

GEORGE: What's the name of this river?

JILL: Waukarusa.

GEORGE: Nice. An Indian name?

(She nods.)

GEORGE: You know what it means?

(She nods again.)

GEORGE: You gonna tell me or do I stop the truck and wait?

JILL: Once there was no water here. One day a spring burst forth, and there was water, and the waters rose. An Indian girl on horseback rode to the edge. She began to ford it. Her horse went in deeper and deeper, and she grew more and more alarmed. Suddenly her horse was swimming and the girl cried out "Wau-ka-ru-sa!"

(She glances at GEORGE.*)*

JILL: "Hip deep."

GEORGE: *(Laughing)* Hip deep!

JILL: That was the last thing anyone ever heard her say, and that became her name in their memories.

GEORGE: Wait a minute. She didn't make it? She *drowned*?

JILL: Swept away.

GEORGE: Nah! You got that part wrong. She made it to the other side, and all her friends laughed, and for the rest of her life they laughed and called her Waukarusa. See?

*(*JILL *laughs a bit.)*

GEORGE: Yeah! Why make things tough on yourself?

JILL: *(Flatly, staring out her window)* Life is harder for some.

*(*GEORGE *glances at her, then back to the road. Her perspective disturbs him.)*

GEORGE: Yeah. I seen that. *(Brief silence)* But I never seen *nobody* trouble *free*. Some people just handle it better than others.

JILL: *(Still muted, flat)* That, too. *(Glancing at* GEORGE*)* Don't you have any other clothes?

GEORGE: Hey, if I had 'em, wouldn't I be wearing 'em? They all went down in the Big Thompson. Everything I owned packed into my Ford. Last night of the season. Big party down in the Canyon. And where am I? Waxing the damn dining room floors. And why me? Because I'm trying to impress Mr

Tony so he'll get me the chef's job in Florida. Three in the morning before I'm driving through the Gorge, looking for all the drunken waitresses before the party breaks up when here comes this jerk waiter named Harvey in his '59 Chevy, brights on, barreling around the curves on this narrow damn dirt road, and me, I'm looking down into the Big Thompson on my right and I'm yelling "Jesus, Jesus, pull up against the mountain, get *over*, Harvey!" But he don't. Can you believe it? He *don't*! And the next thing you know, it's *Wau-ka-roo-saaa*!

(JILL *laughs, and* GEORGE *is delighted to hear it; he laughs, too.*)

GEORGE: Swept away! Everything I owned! Wau-ka-*rooo*-saaaa! I almost drowned! (*His laughter tapers off as the horror of the moment comes back.*) I almost drowned. Me, George Antioch. (*Turns to her, almost whispers*) But I didn't. I'm still alive. (*Shouts at her*) AND SO ARE YOU!

(JILL *is startled;* GEORGE *laughs.*)

GEORGE: Scared ya, huh?

JILL: You? Scare *me*?

(JILL *laughs at the thought.* GEORGE *grabs the C B mike and transmits.*)

GEORGE: Matterhorn, Matterhorn, are you receiving?

(*Lights up dim on* JAY *in same position as when last observed. He does not seem aware of the transmission.*)

JILL: Are you sending? Are you really sending?

GEORGE: This is the Magic Chef shaking and bakin southbound clear to *Mi-a-MEE*! Got the Thin Lady ridin shotgun. Gonna fatten her up. Catch you on the re-bop, Matterhorn, over.

(*He replaces mike, smiles at* JILL, *who stares aghast. Lights out on* JAY.)

JILL: You were sending to Daddy! You idiot! (*Slaps at his arm*)

GEORGE: Whazzamatta wit you? Ya wanna get us killed?

JILL: You're a stupid boy!

GEORGE: Don't say that.

JILL: What's that sign say?

(GEORGE *looks trapped.*)

JILL: Just what I figured from hearing those tapes to your mother. You don't know how to read, and you don't know how to write.

GEORGE: Yeah? Well *you* don't even know how to *eat*! Now how dumb is that? Huh? Even new-born babies know how to *eat*!

JILL: Just shut up! Why don't you just shut up?

(Silence. GEORGE *drives on, resentful. When* JILL *next speaks, her voice is squeezed, strained.)*

JILL: That's what I want to be when I grow up.

GEORGE: *(Still a bit angry)* What?

JILL: A new-born baby. *(Smiling slightly)* Start me out again with a different seed in my mother's egg.

GEORGE: Don't talk dumb.

JILL: Wouldn't it be neat if we all had a Re-set Button? Like a pinball machine or a computer? Go along three, four years, see how things are going—*you can tell by then*—you don't like what you see, PING! You hit your Re-set Button and start all over.

(She smiles to herself as GEORGE *glances over curiously.)*

JILL: I read this science fiction story once. This man falls through a hole in time. He finds himself laying on a sandy beach. He looks around. Nothing. He can't orient himself. He spots a jellyfish washed up. Good, he thinks, I'm up to at least the Paleozoic Era. He walks down the beach. Suddenly a giant pterodactyl swoops down at him. The guy is thrilled. "Aha!" he cries. "I'm in Cretaceous times!"

*(*JILL *stops the story as if it had ended;* GEORGE *glances over impatiently.)*

GEORGE: *So*? Did this terrordackle get him?

JILL: No.

GEORGE: Good! *I thought this was gonna be another Waukarusa.*

JILL: At the last second a twenty foot tylosaurus breaks the water—

GEORGE: I heard of them!

JILL: Leaps like a salmon fifty feet into the sky, and Snap! grabs the pterodactyl by the throat, and they both fall back into the ocean.

GEORGE: Wow!

JILL: Disappear without a trace, like they never happened! In a flash the time traveller is spared and left all alone again.

GEORGE: I had this ride had *bones* of them water dinosaurs, but he didn't show me, so I dunno...

JILL: So after a while the guy falls forward into time, but you know what? Everything changed! He stepped on a clam back on that seventy million year-old beach, *and all the rest of history changed*!

GEORGE: *(Thinks for a while, then:)* I don't get it.

JILL: It's all linked! Because he stepped on the clam, Hitler gets the A-bomb first, drops it on London, and the Nazis win the War!

GEORGE: This is too deep for me. About hip deep. *(He laughs; she doesn't.)* Wau-ka-*ru*-saaa.

JILL: It's all out of our hands. Pure chance. A woman goes berserk in Cherokee County and you end up driving me to the A & P. Jay Cady stops to change a flat tire for Gloria Amberson and I am born. People think they see connections and it makes 'em feel they can out-guess life. But they're *wrong*. The number of permutations is terrifying.

(GEORGE *is staring at her blankly. She realizes she makes no sense to him. She sighs and stares ahead.*)

JILL: Do you think we have anything in common?

GEORGE: Well...

JILL: It doesn't matter.

GEORGE: You lose me sometimes. I'm not unhappy. Unhappy people confuse me.

(JILL *looks at him, looks forward again, covers her face, and sobs.*)

GEORGE: Like this. I don't get this. Have I hurt your feelings? I don't have brothers or sisters. The saddest thing that ever happened to me was losing my father. Nothing else comes close. Maybe if I thought about that for a while I could get on your wavelength.

JILL: Oh stop it! Stop it, shut up! Turn right at this block and shut up. I don't even know why I'm talking to you.

GEORGE: Cause we're in a vehicle.

JILL: What?

GEORGE: Truck, car...only place people feel free to talk personal any more. There's the A & P. Wait'll you see what I'm gonna create out of the junk in this place.

JILL: *(Composing herself)* Are you really going to be our cook?

GEORGE: Yeah. Less you got some opinion on it.

JILL: Why should I care? I don't eat.

GEORGE: *(Smiles slyly)* The Ultimate Challenge.

(*Sound of pick-up pulling to a stop.* GEORGE *mimes opening his door.*)

GEORGE: You coming with me, or not?

(JILL *shakes her head no.*)

GEORGE: C'mon...

JILL: I'm afraid I'd see somebody I know.

GEORGE: What, they got a warrant out for ya?

JILL: I'll wait.

(She waves him off and GEORGE *exits. A light sequence: spot narrows and intensifies around* JILL *and begins to come up again around* JAY, *who is still in the same position in his chair. At this moment, at least in their posture, father and daughter look much alike.)*

JILL: If we could start over even once, it would all be totally different. But we can't. We're locked in time. *(Pause)* That's what I should have said.

(Lights up to half on JAY, *who continues to sit like a statue. Sound:* JAY's *T V crackles with inter-channel static, then dies away. Lights dim out on* JAY, *and then on* JILL. *Blackout)*

END OF ACT ONE

ACT TWO
The Birthday Party

(Spot picks out S J sitting formally, somewhat stiffly, as if for his portrait. He has been cleaned up and looks striking: dignified and intense, vigilant but calm. His "emblem" is safely back in place, slung over his shoulder in its plastic bag. Light spill from S J reveals GUS *and* MONICA: *They sit, curious and silent, drinking aperitifs and observing* S J.)

(In the far left kitchen area a spot on GEORGE, *assiduously hand-whipping some frosting.* JAY *lounges nearby, drink in hand, watching* GEORGE *at work. Spot isolates* JILL *D S C, staring at all the other characters. After a moment, she turns and speaks to the audience.)*

JILL: So George finds out I turn fifteen tomorrow. "Fabulous!" he hollers. "Your party will start on the stroke of midnight! Call all your friends!" and starts baking this cake from scratch. *(She sighs.)* I wasn't in a party mood. Actually, I was borderline suicidal. And the only friends I had left were my father's sworn and mortal enemies, Gus and Monica. Who didn't want to come anyway. *(Pause)* Of such ingredients are disasters made. But George—well, George—

(GEORGE *bursts into song as he bakes: "Born Too Late" by the Ponytails, 1958.)*

GEORGE: "Born too late/to win your heart/to you/I'm just/a kid/who you won't *daaate*/Why was I born too late?" Hey Jill! C'mere! *(He shoves a bowl and spoon at her.)* This'll make your teeth fall out!

JILL: What is it?

GEORGE: What's it look like? Lickins! Left-over frosting from the carrot cake. You can't hedge your bets with frosting—either forget about it, or *glop it on thick*! You like?

JILL: Not bad, George. *(She cleans off the spoon.)*

GEORGE: I use a cream cheese base. Let me tell you somepin: If the Russians had enough cream cheese, they'd be a lot easier to live with. *Save some of that frosting for your father.*

JAY: No no, finish it.

GEORGE: C'mon, take a taste. *Give him a taste.*

(JAY *and* JILL *momentarily freeze; then* JILL *offers the spoon,* JAY *accepts, and they get past the moment.)*

JAY: Too rich for me.

GEORGE: *(Mildly disappointed)* Yeah? Well, that's the thing about cooking—everybody's got a different set of taste buds. *(To* JILL*)* How many we got coming so far?

JILL: So far? Um, nobody.

GEORGE: What? You don't have no...uh...hmm. Gus! Call Gus. You like him, right? And he treated me decent. Give him a call.

(JILL *glances apprehensively at* JAY, *who is staring icily at* GEORGE.)

GEORGE: Oh, it's like that, huh? The thing is, Mr Cady, this cake needs an audience, ya unnerstan what I'm saying? And Jill could sure use a party.

JILL: It would be O K, wouldn't it, Daddy? If we all tried hard?

JAY: All right. As long as I don't have to be polite to them.

GEORGE: That's the spirit!

(JILL *smiles and runs to her room to phone* MONICA. *Lights dim on* JAY *and* GEORGE. *Lights to full on* GUS, S J, *and* MONICA. S J *jumps up from chair.*)

S J: This is not where I am called!

MONICA: Siddown, take a load off.

S J: You are petty disbelievers, confirmed in your ignorance.

MONICA: "Petty"? I think of myself as rather *Grand*.

GUS: "In the Beginning was the Word...."

S J: "...and the Word was with God, and the Word was God."

GUS: You wrote that?

(S J *nods "Yes."*)

GUS: Inspired.

S J: Yes, of course. It all was.

MONICA: You impress me, John, I admit it. You got total instant recall of the entire Bible.

S J: No, no. Barely half.

MONICA: O K, all the good parts. But it *does* tend to dominate your conversation.

GUS: Whadaya expect? He's an Evangelist.

MONICA: I wanna get to know the *real you*, John, assuming that exists. Like, what's your secret for living two thousand years?

S J: I ate the bread at the Last Supper.

GUS: That'll do it.

S J: He warned us. "If anyone eats of this bread, he will live forever."

(GUS *refers to a Bible.*)

S J: I assumed He was speaking metaphorically.

GUS: "The saying spread abroad among the brethren that *this* disciple was not to die."

S J: "Yet the Lord did not say to him that he was not to die, but 'If it is my will that he remain until I come, what is that to you?'"

MONICA: So when He comes, you die?

S J: He is saving me for Armageddon, when I will die alongside every other living creature. This is to fulfill the Scripture: "The Beast was allowed to make war on the Saints and to conquer them."

GUS: Essentially, then, that makes you Beast Bait.

S J: *(Sadly)* Essentially.

MONICA: How much longer do we have?

S J: Before the Final Wrath? It should come any day now.

GUS: You don't sound terribly distraught over that prospect.

S J: *(Shrugging)* "Men have shed the blood of saints and prophets, and thou hast given them blood to drink. It is their due!"

MONICA: Nice guy.

S J: Get it over with. That's the only prayer I have left. I am sick of the struggle. I long for my final reward.

GUS: Which is?

S J: Death. Transfiguration. The New Jerusalem.

(*Sound: The phone rings, and* MONICA *answers it.*)

JILL: Monica—

MONICA: Hi Toots!

GUS: More wine?

(S J *nods, hands him his glass.*)

JILL: I'm having a birthday party!

MONICA: Tomorrow, right?

JILL: No. Tonight! Midnight at my house! Can you and Gus come?

GUS: What is it, luv?

MONICA: *Birthday party for Jill. Tonight, her place.*

GUS: At Cady's? She must be crazy.

MONICA: Honey, I wish you'd told us sooner—

JILL: It's a surprise party! I mean, we just decided, and George baked this beautiful carrot cake—

MONICA: Who's George?

GUS: The busboy's over there?

JILL: He's our cook, just hired. You gotta meet him, Monica. He's so...*chipper*. *(Laughing)* He's the chippest of them all!

MONICA: Does Jay know you're calling us?

JILL: Yes! He's in a great mood since George showed up. He wants to make it up to you, Monica.

GUS: Tell her to have it over here!

MONICA: You know we've got a house guest?

JILL: Bring him.

GUS: I'm not setting foot under the roof of that neolithic loser!

JILL: Monica, if you don't come, who else will?

MONICA: Not to worry, Jilly Pill. We'll be there with bells on.

JILL: Oh, Monica, thank you! I love you! Bye! *(She hangs up.)*

GUS: You're breaking up my evening with Saint John the Evangelist to subject me to Jay Cady?

MONICA: *(Softly)* I love you, too, Jill. *(She hangs up.)*

GUS: Well, *this* should be the gala of the season!

MONICA: Gus, it's the poor kid's birthday.

GUS: I don't care if it's her funeral!

MONICA: Watch your mouth!

GUS: Retract, retract...

MONICA: Tough it out for an hour, will ya? Honest to Pete! One would think you were afraid of Jay Cady.

GUS: Would one? And would one not also think that one had been knocked around enough by that lethal fool, at least for this week?

S J: If you don't mind, I'll turn in now.

MONICA: Not so fast, your Saintliness. We're going to a party. *(A wink and a leer)* Didja bring yer dancin' shoes?

(Blackout. Sound: a clock chimes twelve times, during which JILL walks into a spot.)

JILL: So that's how these people came to be at my birthday party. *(Pause)* When someone behaves badly, it doesn't necessarily mean that's a bad person. Does it? Some of these things...still embarrass me.

(Sound: doorbell ringing. Sound: Paul McCartney's World Without Love *recorded by Peter & Gordon in 1964. Some of the more salient lyrics: "Please lock me away.../I don't care what they say/I can't stay in a world without love." Lights up on* CADY *living room and the guests:* MONICA, GUS, *and* S J. MONICA *greets* JILL *effusively, handing her a little birthday package.)*

MONICA: Hi Toots! Happy Birthday!

(GEORGE is delighted to see GUS again and seems immediately captivated by MONICA.)

GEORGE: Heeey, look who's here! How ya doon, Gus? Who's your date?

MONICA: Monica's the name. And you must be Chef Boy-Ar-Dee.

GUS: George Antioch from Miami.

GEORGE: Ya ever been to the Big Orange?

(MONICA smiles, nods.)

GEORGE: If you could lose the Jailer here, I could show you some good times down there.

(GEORGE notices S J, who is like a dignified animal—always more aware of the periphery of events than of their center. At times he unobtrusively sniffs the air.)

GEORGE: *Don't look now, but I think something followed you in off the street.*

(JAY saunters in; GUS indicates S J.)

GUS: Our guest for the evening. His name is John.

JAY: Your friend drink?

GUS: He likes wine.

JILL: Uh, excuse me...we made some punch.

JAY: Yeah, an she wouldn't let me spike it.

(The others dutifully allow JILL to pour them punch all around, but as soon as decently possible, GUS, JAY, and MONICA begin depleting the bar.)

JAY: He looks a whole lot cleaner than the last time I saw him.

JILL: *Daddy!*

GEORGE: *(Confidentially to MONICA)* *Lemme tell you somepin about these tramps: Even when you clean 'em up, they're still stinkers.*

MONICA: *Careful, he's got ears like a bat.*

GEORGE: *Never mind. Count your silver before he goes.*

(GEORGE *exits to kitchen. Sound:* World Without Love *fades out.*)

JAY: Whadaya say, Preacher? You like the looks of the place?

(S J *takes note of* JAY *for first time.*)

S J: "For you say, I am rich, I have prospered, and I need nothing; not knowing that you are wretched, pitiable, poor, blind, and naked."

(*This brings the conversation to a momentary lull until* JAY *smiles at* MONICA.)

JAY: He don't beat around the bush, do he?

MONICA: You get used to it.

(S J *becomes aware of* JILL, *approaches, and holds her at arm's length while he stares at her. She returns it.* JAY *indicates some concern, but* MONICA *motions not to worry.*)

S J: "My heart is smitten like grass, and withered; I forget to eat my bread." (*He embraces her.*) "Because of my loud groaning my bones cleave to my flesh." (*He glares at the others.*) "Who provides for the raven its prey, when its young ones cry to God and wander about for lack of food?"

(*A pause, then* JAY *pours a drink.*)

JAY: What's he got in that bag?

MONICA: He calls it his emblem.

S J: Emblem? What about it?

GUS: It's all right, John. No one's going to touch it. We just wondered if you could *describe* your emblem.

S J: An eagle, soaring!

JAY: What *is* all this bullshit? What the fuck's an emblem?

S J: "He loved to curse—let curses come on him! He did not like blessing—may it be far from him!" (*More softly*) Remember this when we part.

(JAY's *clearly disturbed by* S J; *he takes his seat in his recliner.* GEORGE *re-enters bearing several trays of silver and dishes and arranges them on coffee table.*)

MONICA: (*To* JAY) Many saints have emblems—objects identified with them.

GUS: Like calling cards.

GEORGE: It's his handle—like Matterhorn!

(JAY *glares at him;* GEORGE *smiles, winks at* MONICA, *and exits.*)

JAY: Are you telling me this flea-bitten lunatic is a *saint*?

JILL: Daddy, *please*?

MONICA: He's an Apostle.

GUS: John the Evangelist, author of the fourth Gospel and the Book of Revelations.

(JAY *considers this and bursts out laughing, scandalizing* JILL.)

JAY: John-Boy, they got a padded room full of you guys up in Topeka.

JILL: Daddy, he's my *guest*, don't you understand?

JAY: Don't you correct me, Ji'Lady, ya hear? *(Back to* S J*)* Tell me, Preacher, you find any bats up in your belfry? *(He laughs.)* I saw you trying to escape. *(To* GUS*)* Seen him right out my bathroom window while I was shaving, seen him going right over the top of that steeple. *(To* MONICA*)* Thought he was a workman till I didn't notice any tools. *(Back to* S J*)* I coulda picked you off without even using my sniperscope.

JILL: Stop being so mean!

JAY: I won't have disrespect! Not in front of people, and not alone!

(JILL *turns away, very upset.*)

JAY: What is he to you anyway? Bible-beating wino transient, hugging you and mooning into your eyes—what the hell is going on here?

JILL: I don't know! *(Pause, then more quietly)* He reminds me of someone.

MONICA: Who, Jill?

JILL: My mother.

JAY: *HIM*? *(He snorts derisively.)*

JILL: When he gets down and peers into my face! And when he hugs me.

JAY: *Everything* reminds you of your mother!

(JILL *flinches, then whispers.*)

JILL: Yes.

JAY: Well you better work on forgettin her or you're gonna be weak and puny your whole life!

(JILL *covers her eyes and stands there, humiliated.*)

MONICA: You hopeless bastard.

(MONICA *puts an arm around* JILL.)

JAY: Jill, I didn't mean that, I—

JILL: *(Whirling on him)* DID TOO!

(*Enter* GEORGE *with a large cake aflame with fifteen candles.*)

GEORGE: Happy Birthday to you, happy birthday to you—everybody! Happy *Birth*day, dear... Jill? *(Glancing around the silent, tension-filled room)* Happy birthday to you. *(He sets the cake down and asks timidly:)* Don't you wanna blow the candles out, Jill?

JILL: Blow em out yourself!

JAY: *(Walking off D L)* Jill, may I please speak with you?

(After some hesitation, she joins him.)

JAY: *I truly did not mean to hurt you. I...try to say things to help, and they come out hurt. I want to turn this around, Jill. That's what this cake is all about. I know you ain't gonna start liking me right away. But maybe, some time down the road, we can look back on tonight as when it—began to get better.*

(Silence; after a while, she nods.)

JAY: George, cut this young lady a piece of that cake.

GEORGE: Yes sir, coming up!

JILL: Wait! *(She crosses over to cake, closes her eyes in a silent wish, and blows out the candles.)*

GEORGE: Attagirl!

(Applause all around as GEORGE cuts a slice for her. When he hands it to her, she blanches. Everyone waits for her to eat. After a brief struggle, she puts the cake back on the table.)

JILL: I'm sorry. *(She runs off to her bedroom.)*

MONICA: Jill!

JILL: I'm sick!

JAY: So am I, Jill! Sick of putting up with this neurotic bullshit!

(MONICA tries to join JILL.)

JAY: Don't go up there, Monica! Ya hear me? I want you to just leave her be.

(MONICA reluctantly accedes.)

JAY: She wants to reject me, let her learn the price of rejection: Solitude.

GEORGE: *(After brief silence)* Mr Cady?

JAY: And *you*! What kind of cook are you, she won't even touch a *cake*?

GEORGE: Maybe she just don't wanna eat in public? Some people don't. Lemme take her up a slice.

JAY: *(For JILL's benefit: loud)* Jill can come down here and eat that cake any time she wants to be *civil*! *(To GEORGE)* *You think she's eating behind my back?*

(GEORGE *shakes no.*)

JAY: Then I'm whipped.

(*He slumps into his recliner and stares;* GEORGE *slips off with cake for* JILL.)

GUS: Well Jay, I want to thank you for another scintillating evening.

(*On* JILL's *level,* GEORGE *discovers her eavesdropping and hisses:*)

GEORGE: *Don't you never learn?*

(*He tries to usher her back inside her room, but she vigorously refuses.*)

MONICA: Any man who banishes his kid from her own party—

JAY: You make overtures, you get rebuffed! So fuck her.

MONICA: Filthy mouth!

JAY: Hypocrite!

MONICA: You treat her like shit!

JAY: *I* decide how she's raised, Monica, not you! Of all people in this world, *especially* not you!

MONICA: Jill! If you're up there snooping, get into your bedroom and go to sleep! Happy Birthday and Good Night!

GEORGE: *C'mon, will ya? Ya never know what these people will say.*

(JILL *now permits* GEORGE *to escort her behind the "closed door" of her room.* S J *has grown increasingly vigilant, moving warily on the stage's periphery. He senses his ancient foe; he unties his emblem, holding it before him as a buckler.*)

S J: He is loose.

MONICA: Honest to God, Jay, *you're* one who ought to be sent to his room.

JAY: Lead the way, Monica. Any time.

(*A brief pause.* MONICA *stares easily at* JAY. GUS *is unflappable.*)

GUS: Sounds like a pretty cut and dried proposition to me. Find out what's in it for you.

(MONICA *smiles and nods slowly at* JAY *by way of confirmation, not assent.*)

MONICA: You'd love that, wouldn't you?

JAY: I doubt it. But *you* sure as hell would never forget it. *Or* regret it.

GUS: Jay, how can someone as predictable as you continue to amaze me?

JAY: Aren't you sick of this bloodless wimp by now, Monica?

MONICA: If I leave Gus, it won't be for some paunchy, middle-aged hick.

JAY: Well...I'd say this party was about over. *(He tries to show* S J *the door.)* C'mon Pops, out you go.

(To JAY's *astonishment,* S J *recoils from him in obvious loathing.)*

JAY: Can you believe this? This *derelict* thinks he's too good for me to touch him.

S J: "You are of your father the Devil and your will is to do your father's desires. He was a murderer from the beginning."

JAY: This garbage has been on my case since he walked through my door. *(To* GUS*)* You bring him round just to antagonize me?

GUS: Jay, *life* antagonizes you.

JAY: You're right! I got this rage in me! I can't get rid of it! *(None seems more startled by this outburst than* JAY, *who refills his drink.)*

MONICA: Well, no one's throwing me out till I get a piece of cake.

GUS: Yes, that might partially redeem this ordeal.

(She cuts a couple pieces and brings one to GUS. *In* JILL's *room* GEORGE *also produces a piece of cake wrapped in a napkin.)*

GEORGE: I brought ya somethin.

*(*JILL *is touched. She carefully places the cake, unsampled, on her bedstand, turns to him, says:)*

JILL: Thank you, George.

(...and gives him a kiss. GEORGE *is, in quick succession, startled, pleased, then apprehensive. When she hears* S J *speaking below,* JILL *creeps back to her listening post, despite* GEORGE's *silent efforts to dissuade her.)*

S J: Come, Abaddon. Are you shy around so long acquaintance? *(To* GUS*)* Do ya smell him? Rotting flesh. Is that *your* emblem, Abaddon? A ripe carcass? *(To* MONICA*)* Wherever I am, he finds me. Then he tries to hide, to sneak up on me. *(Chuckles)* As if the scent of corruption could be perfumed over.

JAY: Is this guy under control?

GUS: Compared to me, or you?

JAY: Hey! Old man! Who you talking to?

S J: Your Father! Abaddon the Destroyer. He finds this house congenial. He waits. He watches. He knows how it all ends, just as I do. "And when they have finished their testimony, the Beast that ascends from the Bottomless Pit will make war upon the Saints and conquer them and *kill* them." Will this be the time, Abaddon?

*(*JAY *looks wonderingly about him, including up toward* JILL's *room.)*

JAY: I look at my house. I've been invaded.

MONICA: You're aware Jill's alone in her bedroom with your cook?

(JAY *waves her off with a "Don't bother me" gesture.*)

MONICA: You're a prize. *(To* GUS*)* What's the kid's name?

GUS: George.

MONICA: Hey George! Tuck her into bed and get on down here!

GEORGE: Listen to her. She can't stand to have me out of her sight.

JILL: You're crazy. *(Calling down)* It's O K, Monica.

MONICA: Says you? *(To* GUS*)* Modern Times.

GEORGE: I don't understand it. Older women just go crazy for me.

JILL: You are so con*ceit*ed!

GEORGE: You know how many times I got propositioned bussing tables last summer?

JILL: No, and I don't want to! What are you doing in my room anyway? No one comes in here. Get out.

GEORGE: Monica says I gotta tuck you into bed.

JILL: You touch me, I'll bite your ear off.

GEORGE: Yeah, be the first good meal you had in a month.

(She hits him with B'ar.)

GEORGE: Hey, you're messing up my cake!

JILL: It's yuck! The cake is yuck and so are you!

GEORGE: I'm yuck, huh? O K. Starve. *(He gets up to leave.)*

JILL: I'm sorry.

GEORGE: No you're not. You're always calling me names. "Stupid yuck." That's not sorry, that's an *observation*.

JILL: You're right. You're so good to me, and I can't even remember how to be nice. It's because I always ache. It makes me ugly.

(GEORGE *sits on the bed with his arm around her. Again he offers her cake and again she refuses, covering her face and sobbing quietly.*)

GUS: John, are we still in imminent peril?

S J: What, from the Fiend? From the Great Coward? *(Laughs, contemptuously dismisses him)* He is like an aging lion on the edge of the herd, stalking only the weak and the injured. None else need fear him.

JAY: Listen, you're what you claim, you got to have powers, right?

S J: Am I to be put to the test again?

JAY: You make claims, you got to back them up. So levitate.

S J: Levitate?

JAY: Yeah, way up high in the middle of the air.

S J: I'm too old for that nonsense.

JAY: O K, Dealer's Choice. Do your specialty. I want a miracle. Now. *(To* GUS*)* *That's the end of that game.*

S J: *(To* MONICA*)* Always with the peasants it comes down to the cheap stunt.

JAY: *(To* MONICA*)* Did I just get called a "peasant"? *(To* S J*)* C'mon, c'mon, you phony bastard. Do something! Speak in tongues!

S J: Ah, the Gift of Tongues. Yes, I was once blessed with the Tongue of Fire. But these days, whatever the language, I hardly understand a word spoken to me. *(Shakes his head sadly)* My gifts have withered away, one by one. It is all I can do now to haul my bones on to the Final Carnage.

JAY: Preacher, you're not showing me much. How bout fortune telling? Can you at least read the future?

S J: Why do you think I'm so miserable?

JAY: So tell me: When am I going to die?

S J: Not as soon as you'd like.

JAY: What's *that* crack 'sposed to mean?

S J: It means you are a man without love, infested with regret, longing for surcease. A man not unlike myself.

*(*JAY *is stunned by this analysis.)*

GUS: He's got *you* down, Jay.

JAY: *(To* GUS *and* MONICA*)* You people can find more goddam ways to infuriate me....

(In JILL's *room* GEORGE *tries once again to entice* JILL *with the cake.)*

GEORGE: Jill, I worked four hours on this, just for you.

(She looks at it.)

GEORGE: Please: Eat this cake.

*(*S J *turns sharply at these words, looking up toward Jill's room. After a moment, she accepts a bite; then takes the rest of the piece and feeds herself.* GEORGE *beams.)*

GEORGE: Good?

(She smiles and nods. Downstairs S J *is recalling the getting of his gifts.)*

S J: That's what the angel said to *me*: "'Take it and eat.' And when I had eaten the cake, my stomach was made bitter, and I was told, 'You must again prophesy about many peoples and nations and tongues and kings.'"

GUS: Tell us how the world ends.

S J: You wish me to perform my Apocalypse? The locusts and the scorpions and the stars falling from the sky? *(Suddenly resonant and powerful)* "Alas! alas! thou great city, thou mighty city, Babylon! In one hour has thy judgment come!" *(Back to "normal" voice)* That one? *(With true loss)* "Fallen, fallen is Babylon the great! It has become a dwelling place of demons, a haunt of every foul spirit, a roost for every filthy and hateful bird." *(Mildly sarcastic)* You like it? How much should I do, the whole nine yards? I plagiarized it, you know. Much of it. For a while *everybody* was doing Apocalypses. Oh, perhaps here and there I may have turned a phrase more gracefully than they: "And in those days men will seek death and will not find it. They will long to die, and death will fly from them." *(With quiet pride)* That was mine.

MONICA: Terrifying. Lovely.

S J: *(Smiling)* It's all a bit dated now, though, isn't it? Since Hiroshima? *You* know how the world ends. *Everybody* does. *(Laughing)* For nearly two millennia I thought they were stars falling from the sky. *(Chuckling ruefully)* The limits of language.

(Silence. JAY *fills his glass.)*

GUS: There's no way out? A sudden burst of wisdom in a great leader?

S J: *(Smiling)* Who can put the genie back in the jar? *(Laughs)* D'ya hear him? Abaddon is laughing.

JAY: *(After a silence)* Preacher, you're downright morbid.

S J: *(With great simplicity)* And you are damned.

JAY: *(Almost sneering)* I can live with it.

MONICA: Jill can't.

*(*JAY *glares at her.)*

MONICA: Will you please let her come down?

JAY: She's doing what she wants, Monica—I don't enter into it.

MONICA: Tell her it's O K.

JAY: *You* tell her. Maybe she'll believe you.

MONICA: Jilly Pill! Come on down and open your present! It's O K!

JILL: No it's not!

(JAY *gives Monica an "I told you so" shrug.* MONICA *gets up and starts for* JILL's *room.*)

JAY: You got gall to spare, Monica, telling me how to raise my kid. Instructing me on my shortcomings. You think I don't know about *your* daughter?

(MONICA *freezes.*)

JAY: You messed her up so bad she's in a *nuthouse!*

MONICA: *(Hurt, to* GUS*)* You *told* him?

GUS: Of course not.

MONICA: *(To* JAY*) Gloria*?

JAY: Never tell a secret to a boozer, Monica. Especially if she's married.

(MONICA, *moving as if wounded, completes her cross to* JILL's *room. She screams at* GEORGE.)

MONICA: GET OUT!

(GEORGE *does so with alacrity, awkwardly joining* GUS *and* JAY.)

MONICA: Why are people so *disgusting*?

(JILL *moves to comfort her.*)

GUS: Actually, it's a very *nice* nuthouse. I've decided the problem was genetic—on my side, of course. *(With some pride)* I can trace the madness in my family back to King Ethelred the Unready.

JAY: *(To* GEORGE*)* You got this? Here's this absolute *failure* of a father— and probably of a husband, too—coming in under *my* roof—which I built with my own hands—

GUS: Oh please don't run that number by again, Jay. You act like this house was your first and last erection.

GEORGE: Uh, Mr Cady. This ain't what I had in mind.

JAY: You'd rather be out in the road, freezing your butt off?

GEORGE: Yes.

JAY: My coat pocket! Take what you need and split.

(As GEORGE *exits S R)*

JAY: You were a dumb idea anyway! *(Noticing* S J*)* Why don't you take this bozo with you?

S J: *(Smiling)* "They are a rebellious house, yet they will know there has been a prophet among them."

JAY: Shut up! Just shut the fuck up, will ya?

(GUS *sips a drink;* JAY *pours another. They are both drunk.* GUS, *always composed, is now practically anesthetized.* JAY *is becoming dangerous. In* JILL's *room* MONICA *composes herself somewhat.*)

MONICA: Open the present.

(JILL *opens the package and finds a wristwatch. She wants to be grateful, but* MONICA's *tension affects her, too.*)

JILL: Thank you, Monica.

MONICA: I couldn't find quite what I was looking for. The selection is so limited out here.

JILL: Yes.

MONICA: *(Floundering a bit)* I wanted more elegance, yet nothing that would accentuate the boniness of your wrist.

(JILL *looks down and away.*)

MONICA: Oh. I've hurt you? You bruise so easily.

(*She hugs* JILL.)

JILL: Monica?

MONICA: Yes?

JILL: Monica, I'm dying here. I don't want to. Help me.

MONICA: Baby, what can I do?

JILL: Adopt me.

MONICA: *Oh God.* *(Pulling away)* No, I cannot adopt you. Not now. Not ever.

JILL: Then I'm dead.

MONICA: Jill, you're dramatizing again. I've told you, don't dramatize.

(JILL *gets teary and* MONICA *holds her. Downstairs* GEORGE *cautiously reenters and tries to cross unobtrusively up to* JILL's *nook. He's wearing his Korea jacket and is ready to leave.*)

JAY: You still hanging around?

GEORGE: Wanna say Bye to Jill.

JAY: While you're up there, tell that *lesbian slut* to keep her hands off my daughter!

(*This is meant to be heard upstairs, and is.* MONICA *springs away from* JILL, *then holds her head.*)

MONICA: Oh that filthy, filthy man.

GUS: Jay, if you insult my wife one more time, I'm gonna cut your balls off and put you in the choir.

JAY: You should know about balls off.

GUS: I always heard you widow men get pussy on the brain. You want her that bad? Ask her nice. Maybe you'll catch her in a good mood. *(Pause)* Then again, maybe she'll take her cigarette holder and poke your eyes out.

(Upstairs GEORGE tentatively peers into JILL's room only to have MONICA snarl:)

MONICA: BEAT IT!

(GEORGE quickly backs off, standing trapped and uneasy outside her room.)

JAY: There are nights I sit in this chair and just dream of ways to make you squeal.

GUS: That's because you're sick, Jay. You need help.

JAY: I didn't need any before *you* came. You and Monica. I can trace all my problems directly to you.

GUS: How convenient.

JAY: We were hacking it before you showed up, Gloria and me. Then you two start dropping all these *names* and *places,* and suddenly my girls are unhappy. My wife starts drawlin like she's back in Virginia, runnin on about her *Tide*water days, how *back*-wahd we all are.

GUS: How ya gonna keep em down on the farm?

JAY: She belonged here, but you don't! And you never will, no matter how you cozy up the Sheriff and the powers that be. You know why? Because you weren't *born* here, didn't go to school here, never hunted in these fields or fought off the weather. And on top of all that, Gus... you talk funny. Truth is, most men I know think you're a faggot.

GUS: Monica! Come on down here so I can fuck you for Jay!

MONICA: *Shut up, Gus!* *My God, my God.*

JAY: Ya hear me, Monica? My wife didn't hate me till she met you!

GUS: Why give Monica all the credit? I like to think I had something to do with it.

JAY: Funny. I've heard that, too.

GUS: No secrets in small towns, eh Jay?

JAY: You admit it?

GUS: Admit what, Jay?

JAY: *You fucked my wife*!

MONICA: *(To JILL, intensely)* You must not believe anything you hear.

(JAY *grabs a baseball bat from behind his chair and threatens* GUS *with it.*)

JAY: *TRUE?*

(*When* GUS *doesn't answer,* JAY *slams the bat to the floor near* GUS's *foot.* GUS *doesn't flinch, but* MONICA *moves to door, only to be blocked by* GEORGE.)

MONICA: *Gus?*

GUS: I thought I was a faggot?

GEORGE: Don't come out, he's getting ugly.

MONICA: Gus! Are you O K?

GUS: Opera bouffe, dear. Nothing to worry about.

JAY: (*Still threatening with bat*) You scum. You never took me seriously.

GUS: Jay, you make it hard.

(JAY *slams the bat into his big chair, then exits in a rage to his bedroom.*)

MONICA: What's going on? What's he doing?

GEORGE: He's in his bedroom—

(*Re-enter* JAY *with pistol.*)

GEORGE: Jesus! The crazy bastard's got a gun!

JILL: (*Stuggling to get past the door*) No Daddy! No no no please!

JAY: (*Yelling to* JILL) Stay in that room!

(MONICA *pushes* JILL *to the bed, then pulls* GEORGE *into the bedroom.*)

MONICA: (*To* GEORGE) Get in here! You gotta take care of her, you understand? No matter what, help her!

(GEORGE *nods, gently restrains* JILL *as* MONICA *cautiously opens the door on the tense stand-off between* JAY *and* GUS. *For the moment,* JAY *holds the gun at his side, pointed down toward the floor.*)

JAY: Last time. Did you screw my wife?

(GUS *merely smiles.* JAY *points the pistol at his head.*)

MONICA: Jay! Don't act stupid!

GUS: (*To* MONICA) Wouldn't you know it? A life of intellectual purity, sullied by a tabloid death.

JAY: You wanna die laughing? Is that your ambition?

MONICA: Jay! Come to your senses!

JAY: (*Turning the gun toward* MONICA) I wouldn't be surprised if you had it on with my wife, too, Monica.

MONICA: That poor woman had one miserable little affair two years before we came here.

JAY: That was the first.

MONICA: That was the *last*, you...you—

JAY: Spit it out, Monica. Give me a reason.

(GUS's *panache crumbles with the gun aimed at* MONICA; *he makes an abortive move on* JAY, *who whirls, holds* GUS *at bay.*)

GUS: Get in that room, Monica, and stay there.

(JILL *briefly escapes* GEORGE, *bursts through bedroom door, and is immediately restrained by* MONICA, *who compels her back toward the bedroom as* JILL *pleads with her father:*)

JILL: Daddy, don't hurt us, please, please, don't be mean to us...

(*Throughout all this,* S J *seems unconcerned with the human events; instead he is intent upon warding off the encroaching spectre of Abaddon.* S J *uses his emblem as a shield. In the bedroom with* GEORGE *and* JILL, MONICA *has already made a decision. She is hugging* JILL, *almost pleading with her.*)

MONICA: Listen to me. I've got to—. Don't hate me, no matter what happens, please don't ever hate me. (*She exits to living room.*)

JILL: Monica!

MONICA: Jay...

GUS: Don't interfere, Monica. Jay isn't going to shoot anyone, are you?

JAY: You people don't realize how hard it's been for me.

MONICA: That's not true, Jay. Gloria and me, we used to talk about it.

JAY: I'll bet you did. You talked about what we did in bed.

GUS: (*Helpfully*) More about what you didn't.

(JAY *whirls away from* MONICA *and points the gun furiously toward* GUS's *head.*)

MONICA: JAY! Gus, you goddamn fool—

GUS: Don't worry, darling. Jay has a healthy fear of jail. Isn't that right, Jay? Who wants to be buggered by hordes of weightlifting felons?

MONICA: SHUT UP!

JAY: You're right. If I take you out, I'll have to take us all out. I could do it. Think I couldn't?

MONICA: Jay. It's Gus you want to hurt, isn't it?

(JAY *is wary, a bit confused.*)

MONICA: Get rid of the gun, Jay, and we'll go hurt Gus.

GUS: Monica. Don't do this. Please don't.

(MONICA *turns on* GUS *and slaps him.*)

MONICA: You fool! You fool! You provoke him!

(MONICA *abruptly exits U R to* JAY's *bedroom.*)

(JAY *seems momentarily stunned by this turn, then smiles and follows* MONICA *off. He slams the bedroom door and locks it.*)

(GUS *charges after them, trying to force the door and screaming:*)

GUS: Monica! (*He backs away, dazed. He wanders slowly through the living room trying aloud to work out an appropriate response.*) I could kill him. Never mind the details, I could do it. Crime of passion. Be out again in maybe twenty years. (*Reluctantly rejects that*) I'm not that stupid. God help me, I'm not that stupid. (*He slumps into the La-Z-Boy.*) I could wait till she comes out, then beat her. Stupid. She thinks she's saving my life, surrendering her virtue to a higher good, etcetera etcetera. Like this is a fucking opera. (*A long silence*) I have no passion.

(*He notices* S J *staring at him.* S J *has avoided these altercations, content to bear witness without response.*)

GUS: You. What would you do?

(S J *sadly, silently, shakes his head.*)

GUS: Got nothing to say now, huh? Then what good are you with all your ranting and raving?

S J: (*Quietly, humbly*) "If the Lord had not been my help, my soul would soon have dwelt in the land of silence."

(*Upstairs* JILL *is interpreting the silence that has fallen below.*)

JILL: Monica's with my Daddy.

GEORGE: No!

JILL: Yes. And Gus did it with my mother.

GEORGE: Gus didn't say that!

JILL: He didn't deny it.

(*She looks* GEORGE *in the eye.*)

JILL: You see what people are like?

GEORGE: Look, I...I think everything's gonna be O K.

JILL: You're blind, and deaf. And dumb, George.

GEORGE: I *have* to think that way! You rather I think like you and suffer?

JILL: *I* don't want to think like me! But here I got no choice. Someplace else maybe I could think like you, or like the Queen of Sheba or a million other people, but not *here*! Here I'm dead!

GEORGE: Jill, I see it's tough for you, I see that, sure. But in a couple more years you'll be—

JILL: Dead! I don't *have* a couple of years. My father's crazy and I'm getting there. I'm afraid to sleep. I keep thinking he'll come home drunk some night and kick the door down and shoot me in the head or rape me—

GEORGE: That's about enough of that talk! Your dad's doing the best he can, and he's not like you're making him out to be.

JILL: You rode with him. Did he look away from the highway and threaten to drive you into a telephone pole?

(GEORGE *looks trapped.*)

JILL: You don't think he's played that trick with me before? *(She slaps* GEORGE *lightly in the face a couple times—taps, really.)* Wake up, George. Are you lisnen? Get me out of here. Tonight.

GEORGE: Now don't get hysterical.

JILL: I'm going with you. We won't discuss it. I'll be your sister. People ask, you tell 'em, that's my kid sister. Call me anything you like, but *don't leave me here*!

GEORGE: That's a hell of a thing you're asking me, Jill. Your father would hunt me down and string me up.

JILL: No! He hates me! He'd be thrilled to get rid of me!

GEORGE: You're too young. Don't you know they got laws covering this?

JILL: *(Hesitantly)* I could teach you to read.

GEORGE: *(Defensive)* Who needs it? I do O K.

JILL: O K. I won't hang around. Just get me to another state, another town, anyplace else. *(Slapping at him for real, crying with frustration)* Don't make me beg! Help me, you stupid boy!

(*By way of restraining her, he hugs her. She clings to him and sobs.* GEORGE *looks perplexed and miserable. In the living room* S J *seems conscious of the pain from upstairs and is ready to climb to* JILL's *room when* GUS *buttonholes him with his drunken despair.*)

GUS: You know what I wish I could do? I wish I could wax poetic. *(He smiles.) You* can. I've heard you. But that's because you're crazy. It's harder for sane men. *(Pause)* These are not poetic times, are they? *Are they*?

S J: I suppose that's in the eye of the beholder.

GUS: Well, this beholder says things are *tawdry*! *Tacky*! *(Finishes his drink, adds:)* Horrific. Apocalyptic. *(Pause)* What's that add up to, will you tell me? A tacky apocalypse? The end of the world as a frayed melodrama on the late late show? One last hysterical tabloid headline before we all fry?

(GUS becomes aware of S J staring at him compassionately and screams:)

GUS: What are you staring at? Fuckin ravin useless lunatic like the other one in there—*what are you staring at*?

S J: A man born without faith who lives without hope. And lives well.

GUS: There you go. Living well, the best revenge. That's what they say, isn't it? *(Pause)* And what *is* "well"? For that matter, what is truth? Pontius Pilate asked Jesus that, didn't he? How come Jesus didn't answer? Didn't he *know*?

S J: "He who teaches men knowledge knows the thoughts of man are but a breath."

GUS: I suppose I should go shoot myself. Except I know I'll feel better in the morning after a hot bath. *(He laughs softly, shakily moves under the deer head mounted in JAY's living room. He stands on a stool so that the buck's horns appear to be his own.)* Take a picture. Send it to *Cuckold's Digest*.

(This pains S J, who crosses and takes GUS's hand.)

S J: Stand down. Please.

(GUS obediently climbs down; S J embraces him. GUS instinctively recoils at first, then allows S J to hug him. For a moment, GUS rests his head on S J's shoulder; then he gently pulls back.)

GUS: I've got to get Monica out of this town.

S J: Yes, someplace where she's happy.

GUS: That narrows it down fast. *(Pause, then mutters:)* I can't stay here. Send her home.

(GUS exits. S J stares after him a moment, then crosses to JILL's room, where GEORGE is still comforting her. They look up at S J with some apprehension. S J thrusts out his emblem, the plastic-wrapped package.)

S J: For you. For your birthday.

(She hesitantly takes the package.)

JILL: But...thank you, but this is yours.

S J: Nothing is mine.

(She tentatively starts to unwrap it.)

S J: No. Not yet.

GEORGE: Give presents you can't unwrap—

JILL: Hush.

S J: I'm sorry I stole from you, young man. You must now forgive me and take her with you, quickly.

(GEORGE *takes him aside.*)

GEORGE: *Listen you, whoever you are. The people around here are maniacs. I run off with this little girl, and they catch me, they'll tear me to pieces.*

S J: You must! Is it not written that "the woman was given the two wings of the great eagle that she might fly from the serpent into the wilderness, to the place where she is to be nourished for a time, and times, and half a time"? *You are her eagle!*

(GEORGE *looks doubtfully at* JILL, *which incenses and humiliates her.*)

JILL: Get out of here, George. Get away. You make me feel ugly.

(S J *approaches her, takes her face in his hands.*)

S J: "The serpent poured water like a river out of his mouth after the woman, to sweep her away with the flood. But the earth came to the help of the woman, and the earth opened its mouth and swallowed the river." (*To* GEORGE, *commandingly, accusingly*) Be the earth to her!

GEORGE: Yeah? Yeah? You go my bail?

(*To* GEORGE's *astonishment*, S J *reaches out and slaps his face and snarls:*)

S J: You are less than she deserves.

(S J *stalks down to the living room, leaving* GEORGE *in a state of anger, shock, and shame. He turns on* JILL *and snaps:*)

GEORGE: Get your things. Let's go.

(*She starts to object to his curtness, but doesn't. Quickly she throws a few things into a bag, hesitating only over her stuffed koala bear. She leaves it.* GEORGE *crosses down to* S J *in living room.*)

GEORGE: *I'm taking Cady's pick-up as far as Joplin. Tell him he should not persecute me for Grand Theft Auto, the truck's at the bus station.*

(S J *nods, then embraces* GEORGE *briefly by way of appreciation.*)

GEORGE: *Everybody wants me to be the hero. I don't even know this girl. What happens when we get to Miami?*

S J: *Take her to your mother's.*

GEORGE: *Yeah. Sure. She'd fatten her up.*

(JILL *joins them in living room. She carries one small suitcase and the emblem, and she is staring apprehensively toward* JAY's *bedroom.*)

JILL: *Let's go.* (To S J) *Will I see you again?*

S J: *"I will not leave you desolate; I will come to you."*

(She embraces him, then recoils in fright when MONICA appears from bedroom. JILL motions her to be silent, and MONICA understands. She looks emotionally and physically battered. Her lower lip is swollen and there is the start of a bruise under her eye.)

JILL: *I've got to go!*

MONICA: *I know. Give me a hug.*

(JILL can't until GEORGE prods her.)

GEORGE: *G'wan we got time for that.*

(JILL allows herself to be hugged.)

MONICA: *You promised not to hate me.*

(MONICA is on her knees. JILL breaks away and hisses to GEORGE:)

JILL: *Now!*

(GEORGE and JILL exit. MONICA slowly, stiffly struggles to her feet. She tries to head for the closet, for her coat, for an exit. But she's too drained. She falls back onto JAY's recliner and covers her eyes. Sound of pick-up truck starting and pulling away. Soon thereafter MONICA mumbles....)

MONICA: Gus home?

S J: Yes.

MONICA: Gus. Oh Gus. You're all there is to love. (She sighs, then a small smile.) That pig in the bedroom is right about Gus. He wants to die with a bon mot on his lips. As if anybody will hear but me. As if anybody else cared.

S J: Obviously he lives only for you.

MONICA: Yes?

(S J nods.)

MONICA: Am I disgusting?

S J: We are dust.

MONICA: Dust. I'm more than that. Dust...doesn't hurt.

(S J leans her back in the recliner, then gently rubs her hand.)

MONICA: That vicious bastard threw me out of this chair once.

S J: He shall not do so *twice*.

(After a moment, an involuntary groan escapes MONICA, and in a voice filled with regret and self-loathing, cries out:)

MONICA: Jill! Oh, Jill! What must my darling think of me now?

(S J *stands behind her chair, gently rubbing her temples, as lights dim on* S J *and* MONICA.)

(*Lights up on the pick-up truck windshield.* GEORGE *and* JILL *are lit from low with a greenish dashboard sort of light.* GEORGE *is driving tensely, glancing frequently into his rear and side mirrors.* JILL *stares straight ahead, clutching* S J*'s gift.*)

GEORGE: That's how he does it.

JILL: Who? What?

GEORGE: Your father. When he scares you by not looking at the road. You think he's staring at *you*, but he's really staring out your side mirror. Tricky, but it can be done on a straight road.

JILL: Yes. I figured it out, too. It still scared me. *(Pause)* I'll have to call him.

GEORGE: What for?

JILL: It feels unfinished.

GEORGE: At least wait'll we're safe in Miami.

JILL: Look! *(Points out a passing sign; smiles)* If you could read that sign, you'd know we were "Welcome to Missouri."

GEORGE: Yeah? Well, that's that. Now I've done it for sure.

JILL: What?

GEORGE: Crossed a state line with an underaged girl. A Federal offense.

JILL: You're really scared, aren't you?

GEORGE: Whadaya think? I just got sprung from one jail and now I'm risking Attica or worse—for you!

JILL: For me?

GEORGE: Yeah, you!

JILL: Thank you, George. You're brave, and you're kind.

GEORGE: I am?

(She nods; he grins.)

GEORGE: Hey, what the heck, you were going my way.

(She laughs.)

GEORGE: That's pretty. Your laugh is pretty.

(A moment of mutual shyness, broken when GEORGE *asks:)*

GEORGE: What did you wish for?

(She looks at him questioningly.)

GEORGE: I saw you close your eyes and make a wish before you blew out the candles on the cake. What did you wish for?

JILL: *(Smiles)* This.

GEORGE: *(Laughs)* See? It works! When you gonna open your present?

(She looks as if she'd forgotten it, though she's clutched it throughout.)

JILL: I'm scared.

GEORGE: Scared? Go wan...the old guy already told you what it is. A picture of an eagle, remember?

JILL: Soaring. *(She takes a deep breath, relaxes, and unwraps the plastic. She finds a rolled-up 8 x 10 photograph.)* Turn the light on.

(Interior light up. JILL's puzzled.)

JILL: It's a photograph of a bride. She's so beautiful. She shines.

(GEORGE steals glances from the road to the photo; he too is impressed.)

GEORGE: Gorgeous. What is she, some movie star?

JILL: George. That's Mother. That's my mother when she got married.

GEORGE: You sure?

JILL: Yes! That's what Mother looked like before he broke her down!

GEORGE: The ole guy musta swiped it from your house? No no, he had it all along, fought em like a maniac when they kept it from him in the jail... what's going on here?

JILL: George. Look what my father did to that woman.

GEORGE: Now he didn't do nothin, Jill. Years do it. Time.

JILL: He broke her and killed her and I hate his insides. *(As she continues to stare at the photo, she begins to weep silently, her mouth open and frozen. Finally she wails...)* She was so beautiful!

(GEORGE moves as if to pull the truck to a stop by the side of the road.)

JILL: NO! No. Keep driving. Keep pointing me away from there.

(Lights and sound dim out on JILL and GEORGE. Lights up full on CADY living room. MONICA continues to sleep peacefully in the recliner. JAY remains offstage in his bedroom. S J, who has been watching over MONICA, now seems deep in thought. He paces a small area, fretfully muttering:)

S J: "Those whom I love, I reprove and chasten. Those whom I love, I reprove and chasten...." *(Slowly he stares coldly upward and speaks with deep rebuke:)* Not a pleasant quality in you.

(Sound: a phone rings. Lights up on a pay phone. JILL is calling. GEORGE stands near her looking full of misgivings. MONICA stirs. She and S J are within an arm's reach of the phone, but neither moves.)

JILL: Nobody answers. Shall I hang up?

GEORGE: Yeah. He's asleep. He'll be mean.

(She starts to hang up, but freezes with indecision.)

JAY: *(Offstage)* Where's the phone? Jill, answer the goddam phone!

(At his voice MONICA orients herself. A moment later JAY stumbles in from the bedroom, clad in his underwear. It takes a moment for him to identify S J and MONICA.)

JAY: Your arm broke, Monica? Get the phone.

(They stare, unflinching, as the phone continues to ring. GEORGE panics.)

GEORGE: Hang up! Hang up!

(He reaches over and breaks connection. Phone goes silent as JAY and MONICA continue to glare at one another.)

JAY: You do like that chair, don't you, Monica?

MONICA: It stinks. Of you.

(MONICA, assisted by S J, gets up.)

S J: Shall I help you home?

MONICA: No. I'm all right. *(Nevertheless she leans on him as he escorts her toward the front door.)* You'll stay with us?

S J: For now it is best you be alone with your husband.

MONICA: You hear that, Jay? I have someone to be alone *with*. You don't. You're going to sit here, all all alone, quarantined like a repulsive contagious disease. And here you'll stay till your sickness runs its course and there'll be nothing left of you but a nauseating stain on your glorious chair.

(She exits with S J. JAY reflexively pours himself another drink. In the phone booth spot, JILL redials.)

GEORGE: Let him go, can't you just let him go?

JILL: No.

(JAY, alone now, is a different person. His rage is gone. What remains is confusion and humility. Sound: the phone rings. JAY picks up.)

JAY: Cady.

JILL: Dad?

JAY: Jill? That you? Where you at?

JILL: I'm gone. Don't try to find me just because you think you're supposed to. That old man, Steeple Jack? Is he still there?

JAY: *(Looking around)* I'm not sure.

JILL: Find him. Ask him where your truck is. He'll tell you. But that's *all* he knows, so don't badger him.

JAY: Jill. Come home. I need you.

JILL: It'll be a long, long time before I can forgive you. But I won't stop working at it.

(JILL *hangs up. Lights out on* JILL *and* GEORGE. JAY *stares at the receiver, then hangs up. He leans back in his recliner. Enter* S J.)

JAY: She's gone. *(Pause)* Will she be all right?

(S J *stares silently.*)

JAY: If you know, please tell me.

S J: "She will hunger no more, neither thirst any more. He will guide her to springs of living water, and God will wipe away every tear from her eyes."

JAY: *(Nods, seems comforted)* I hope she'll be happier than me.

S J: She already is. *(Pause)* In this there is the illusion of progress.

JAY: I'll bet if you totalled up all the time I've been really happy during this miserable life of mine, it would work out to about six days and twenty nights. *(Smiles ruefully)* I've been robbed.

S J: Millions have had less. *Billions.*

JAY: Why was I born? *(Silence)* Hmm? To build a jail? This house? That girl?

S J: All that.

JAY: And nothing more? *(Silence)* I need some reason to live.

S J: Reasons are scarce. You're too greedy.

(JAY *seems "dreamy," remote. He picks up his phone and dials.*)

JAY: How much is a one-way first class ticket to Geneva, Switzerland? *(Pause)* Book one for Jay Cady, one week from today. *(He hangs up.)* Fly direct to Geneva. Rent a Porsche. Drive along Lake Leman, then up the Rhone Valley to Visp. Take a right and down to Zermatt. Get out. Take a deep breath. I'm there. The Matterhorn. The Swiss slope. I'm going to climb it. I've always wanted to. Now I will.

S J: *(Without belief or enthusiasm)* Splendid. Do that.

JAY: No encumbrances. Free and clear again... I wasn't meant for responsibilities.

(JAY slips into a numb sort of travelogue for Switzerland, during which S J calmly exits out the front door.)

JAY: The Swiss are a magnificent nation. The most intelligent people in the world today. Smarter even than the Orientals.

(Lights dim on JAY as his speech grows more introspective and slurred. The effect is of him fading away, frozen in place.)

JAY: They have it figured out, those people. Know the combination of the lock. Hold the money and lease it out. Chocolate. A major industry. Watches: a trouble spot. The Japanese are winning, all across the board. Make yourself invulnerable! Mountains! Barricade yourself within mountains! Drink in the grandeur surrounding you, and laugh at them all. They were never so real, all those people.

(Lights out on JAY. Lights up on the steeple. S J slowly opens the shutters and peers down at the town.)

S J: And who shall comfort me? What cheer for the *Beast Bait*? For this, so long and hard a life? To be slaughtered by my ancient foe? Abaddon victorious.

(Lights up on GEORGE and JILL, tickets in hand, waiting to board their bus. We do not hear him, but GEORGE is animatedly telling a story which is making JILL laugh. He suddenly notices something and races offstage, leaving JILL staring after him with genuine affection.)

S J: Yet knowing all this, still I am required to wander the earth, prattling about Love, when everything within me wants to scream, "Live like pigs! Die in your filth!" And yet I do it, and *will* do it, and will *believe* it when I do it. And sometimes others believe me, and there is some new love in the world for a moment or two. The species perpetuates itself and trudges on toward Armageddon, as it must. And *there* is all the comfort I am permitted.

(He pulls the shutters closed. Lights out on steeple. Sound of bus idling. It is boarding time for GEORGE and JILL. He races back onstage.)

GEORGE: Holy Cow, this bus has got windows in the *roof*! You can see the stars! *(Grabs her suitcase and races off again, yelling back:)* C'mon Jill, we're boarding!

(JILL follows, smiling with excitement and relief and hope. Just before she exits, the sound of the bus fades out. Silence. JILL turns to the audience and declares:)

JILL: And that is how I heard my mother say, "That's enough. You can live now."

(She smiles and hurriedly exits to catch up with GEORGE. Blackout)

END OF PLAY

THE PEER PANEL

THE PEER PANEL premiered at the Indiana University Studio Theatre on 26 March 1999. The cast and creative contributors were:

PENNY PINCHBEAK . . . . .Kelly Ann Ford
RAUL TRUJILLO . . . . .Abdul-Khaliq Murtadha
LYNDON MACILVANE . . . . Jason Ruben Marr
X Y ZAMBEZI . . . . .Teresa Long
CHARLOTTE BRILL . . . . Laura Cronk
WALTER CHANG . . . . Michael Lindstrom

Director . . . . .C Russell Muth
Set design . . . . I Christopher Berg
Costume design . . . . Sarah Conyers-Conte
Lighting design . . . . .Robert A Shakespeare

Two readings assisted in the development of THE PEER PANEL. The author would like to acknowledge the assistance of Robert Brustein of the American Repertory Theatre and reading director Timothy Banker.
He is further indebted to Donovan Marley of the Denver Center Theater Company for including THE PEER PANEL in the 1998 U S WEST TheaterFest under the direction of Anthony Powell.

THE PEER PANEL won the Theater Memphis National Play Competition in 1997.

CHARACTERS AND SETTING:

PENNY PINCHBEAK, *white female, mid-to-late twenties*
RAUL TRUJILLO, *Latino male, mid-twenties*
LYNDON MACILVANE, *white male, forty to forty-five*
X Y ZAMBEZI *(also known as* YVONNE BROWN), *African-American female, twenty-five to thirty*
CHARLOTTE BRILL, *white female, thirty to thirty-five*
WALTER CHANG (also known as YOJIMBO), *Asian-American male, mid-twenties*

A drab conference room in a lower Manhattan office building. Also, simple suggestions of a couple fast-food eateries—a few cheap tables and chairs should suffice.

ACT ONE: a Thursday morning from 9 A M till 1 P M
ACT TWO: the next day, Friday, from 3 to 4 P M

Suggest a late Fall, early Winter atmosphere.

Author's Note: It is customary to issue a disclaimer that such and such is a work of fiction and that any resemblance to actual people, living or dead, is purely coincidental. This is that disclaimer. I include it only because I must add an additional disclaimer. In the course of this play, I have had to dream up not only fictional playwrights but fictional titles and fictional synopses as well. I strongly suspect that for every synopsis I've concocted there is somewhere out there an actual play that resembles my imaginary one. To all those who come across THE PEER PANEL and suspect that I have somehow battened upon their very own unique idea: You are mistaken. Conversely, anyone who likes any of these synopses should feel free to go ahead and write that play, and I wish you well with it.

This play is dedicated to the memory of Joseph Papp.

ACT ONE

(Lights up on a nondescript downtown Manhattan office room—a 1930's vintage feel to it though it is a little before 9 A M on a Thursday morning in this year. There's a cheap conference table with half a dozen functional-looking chairs scattered around it and piles of scripts with accompanying files laid atop it. Waste basket. Small table with a coffee-maker and requisite accouterments. Opening for door upstage right leading out into a common hallway. Maybe one five-drawer metal cabinet upstage. Nothing adorning the drab upstage walls. This is a place where business is conducted when there is no other place to conduct business.)

(PENNY PINCHBEAK, Administrative Director for the New York Playwrights Endowment Council [NYPEC, or "Nigh-peck" as the acronym is usually pronounced], is fussing around with the files and the coffee-maker. She's in her mid to late twenties, casually but tastefully dressed, with the air of a hostess not quite certain she's ready for the first guest. Sure enough, she discovers she's one coffee cup short and the donuts are not in place. A bit exasperated, she exits U S R. After a few seconds RAUL TRUJILLO appears in the doorway; looks around tentatively.)

RAUL: Hello?

(He looks for a room number or identifying title above the door in the hallway. He eases himself cautiously into the room; glances at the scripts on the table, seems somewhat reassured. He takes a chair. But sitting feels wrong. He stands and just waits self-consciously for anyone to appear. In a few more seconds someone does: LYNDON MACILVANE, a rather handsome man some fifteen to twenty years older than RAUL, and far more self-assured. What he says to the bewildered RAUL sounds like:)

LYNDON: Nigh-peck?

RAUL: Uh...Raul.

LYNDON: Raul Trujillo? DREAMS OF DEAD OCTOBERS?

(RAUL smiles, nods. LYNDON shakes hands.)

LYNDON: Beautiful piece of work. Wish I could write like that. I'm just too literal.

RAUL: No, no...I mean, you're too kind.

LYNDON: Lyndon. Lyndon MacIlvane.

RAUL: Yes, I know.

(LYNDON *seems unsurprised by this; he inspects his surroundings.*)

LYNDON: God. Must *everything* about the Theater be so threadbare? Even the rooms where they dole out the money? (*Smiles at* RAUL) I suppose it serves to remind one of the monastic purity of our chosen calling.

RAUL: Have you heard who else is on our panel?

LYNDON: No, but my guess is that at least two out of the remaining three will be women. Of them, at least one will be of the same-sex amorous persuasion. Then of course we'll need the requisite African-American. You've got the Hispanic bloc covered. And, I don't know, who have I forgotten? Does that add up to five?

RAUL: (*Smiling*) You've done this before?

LYNDON: Have I not? And you, I surmise, are a virgin in these matters?

RAUL: And should have remained one. They never told me I'd have to read three hundred manuscripts.

LYNDON: Well, portions thereof, at least. (*Pause*) Good Lord. You didn't actually...*read* them?

RAUL: Of course.

LYNDON: Cover to cover?

RAUL: You didn't?

LYNDON: Are you crazy?

RAUL: But they're paying us to read them.

LYNDON: Three dollars and thirty-three cents per script? How long did it take you, on average, to get through one of these plays?

RAUL: Well...average? Maybe an hour and a half.

LYNDON: (*Pulls out a pocket calculator*) Let's see, one thousand dollars remuneration divided by your four-hundred and fifty man-hours works out to—the princely wage of two dollars and twenty-two cents per hour. Is that top dollar in Puerto Rico?

(RAUL *decides he doesn't like* LYNDON. LYNDON *forgives him.*)

LYNDON: Ah. Value judgments are being made. Rhetoric about Honor and Integrity is being suppressed—for which I thank you. Your initial respect for my hard-won reputation is being eroded by the sudden conviction that you are in the presence of an asshole.

(LYNDON *smiles charmingly;* RAUL *doesn't.*)

LYNDON: When you open a half-gallon of milk and you take a sip and your tastebuds wither and your stomach convulses, do you then drain the container so you can be *positive* that milk has gone bad?

RAUL: A playwright's work is worthy of more consideration than the secretions of a cow.

LYNDON: You think so? *(Picks up a script, at random)* SUCK MY SACRED PARTS by Winnifred Tobler. You read this? Cover to cover?

RAUL: The vampire archetype as lesbian metaphor, yes.

LYNDON: Not even played for laughs! Straight up serious!

RAUL: A very bad play, yes. Your point?

LYNDON: Point: The secretions of a cow are infinitely worthier. Milk nourishes. Bad plays deplete.

RAUL: But Lyndon, if I may?

(LYNDON *nods, accepting the first name form of address.*)

RAUL: She didn't set out to write poorly. You must know that she worked just as hard to turn out her failure as you did to produce your successes. *(Beat)* I felt compelled to finish it out of respect for her labors.

LYNDON: That woman wasted months out of her life on that god-forsaken dreck. So be it: The punishment fits the crime. But. She then imposed it upon the working life of one of America's most brilliant young playwrights—you, sir—invading his mind for an hour and a half with her lesbian drool, time which might well have been spent—by you, sir—in the creation of a heartbreakingly lovely page of playscript, perhaps a page which would have redounded to the credit of us all for the duration of the American theater—or till next January, whichever comes first. *(Beat)* For that crime, the theft of your creative life, her fingers should be broken one by one.

RAUL: *(Smiling)* You mustn't waste your best speeches on an audience of one.

LYNDON: Why not? One discriminating auditor is worth a week of rabble. *(Beat)* In any case, we're stuck here for the next two days. We owe it to each other to be amusing.

(*Enter* PENNY PINCHBEAK, *carrying another cup and saucer and a couple boxes of donuts. She seems momentarily startled to see two panelists already in place.*)

PENNY: Oh! We're arriving.

(RAUL *and* LYNDON *smile, murmur politely:*)

RAUL:	LYNDON:
Hello.	Morning.

(PENNY *sets out the cups and donuts at the same time she's shaking hands.*)

PENNY: Penny, Penny Pinchbeak, feel free to smile, accident of marriage, you know, couldn't be helped, donuts? Plenty of coffee, shall I serve?

RAUL: Raul Trujillo...thank you, I'll help myself, thanks.

LYNDON: Lyndon MacIlvane.

PENNY: *(Fame-smitten)* This *is* an honor, sir, I can't tell you how thrilled Nigh-peck is to have you contribute—well, virtually contribute—your valuable time to our organization.

LYNDON: One does what one can. Any glazed?

(She instantly produces the desired donut, tissue-wrapped, from the box.)

LYNDON: Ah. *(Savors the donut)*

PENNY: I studied your plays in college. I never thought I'd actually—

LYNDON: *(To* RAUL*)* You know you can't find these things anywhere in Europe?

PENNY: —actually one day get to—

LYNDON: And *they* call *us* barbaric. *(Sips his coffee)*

*(*PENNY *offers the box to* RAUL.*)*

PENNY: Mr Trujillo?

RAUL: Later, perhaps. Please call me Raul.

PENNY: I've heard excellent things about your work. Never quite caught up with it yet, but—

RAUL: You have to move fast to catch my stuff. Two weekends, over and out.

LYNDON: Ephemera, ephemera. *(To their stares)* Our common lot. Even the print-mongers have the shelf-life of a may-fly. *Ars longis, vita brevis* my ass. *(To their continuing stares)* I'm not a morning person.

(In the hallway O S. U R the voices of CHARLOTTE BRILL *and* X Y ZAMBEZI *can be heard.)*

CHARLOTTE: There's four-two-eight, four-three-one—what's the number we're looking for again?

X Y ZAMBEZI: *(O S)* Four thirty-five, I believe.

*(*PENNY *moves officiously to the doorway.)*

PENNY: You're looking for Nigh-peck?

(As PENNY *orients and greets the women panelists,* RAUL *and* LYNDON *have a simultaneous sotto-voce aside:)*

CHARLOTTE: *(Offstage)* Yes...we're here?	RAUL: What is this thing you all keep saying? This "Nigh-peck" thing? I'm lost.

PENNY: Absolutely! Welcome!

(The women enter.)

CHARLOTTE: You must be Penny?

PENNY: I am indeed. And I'm guessing you're Charlotte. and you're... *(She hesitates.)*

LYNDON: Oh. Acronym-speak. New York Playwrights Endowment Council.

RAUL: Ah...N-Y-P-E-C. Nigh-peck.

LYNDON: Relatively new group. Replaces another acronym that fell out of favor. As will this one, eventually.

X Y ZAMBEZI: *(Not smiling)* Zambezi. X Y Zambezi.

PENNY: Of course. Well. We very nearly have a quorum. Have any of you met?

CHARLOTTE: *(To* LYNDON, *shaking hands)* Charlotte Brill. Met you briefly at the Dramatists Guild reception last October.

LYNDON: Ah yes, for that season's playwrights, God rest their souls.

RAUL: Raul Trujillo. *(He shakes her hand.)*

CHARLOTTE: Caught your production at INTAR. Very impressive.

RAUL: Thanks. They did well. Hard workers.

(The men smile with introductory expectations at the rather short African-American woman staring back at them. Into the breach:)

PENNY: X Y Zambezi. Raul Trujillo and Lyndon MacIlvane.

LYNDON: How do you do?

(She smiles noncommittally, makes no move to shake hands.)

RAUL: I connect you with Woodie King's people—New Federal Theater?

X Y ZAMBEZI: If we had more options, I'd say "Lucky guess." But we don't. So I won't.

(This response induces a strained chill for a moment or two before CHARLOTTE *tries to lighten it up.)*

CHARLOTTE: Options are scarce for one and all these days.

LYNDON: Are they not?

X Y ZAMBEZI: Surely not for you, Mr MacIlvane?

LYNDON: I've never been more than one loyal producer away from total obscurity in my entire career. Nor do I know anyone who isn't.

PENNY: Which is where we come in, isn't it?

(The playwrights don't get it.)

PENNY: The Funding apparatus? NYPEC, N E A...

(Now, general recognition from the others—ad-libs of concord: "Oh," "Of course," "Thank God," etc.)

PENNY: We here at NYPEC like to think of ourselves as a kind of safety net for talent—something to sustain until the producing organizations catch up.

CHARLOTTE: Really not a matter of "catching up," though, is it? I mean, it's not like they don't know who's got the goods. It's just about maximizing profits and minimizing risks.

LYNDON: The Producer's Mantra.

CHARLOTTE: Jellyfish, all of 'em.

LYNDON: When will medicine perfect backbone transplants, eh?

X Y ZAMBEZI: I think we should resist the easy laugh at their expense. Don't you? *(Beat)* Why should a producer take a flyer on me... *(To* LYNDON*)* ...when he can take you to the bank?

LYNDON: You flatter me. I think. You must be aware that my last three shows have not proven to be terribly bankable. Aren't you? If not, let me assure you that your ignorance is not my bliss.

PENNY: *(Into the awkwardness)* Donuts, anyone?

*(*ZAMBEZI *ignores her;* CHARLOTTE *takes one.)*

PENNY: Plenty of fresh coffee, too. Please help yourself. I'm wondering if our fifth panelist hasn't gotten on the wrong subway? Perhaps I should make a call...?

RAUL: I would just like to say...

(All turn, but he's focused on PENNY.*)*

RAUL: ...that you, and people like you, have probably saved my life. Literally. Certainly my creative life. I want to thank you.

PENNY: Oh my, I...I don't...we've never even funded you yet, have we, Raul?

CHARLOTTE: *(Laughing)* He's looking ahead.

RAUL: Others have. I never actually meet them. Maybe you will. Tell them what I said. I know it sounds funny, maybe even— *(With a glance at* CHARLOTTE*)* —sycophantic. But as I stand before you, I swear I owe my life to the N E A. I want somebody to know.

PENNY: Well, I...I *do* know people in Washington who would be...touched and, gratified, to hear that. I'll pass it along. Thank you.

CHARLOTTE: God knows we all make a hell of a lot more off grants and prizes than we do off productions.

X Y ZAMBEZI: I don't know about "all."

LYNDON: Sorry, I'm a bit slow at this hour. Was that directed my way?

X Y ZAMBEZI: I don't know. Does that shoe fit?

LYNDON: Well, now that you jog my memory, I do remember a Guggenheim back there somewhere around the time of my first production.

X Y ZAMBEZI: Followed immediately by your first Pulitzer and your first Tony.

LYNDON: Quite right, thank you. Since then I've not applied for foundation largesse. I deem it unseemly to compete for this limited funding with rank novices and unknowns. Does this in some way trouble you?

X Y ZAMBEZI: Do I seem troubled?

LYNDON: Wrong word. "Sick with jealousy" comes closer, I think.

X Y ZAMBEZI: Why are you even here? Slumming with nonentities such as us?

PENNY: Excuse me, but we are *extremely* grateful for Mr MacIlvane's participation.

LYNDON: That's all right. I'm here, Miss—what was it? Miss X? Because I *ought* to be here. I'm here for the same reason Mr Trujillo there assiduously read every last stinking page of our three hundred unrecognized masterpieces—just as, I'm sure, *you* did, no? In a word, I'm obligated to my profession. Got it?

X Y ZAMBEZI: In other words, *noblesse oblige*.

(CHARLOTTE *laughs, then cuts it off abruptly as indiscreet—but she's enjoying the tension. She reaches for another donut.*)

CHARLOTTE: Excuse me. I'm just here for the donuts.

(*An Asian-American man appears in the open doorway upstage. This is the fifth panelist,* WALTER CHANG, *also known as* YOJIMBO.)

WALTER: Ka-nock ka-nock?

(*All turn.*)

WALTER: Anybody order egg rolls?

PENNY: Mr Chang?

WALTER: Correction, oh otherwise knowledgeable White Lady. I have shed the colonialist bondage of my parentally-imposed moniker. The confining chrysalis that was Walter Chang has *burst*. Before you, aspiring towards the resplendent, stands YOJIMBO. *(He strikes a samurai-like pose.)*

(RAUL and PENNY appear befuddled; CHARLOTTE seems mildly amused; X Y ZAMBEZI is rather intrigued; and LYNDON is thoroughly put off.)

LYNDON: Yojimbo. Hasn't that name already been taken?

WALTER: You think Kurosawa cares? I'm not re-issuing his movie, just delivering an *homage* to Toshiro Mifune. *(He sighs.)* What a mensch.

PENNY: Uh, can I assume you already know everybody, Mister...Yojimbo?

WALTER: Why would you assume that? I'm simply wildly successful at overcoming my natural shyness. *(Studying* LYNDON*)* You look familiar. Haven't I spotted you gazing up at me from the Arts and Leisure section on various occasions?

PENNY: Lyndon MacIlvane.

(WALTER/YOJIMBO rather girlishly offers his hand, forcing LYNDON to overcome his reticence.)

WALTER: Oooo, a *real* Arthur. Charmed.

PENNY: Charlotte Brill.

WALTER: Chelsea Women's Project?

(CHARLOTTE smiles, nods.)

WALTER: And how *are* the girls?

CHARLOTTE: *(Not intended maliciously)* Drop by sometime and see for yourself. Who knows, we may have an opening for you.

WALTER: Never saw an opening I didn't like. And is this— *(Indicating* ZAMBEZI*)* —one of your Thespian colleagues?

CHARLOTTE: We'd love to have her.

WALTER: Well, I should *think*. And you are?

X Y ZAMBEZI: X Y Zambezi.

WALTER: LOVE IT! Initials X-Y-Z! How could I not have thought of that? I'm *mad* with jealousy. I may have to run off and simply reconfigure my newly assumed persona.

LYNDON: Oh, *would* you?

(WALTER casts an arch look his way.)

LYNDON: *This* persona's exhausting.

X Y ZAMBEZI: He's right. You're fogging up the windows.

WALTER: People! *(Clapping his hands as if to get the attention of unruly students)* Have we forgotten our Shakespeare? *Life* is *Theater*!

RAUL: It's just that we have some serious work to do.

WALTER: And you would be...?

RAUL: Raul Trujillo.

WALTER: Ola, Raul. *(Ignores him, turns to* PENNY*)* And you? Are you the Chef responsible for concocting this demographically impeccable bouillabaisse?

PENNY: My name is Penny Pinchbeak. I'm the Administrative Director of the New York Playwrights Endowment Council, and I'm not sure I understand the thrust of the rest of your question?

WALTER: I've applied for about fifty of these and similar grants, and I've been rejected about forty-nine times. I've always wondered who was the Judge and the Jury invalidating my art and who decreed them into existence. Now, suddenly, *I'm* the Judge and the Jury when in reality I'd much rather have the money that I will be doling out to how many lucky people?

PENNY: Uh, three.

WALTER: Yes, three lucky winners, none of whom will be me. Do you see? Through no perceivable effort or for that matter *merit* on my part, I've been magically transformed from Rejected Supplicant to Walter de Medici, Patron of the Arts. *(To the others, generally)* Isn't life odd?

CHARLOTTE: Interesting issue. Once I got over being flattered—somewhere midway through the hundred-and-eighty-ninth script, I believe—I began wondering how I got into this.

PENNY: I see. Well, nothing terribly mysterious, I'm afraid. We have numerous consultants in the field—previous panelists on this and other funding entities, professionals from all areas of the theater—and each of your names...surfaced.

CHARLOTTE: How exciting! Secret admirers.

WALTER: Mysterious Benefactors, like in Dickens.

CHARLOTTE: A coven of Magwitches.

WALTER: And this Rainbow Coalition effect? That's pure happenstance? The gender equity?

X Y ZAMBEZI: *Near* equity.

WALTER: *(To* ZAMBEZI*)* Close enough for Rock 'n Roll, Dearie, especially when you factor in my Tiresias-like versatilities. *(Back to* PENNY*)* Surely your various consultants didn't come up with this ethnic balance all by their lonesome little selves? I mean, who's missing? Eskimos? Hasidic Jews?

PENNY: It's incumbent upon us to be as representative as possible.

WALTER: Yes, but the mechanism?

PENNY: A subcommittee of the Board of Advisors comprised of artists from communities of color, O K? They make recommendations from the names submitted.

RAUL: *(To* WALTER*)* What is your *point*? Why are you badgering this woman?

WALTER: The issue, one to which I'm surprised *you* are not sensitized, is racial tokenism.

RAUL: Meaning? I mean, are you surprised to be included? Or did you expect an entire room full of gay Chinese?

WALTER: You've seen my loft?

RAUL: Look. I don't know anything about you or your work. For some reason somebody apparently thought you were fit for this function. Maybe they were right, maybe they were misguided. Same for all of us. Fate has thrown us together, O K? We have a service to perform. Let's get on with it and get done with it.

LYNDON: Hear hear.

WALTER: *(To* RAUL*)* You're cute when you're mad.

RAUL: You're not amusing.

WALTER: And your sphincter needs loosening.

RAUL: In your dreams.

PENNY: Ex*cuse* me. *(Beat)* One expects a certain amount of contentiousness on these panels. But generally not until the plays themselves are considered. And even then I would strongly dissuade you in the name of common civility from engaging in any sort of *ad hominem* vituperation.

(The panelists seem a bit chastened, but sullenly so, and no apologies are exchanged. PENNY *accepts the silence as a step in the right direction.)*

PENNY: Let me summarize where we are at this point and offer a couple procedural suggestions. Then I'll step out of your way and let you get down to work. *(Beat)* At this juncture we have winnowed our original three-hundred-and-six applicants down to fifty-three. Each of the remaining scripts has been recommended for second round status by at least two of you.

LYNDON: Hold it. Hold it right there, please. I don't wish to jump the gun on this process. But am I to understand that at least two people in this room have given a preliminary thumbs up to SUCK MY SACRED PARTS? *(He glares around the room.)* Would the guilty parties care to identify themselves?

PENNY: Uh, Mr MacIlvane...

LYNDON: It wasn't Trujillo. And you have my blood oath that it wasn't me.

PENNY: Mr MacIlvane, sir, there will be time enough for such specificity. Would you be good enough to allow me to finish this orientation?

LYNDON: Appalling...

PENNY: At this point in your consideration we permit you to study the resumes and bios the candidates submitted with their applications. Those are the folders you see arrayed before you on the table.

X Y ZAMBEZI: Excuse me.

PENNY: Yes?

X Y ZAMBEZI: Why do we need to know who these people are and what they've done, or not yet done? Aren't we rewarding quality of script rather than career achievement?

PENNY: Yes. Absolutely.

X Y ZAMBEZI: So why not blind submissions? Let the scripts stand or fall on their own merits?

PENNY: Well...we did it that way last year.

X Y ZAMBEZI: And?

PENNY: We decided not to do it that way this year.

(ZAMBEZI *exchanges a look with* CHARLOTTE.)

X Y ZAMBEZI: Ye-ess...?

PENNY: I'm not at liberty to discuss the intricacies of the Governing Board's deliberations on this matter. I *will* say that the issue of continuing blind submissions was hotly contested. One faction felt that procedure was seriously flawed. They won the day, at least for this year. A compromise of sorts was reached by the decision to withhold biographical and career information until the scripts advanced on their merits alone to this round. (*Looking around, conscious that her explanation leaves something to be desired*) There are valid arguments to be made on both sides of this matter, and my personal feelings are simply not relevant at this point. Nor, frankly, are yours. This is this year's solution.

CHARLOTTE: Are we really down to just three recipients this year? Is that what I heard you say earlier?

PENNY: Yes, regrettably, but we've increased the funding per grant from ten thousand to fifteen thousand.

CHARLOTTE: And cut the number of recipients in half, yes? Didn't you pass out six of these last year?

PENNY: A consequence of the Legislature slashing our funding from sixty thousand to forty-five thousand.

X Y ZAMBEZI: When Nigh-RAPP was running things—

RAUL: Acronym help?

LYNDON: New York Regional Artists and Playwrights Program.

(RAUL *nods.*)

X Y ZAMBEZI: —they were passing around twenty of these at ten grand per.

CHARLOTTE: So. Down from two hundred K to forty-five in three years. Ouch.

PENNY: I think we all discern the trend. *(Beat)* In my business a good memory can be clinically depressing.

WALTER: *You* must have even less job security than a playwright.

PENNY: Don't cry for me, Argentina. I suggest you make every effort to agree upon ten finalists by the end of this day. Take those scripts home this evening, review them, and winnow them down to the three winners tomorrow. Any questions?

WALTER: Does NYPEC provide lunch?

PENNY: Nigh-peck provides the phone number of a good delivery pizzeria. Anything else? *(Brief silence)* My office is down the hall in room four-fifty-seven in the event you require input on policy or procedures. Let me tell you again how much your time and collective wisdom is appreciated. I wish we could reimburse you more generously for these time-consuming and energy-draining labors—and especially for your sacrifices in the form of disruptions to your own work.

WALTER: Personally, I welcome *any* excuse to avoid my work.

CHARLOTTE: *(Laughing)* Especially one that makes us feel so full of Charity.

WALTER: Yes! When will I ever have another occasion to toss around forty-five grand like Lord Bountiful?

PENNY: All right, then. *(Standing, smiling)* Try not to hurl anything heavier than imprecations.

(Panelists chuckle a bit warily as PENNY *exits. The panelists contemplate each other for a moment.)*

LYNDON: Should we elect a Moderator?

CHARLOTTE, WALTER, & X Y ZAMBEZI: No.

LYNDON: Ah. A roomful of anarchists. Oh, happy day.

(Quick fade to blackout)

(Lights up. The panelists have rearranged themselves around the room to suggest the passage of time. Tension is palpable.)

WALTER: *(To* LYNDON*)* How is it possible for you *not* to read it as a comedy?

LYNDON: Because it's not *funny*!

CHARLOTTE: I beg to differ. I laughed all the way through it, starting with the title. I mean, really, SUCK MY SACRED PARTS?

LYNDON: *(To* ZAMBEZI, *too aggressively)* Did *you* think it was funny?

X Y ZAMBEZI: *(She didn't.)* Well...maybe I just didn't get it?

LYNDON: Playwright's fault! Not yours! She's got to *make* you get it. *(To* RAUL*)* Did *you* think it was funny?

*(*RAUL *gestures a bit haplessly.)*

LYNDON: No! You didn't. I *know* you didn't. Because you're a man of taste and discernment.

WALTER: Oh, point taken, point rejected. Agree with you or get lumped in with the unwashed masses?

LYNDON: *(Throwing the script in front of* WALTER*)* Find me a funny page! Show me a joke!

WALTER: I will not be bullied by some testosterone-crazed homophobe!

CHARLOTTE: *(Placatingly)* Perhaps if you understood some of the frames of reference...

LYNDON: Frames of reference!? It's a ninety-three page paean to cunnilingus! I mean, I like muff-diving as much as the next man, but...

X Y ZAMBEZI: Maybe we should just move on.

CHARLOTTE: Agreed. Table it for now.

LYNDON: Oh no. No. We need a benchmark here, and this particular piece of pustulance is it. I want an up-down vote now: Is this to be a finalist or not? All in favor signify by raising your hand.

X Y ZAMBEZI: Excuse me, but did somebody ordain you Czar of this panel?

WALTER: Exactly. The majority voted against any moderator. I realize that as a straight middle-aged white male you believe authority to be your divine birthright, but—

LYNDON: Standards!

WALTER: —but those days are *gone*!

LYNDON: It's not about Authority, it's about *Standards*!

X Y ZAMBEZI: Paternalistically imposed.

RAUL: What does a vote on any of these scripts signify at this stage? Will somebody enlighten me? Does a simple majority vote mean it remains under consideration as one of the ten finalists?

CHARLOTTE: Yes.

LYNDON: No.

RAUL: Maybe we need some procedural guidance on this from Penny.

X Y ZAMBEZI: Why? So we can hear how they did it *last* year? *(Beat)* Didn't she make it pretty clear? Nobody has an operator's manual on how this is done. We have to invent it.

RAUL: O K, a suggestion, then. Dispense with numerical majorities and just keep a running count on straight-up votes over each script. In other words, even four positive votes don't mean a thing if at the end of the day ten other scripts have generated five votes.

WALTER: Unanimity on ten scripts from *this* panel?

RAUL: Suppose we only get it on three scripts? *(Beat)* We wouldn't have to come back tomorrow.

X Y ZAMBEZI: *That* I can get behind.

LYNDON: So? Let's vote.

RAUL: Will those who wish to have Winnifred Tobler's SUCK MY SACRED PARTS remain under consideration for a Nigh-peck grant so signify by raising their right hand.

WALTER: Why must it always be the *right* hand?

X Y ZAMBEZI: Why can't we have secret ballots?

LYNDON: Because that's chickenshit?

(A weary sigh escapes RAUL.)

CHARLOTTE: We finally get a lesbian play that doesn't take itself deadly serious. For that, I vote Yes. *(She raises her hand.)*

WALTER: One left hand for Sister Winnifred.

LYNDON: O K, two votes, case closed. Next!

X Y ZAMBEZI: Wait. *(Staring at LYNDON, she too raises her hand. He briefly returns her stare, then rather mirthlessly smiles.)*

RAUL: Last call. *(Beat)* Three. O K. Now we're rolling. *(He makes the appropriate note on his roster.)* Shall we just proceed down the list Penny's left us?

CHARLOTTE: What was her organizing principle here? Clearly not alphabetical.

WALTER: Do we have to just go top to bottom? That's so *li*near.

LYNDON: Why don't we each just go around and talk about the ones we want to talk about? That way we'd establish, sort of *de facto*, the ones not worth a lot of discussion.

X Y ZAMBEZI: Theoretically.

LYNDON: Meaning?

X Y ZAMBEZI: Oh, never mind. Lead off.

(He glances around, sees no overt disapproval, takes a stab at it.)

LYNDON: Well, if anybody here values superb dialogue, sustained atmospherics, confident structure, and plays with something to say that need to be said—

X Y ZAMBEZI: Quit top-loading.

LYNDON: I beg your pardon?

X Y ZAMBEZI: You're not nominating somebody for president. You're not selling us a car. Just tell us what play you want to talk about.

LYNDON: *(After first repressing a rejoinder)* BLISTERS. Remy Sinclair.

RAUL: Skillfully done. The man's a pro.

CHARLOTTE: Well precisely. He's a highly visible, politically influential, thoroughly well-compensated professional. Why does he need this?

WALTER: Where's his file? Are these alphabetical? —O K, got it. *(He reads.)* This man's won three Obies.

LYNDON: Each well-deserved.

WALTER: And he's a former Chair of the Theater Department at N Y U.

LYNDON: The punishment fits the crime.

(Noting RAUL's smile)

LYNDON: As I am wont to say.

X Y ZAMBEZI: It strikes me that if Mr MacIlvane were not gracing us with his presence, Mr Sinclair would be in his seat.

WALTER: Unless he sat there *last* year.

RAUL: Shouldn't we be talking about his *play*?

LYNDON: Well, that's a novel thought. Thank you, Raul. *(To ZAMBEZI)* Weren't you filibustering Penny back there about rewarding quality of script rather than career achievement? Now you want to punish this man and ignore the value of his script precisely because of his career achievement? You see no contradiction in this?

X Y ZAMBEZI: And aren't you the noble soul who was above snatching grant money from the mouths of the less fortunate? Or, as you so graciously put it, the "rank novices and unknowns"? And now you want to permit your friend to do just that?

LYNDON: Excuse me? My "friend"?

X Y ZAMBEZI: So I presume.

LYNDON: Which makes you an outrageously presumptuous young woman! *(To* WALTER*)* Where does it say in his bio that I'm his friend? Does it list me as a reference?

WALTER: It's a plausible assumption, isn't it? You're roughly the same age, worked for the same producers...

LYNDON: That would make him *not* my friend. That would make him my rival. Possibly my enemy. How long have you been in this business?

RAUL: Please, *please.* Is every script discussed going to generate this degree of contentiousness? If so, would somebody just do me a favor and kill me right now?

(A beat, during which LYNDON *finds the file on Winnifred Tobler)*

WALTER: *(Parodying Rodney King's plea)* Can't we all just get along?

RAUL: *(With razors in his voice)* I despise the slovenly cynicism that question now elicits.

WALTER: That's because you Latinos are *so romantic.*

LYNDON: *(Studying Tobler's file)* Fascinating. *(Beat)* Charlotte, did you realize that Winnifred Tobler, your paragon of Lesbian wit, mastered her craft in a workshop sponsored by—my word—the Chelsea Women's Project? Hmm? *(Beat)* She says here that *you* conducted that workshop. *(Lays aside the file)* Small world, isn't it?

(Blackout)

(Lights up. The panelists are slumped back in their seats in postures suggesting sullenness and anger. Nobody looks at anybody. Nobody moves for about five seconds until CHARLOTTE *lights a cigarette.)*

LYNDON: Put it out.

(She glares at him. He points to a NO SMOKING sign.)

LYNDON: Please.

(She extinguishes it.)

WALTER: Surely there must be somebody in this room who is absolutely in love with one of these plays and does *not* have a vested interest in the playwright? *(Silence)* Raul? Help us out here.

RAUL: Is it my turn to be shouted down and my taste derided?

LYNDON: Can't we agree that people of good will can disagree on these things? Can't we rise to a level of common civility?

CHARLOTTE: This? From you?

RAUL: Let's agree to get through two more, then break for lunch. Is that an attainable goal?

X Y ZAMBEZI: Food as an incentive. That could work for me.

WALTER: Moi aussi.

RAUL: O K. How do people feel about Julia Novack's adaptation of IPHIGENIA AT AULIS?

CHARLOTTE: Brilliant. *(To* LYNDON*)* And no, I never worked with her. *(To the others)* The language is astonishing. The reconceptualization of Euripides actually ameliorated my long-standing contempt for that misogynistic bastard.

WALTER: Euripides was a bastard? I had no idea.

X Y ZAMBEZI: It improves on the original. No doubt. Especially the ending. In Euripides you get her little Pollyanna flip-flop into cheerful martyrdom. Always made me sick.

LYNDON: And you find Novack's ending...salutary?

X Y ZAMBEZI: Oh, and I suppose *you've* got a problem with it?

(She and CHARLOTTE *exchange what can only be called a knowing smirk.)*

LYNDON: Problem? Why should I have a problem with it? Raul? Should I have a problem with it?

RAUL: Lyndon...civility. Civility.

LYNDON: Am I being uncivil? Hmmm? I don't think so. Hmmm? *(He looks around the table. The others regard him warily.)* I simply would like to raise one little Point of Order with regard to Miz Novack's "reconceptualization" of Euripides. If I may? *(Beat)* Iphigenia...did *not*...CASTRATE AGAMEMNON!!!

(CHARLOTTE *tries to contain herself; succeeds momentarily; then erupts:)*

CHARLOTTE: She *should* have! *(Beat)* Daddy's trying to kill her, the militaristic fuck! In public! For the greater good of the war effort! I say the daughter gets to cut off his balls and make Clytemnestra serve them up with the mouzaka!

(LYNDON, *elbows on the table, rests his head in his hands and mutters...*)

LYNDON: God help us. God help western civilization.

WALTER: Oh, fuck western civilization! What good's it ever done anybody?

X Y ZAMBEZI: Amen. Bury it. Start over. New cast. New director. Clean.

CHARLOTTE: *(To* LYNDON*)* You're appalled that the old myths have been transgressed. I say they *must* be transgressed. The old myths are burdensome, dictatorial, depleted. Eviscerate them!

LYNDON: To be replaced with...what?

CHARLOTTE: LIFE! For god's sake, man, read Artaud. Study Grotowski. Go see Robert Wilson.

LYNDON: How dare you condescend to me?!

CHARLOTTE: *Your* Theater is *dead*! Learn a new one, or go away!

LYNDON: *(After a long regard of her)* You supercilious cunt.

RAUL: *Dios mio...*

LYNDON: What have you produced? Other than the cheapest of cheap rhetoric?

(RAUL *intercedes quietly in a neutral, informative way.*)

RAUL: When I was twenty-one, I discovered that the Greeks pronounce "If-a-jen-*I*-a" "If-a-*gain*-ya." Ever since I've been insecure about all Greek tragedy. I keep worrying about what else I've got wrong. How else have we diminished it? Two thousand five hundred years is a long time to keep making sense. *(Beat)* Shall we vote on this?

LYNDON: I want to go on record. I intend to vote against every translation or adaptation.

WALTER: Just like that? With no regard for the level of achievement?

LYNDON: Translators are to real playwrights what Rosie Ruiz was to real marathoners.

X Y ZAMBEZI: *What* is the man *talk*ing about?

RAUL: I think he's suggesting that translators sneak in at the end of the creative race and pretend they were there at the start. *(To* LYNDON*)* Right?

(LYNDON *nods.*)

RAUL: Vote on Julia Novack's AULIS: in favor?

(*All but* LYNDON *raise their hands.* RAUL *records it.* PENNY *appears in doorway.*)

PENNY: How's it going, everybody?

CHARLOTTE: No homicides yet.

PENNY: Well, that's encouraging. Aren't you going to break for lunch?

LYNDON   RAUL:
Yes.   Soon.

WALTER: Have to do one more.

LYNDON: Must we?

RAUL: That was the plan. Are you that hungry?

LYNDON: Not at all. I've completely lost my appetite. But I've acquired a desperate craving for a shot of Tequila. A double, I think.

WALTER: Speaking of "doubles"—thank you for that segue, Lyndon—could we talk about DOUBLE DADS by Lester diGiovanni?

PENNY: May I sit in on this?

WALTER: Frankly, I'd rather you didn't.

PENNY: Oh?

WALTER: I fear that at this point administrative oversight might disrupt the exquisite chemistry our little group has so painfully achieved.

PENNY: Oh. Well. I understand. Uh...I'll just...take my own lunch break now. If you'll check in with me at the end of the day?

CHARLOTTE: Certainly.

PENNY: And of course, if you need help with anything...

WALTER: Bye-bye.

(PENNY waves and exits.)

RAUL: Let's see...DOUBLE DADS. *(Consulting his extensive notes)* Two gay men want to adopt a little boy. Homophobic judge prohibits them. Situation resolved when one of the gays gets AIDS and dies. Understanding female judge then rules it's O K for surviving gay to adopt. He does, and re-names the tyke after his dead lover.

(There is a stunned silence after this synopsis as all stare at WALTER.)

WALTER: Well, I wept. *Gey*sers. I was inconsolably distraught for a solid week after this, this ca*thar*sis.

(They continue to stare at him until RAUL gently points out:)

RAUL: This play is not even one of our fifty-three Second Rounders.

WALTER: An atrocious oversight! Unforgivable! It *must* be salvaged from the slag-heap.

CHARLOTTE: *(After a beat)* Why?

WALTER: *You* of all people must ask?

CHARLOTTE: I'm afraid I must.

WALTER: *(Bursts into tears)* You heartless hollow *things*!

CHARLOTTE: Oh, get a grip. It's the worst kind of gay soap-operatic masturbation.

WALTER: Stop it! Stop it! How can you *talk* like that?

CHARLOTTE: Possibly because I'm not having sex with Lester diGiovanni.

(WALTER *stops weeping, glares at her accusingly.*)

CHARLOTTE: Oh please. Don't bother taking umbrage, Walter. We're all in Show Biz here.

(WALTER *composes himself.*)

LYNDON: Christ...

WALTER: Yes! Who said, "Judge not lest ye be judged!" *(Beat)* Lester is a dedicated artiste, a genuine poet, even if only recognized within his own coterie. And he *is* dying. And he desperately needs this money for medicine. And yes, I love him. And by some miracle I'm in a position here to try to help him. Should I not? Should I *not*?

(Silence)

RAUL: No. You should not. *(Beat)* Re-convene at one-thirty?

(All nod and otherwise signal agreement except for WALTER, *who remains seated as the others file out. Fade to blackout)*

(Lights up on a simple round white table and two wire-frame white chairs. Enter CHARLOTTE *&* X Y ZAMBEZI *carrying trays with salads and drinks.)*

CHARLOTTE: Aren't I the culinary fraud? Here I am with my little tossed salad and my lo-cal dressing, pretending I didn't spend the whole morning cramming my face with powder donuts.

(They sit.)

X Y ZAMBEZI: Well, I hope you're happy. You shamed me out of the chili dog.

CHARLOTTE: Listen, if you'd rather go to K F C like you suggested...

X Y ZAMBEZI: I'm here. With what passes for food. *(Starts eating)* Anyway, you saw those lines at the chicken shack. Forget it.

CHARLOTTE: *(After a moment)* Listen. You know I have to ask it. Can I?

X Y ZAMBEZI: Go for it, girl.

CHARLOTTE: The name thing.

X Y ZAMBEZI: Yeah.

CHARLOTTE: I can't call you "X".

X Y ZAMBEZI: Yvonne.

CHARLOTTE: Yvonne?

X Y ZAMBEZI: I grew up with that. My friends still use it. My mama, of course.

CHARLOTTE: It's lovely. Why change it?

X Y ZAMBEZI: Didn't you absorb our Asian friend's rap on the slavery of given names? Something about colonialism and bondage and all that shit?

CHARLOTTE: God, he's pathetic.

(ZAMBEZI's noncommittal.)

CHARLOTTE: I'm sorry, that's my assessment of the creature. You ever catch his act?

(ZAMBEZI indicates "No.")

CHARLOTTE: The most self-indulgent kind of performance art. Nudity, of course. Yellow finger-paint everywhere, then streaked with blood.

X Y ZAMBEZI: *(Indicating the food: Enough)* Please.

CHARLOTTE: So. "Yvonne Zambezi"?

X Y ZAMBEZI: Brown. Yvonne Brown. Descriptive, huh? Accurate. *Prosaic.* *(Beat)* On my first play I used that name, the one my mama gave me, the one I answered to my whole life. I got one review. One guy came, sort of the neighborhood beat theater reporter. He crucified me.

CHARLOTTE: *(Been there)* Yeah.

X Y ZAMBEZI: Destroyed the play and, oh, by the way, destroyed Yvonne Brown. He made me never want to hear or *read* my name again.

CHARLOTTE: *(Of the unknown critic)* Rot in hell.

X Y ZAMBEZI: So. Time for a pen name. I wanted genderlessness. A name that meant everything to me but gave nothing away to the outside world. A name about origins. My mama's people come from the Cape of Good Hope. A Bantu tribe called the Xhosa. *(Pronounced Ko-sä)*

CHARLOTTE: "X...?"

X Y ZAMBEZI: X-H-O-S-A.

CHARLOTTE: And your father?

X Y ZAMBEZI: Nigerian origins. Yoruba.

CHARLOTTE: Y. Got it. And the "Z"?

X Y ZAMBEZI: After the African river, of course. I like the sound. And there was the initial joke, too. And definitive closure, you know?

CHARLOTTE: *(Smiling)* X, Y, and Zed. *(Beat)* Suddenly I feel so banal. *(Beat)* Sometimes I think that's why I became a dyke. To escape the banal.

X Y ZAMBEZI: Yeah. 'Cept now *all* the ladies seem to do that thang.

(CHARLOTTE *laughs; then, matter-of-factly curious:*)

CHARLOTTE: You too?

X Y ZAMBEZI: In a pinch.

CHARLOTTE: You feeling the pinch these days?

X Y ZAMBEZI: Uh-uh. Putting it all into my work.

CHARLOTTE: Get out. "All"?

X Y ZAMBEZI: Every other Saturday...

CHARLOTTE: Yeah?

X Y ZAMBEZI: Got a pretty black man who does me right.

CHARLOTTE: Twice a month? That holds you?

(ZAMBEZI's *silence and averted gaze signals an end to this line of inquiry.*)

CHARLOTTE: Oops. *(Beat)* So who do you like? *(Beat)* Writers.

X Y ZAMBEZI: Adrienne Kennedy. My idol. Not that I try to write like her. I mean, I *did* try, once, in that first play by my former Yvonne Brown self. Never again. You?

CHARLOTTE: I admire no one, least of all myself.

X Y ZAMBEZI: But you get a lot of stuff done?

CHARLOTTE: The *girls*. They take me along for the ride—you know, down at the Women's Project. I can't write worth a shit most of the time. But a few of them are good, *really* good. They humor me because I'm still willing to paint flats and run lights and be a techie for them when I have to. *(Beat)* You look so *shocked*. What'd I say?

X Y ZAMBEZI: That...you're no good.

CHARLOTTE: *No* I didn't. I said "I can't *write*." It wasn't a statement of personal worth.

X Y ZAMBEZI: See...for me, it would have been.

CHARLOTTE: No doubt. That's why you're at the mercy of every asshole with a word processor calling himself a critic. *(Beat)* Look. Here's where it's at. I'm a minor talent preaching to the Congregation, O K? I grind something out every few years so my friends can have a convenient label to hang on me, which makes it safe for them to invite me to their parties, which can be *real* works of art. I'm having a *great time*, Yvonne. Are you? *(Silence)* Who knows how much longer this ride will last? A couple more years, maybe?

X Y ZAMBEZI: So. That's it?

CHARLOTTE: Yeah. That's it. What else do you want? Riches? In theater? Fame? Grow up. Nobody gets famous this side of television. So what's left?

X Y ZAMBEZI: Art?

CHARLOTTE: No, Yvonne. I'll tell you what I told that dickhead MacIlvane. *Life's* left. Art fart. It's a Will-'o-the-wisp. It'll steal your soul, and that's a bad trade. We're here...to live.

X Y ZAMBEZI: I *do* live. When I'm writing. That's when I come alive. The rest of the time, this life you go on about...where is it?

CHARLOTTE: Northern Italy. A villa near Lake Como. When New York finally spits me out like an avocado seed, I intend to take root in the guest house of some perverse old European duchess with seventeen generations of inherited wealth behind her. Stomp grapes. Make wine. Drink it up. *(Standing to go)* Ready?

*(*ZAMBEZI *stands.)*

X Y ZAMBEZI: You and I...we're very, very different.

CHARLOTTE: For now, girl.

(They exit. Crossfade light opposite them to LYNDON *talking into a cellular phone.)*

LYNDON: How's it going? How's it *going?* I'm stuck on the Peer Panel from Hell, that's how it's going. I *know* you told me, Harvey. Prescient as always. "Prescient." Forget it. So here I am, the only white male on this thing, and I may well be old enough to be everyone's *father*. This age thing, it's getting eerie, Harvey. Is there some kind of vigilante death squad of critics out there, roaming around killing every playwright above twenty-three? I'm feeling like George Bernard Shaw, for crissake....

*(*PENNY *enters, close enough not only to see him, but to hear him. She's carrying a tray and looking for a place to sit, preferably out of earshot. But there's no place to go.)*

LYNDON: ...yeah, the designated male oppressor neo-colonialist over-rated has-been. I mean, Jesus, it's bad enough I have to plow through all these shitty scripts, but now I have to defend the two or three decent ones from the onslaught of these absolutely conscienceless self-promoters trying to skim some gravy for their boyfriends and girlfriends. *(Waving his glass to an unseen waitress)* Yo! Miss! Ma'am? Señorita! Un otro vez, por favor. Tequila, sí. *(Spots* PENNY*)* Penny! You look lost. Join me. Harvey? You still there?

PENNY: You're busy, I don't want to intrude.

LYNDON: *(Indicating his table, two seats)* I've got the only empty chair in this joint. Don't be proud.

(She sits.)

LYNDON: Harvey? Gotta run. And listen, don't forget to call LoCicero. Send him the Guild contract and tell him he doesn't like the LORT numbers, he can kiss my ass, I'm not some pimple-face fresh out of Yale Rep, O K? Right. Later.

(He signs off and looks at PENNY, *who seems flustered.)*

PENNY: These places are so mobbed at lunch-time...

LYNDON: What're ya drinking? Get you a Scotch?

PENNY: Oh no, not for me, thanks.

LYNDON: You caught me talking to my agent.

PENNY: So I gathered.

LYNDON: You're disconcerted.

PENNY: Am I?

LYNDON: He expects me to take that tone to him. So I do. It amuses him. It puts him at his ease. It reinforces his certitudes. So I adopt the patois.

(She smiles noncommittally.)

LYNDON: Don't you ever find yourself engaging in reflexive mimicry?

PENNY: I'm not sure I...

LYNDON: You talk to your mother the same way you talk to your husband?

PENNY: Oh. No. Not at all.

LYNDON: Then to that extent you're a playwright.

PENNY: I reflect the other character...?

LYNDON: In your duologue. Yes. You re-invent yourself to make each particular scene in your life flow more smoothly.

PENNY: That sounds...duplicitous, somehow.

LYNDON: All the world's a stage, Penny.

PENNY: Don't you lose sight of who you are? *Really* are?

LYNDON: *(Laughing)* There is no there there, Gertrude. I am the yin and the yang. I am the Laurel and the Hardy. My name is Legion. I am the World.

PENNY: I guess that's why you became a playwright.

LYNDON: Why?

PENNY: Natural chameleon.

LYNDON: I became a playwright so I could get laid. *(Smiles)* Actually, first I tried to become an actor in order to accomplish that. Didn't work.

PENNY: Why's that?

LYNDON: I got tired of throwing up while waiting for my entrance cues.

PENNY: Stage fright. Yes. How do they do it, actors? Overcome the fear?

LYNDON: Wouldn't know, Penny. I've never understood actors. I can scarcely speak to them.

PENNY: But you married one.

LYNDON: Two. I married two.

PENNY: Oh, I didn't realize...

LYNDON: Divorced one. Dying to divorce the other.

PENNY: Oh, I'm sorry, I....

LYNDON: Can't do it. She'll pick my bones clean. She'll tie me up in the courts for years. She's even threatened to claim *she* wrote my plays.

PENNY: No...

LYNDON: A savage, this woman. Until my fifth year of marriage to her, I never fully understood the plays of August Strindberg.

PENNY: What a pity we can't all be happy.

LYNDON: Are you?

PENNY: Happy? Me? Uh...sporadically.

LYNDON: And what makes you happy?

PENNY: *(Smiling)* My little boy. Jacob. He's four. Everyday when I leave him at the day care, I have to go into a restroom and cry for ten minutes.

LYNDON: Oof. That kind of love is exhausting. And transient. Enjoy it. *(Looking around)* God damn it, where's my drink?

PENNY: I should be getting back.

LYNDON: You like your job?

PENNY: I like having one.

LYNDON: I'll bet. Arts administration. Here today, gone tomorrow.

PENNY: Not if you're resourceful. I'd say that on average our careers last considerably longer than that of your typical playwright.

LYNDON: Who could not make that claim? Playwrights are Kleenex. Critics snot all over us and flush us down the toilet. *(Beat)* Why are you looking at me like that?

PENNY: You're one of the four or five most successful playwrights in America. Yet you talk like...well....

LYNDON: An embittered failure? You want to know what William Shakespeare's last words were? *(Beat)* "Twenty-two of my plays are out of print already! Fuck 'em all!" *(Beat)* No playwright ever died happy.

PENNY: I'm not sure that death is a jolly occasion for any of us.

LYNDON: You're right. Forgive my unmannerly and unmanful whining. Something about sitting around in that dingy room, listening to the putative future of the Theater as embodied in that peer panel. The venality. The mendacity. All those great old Tennessee Williams words spring to the lip.

PENNY: Mr MacIlvane. You're an artist. Haggling over money depresses you.

(He laughs.)

PENNY: No, you scoff, but I know it's true. You aspire to Art, and eventually it collides with filthy lucre, and you feel somehow besmirched, maybe even a bit of a failure. Why should someone of your stature have to flog himself like any other commodity, like you were dog food or toilet paper?

LYNDON: Kleenex.

PENNY: Yes. Kleenex. That's why I like my job. I have no talent. But I'm in a position to nurture it in others. I'm a poor woman, but I'm the closest thing we've got to Catherine de Medici. Sure, grantsmanship can be a grubby impulse. But at least we don't ask, Will it sell? We just ask, Is it Art? If it is, we reward it. Not with much, not with nearly enough, and for so very few, yes. But those few—like Raul today, earlier—they get the message: You count. You matter. We need you. Please don't lose hope. Don't be faint of heart. Work. Produce. *(She stands.)*

LYNDON: *(Not maliciously)* Why do I suddenly feel like Uncle Vanya? *(Standing)* Good lord. I'm still cold sober. How shall I endure the smirking hostilities of my jejune peerage?

PENNY: Offer it up to Dionysus.

LYNDON: *(Offering her his arm)* The charade reconvenes.

(PENNY *takes his arm and exits with* LYNDON. *Crossfade light to* RAUL, *sitting by himself at one of the round little tables, scribbling away on a pad. He does this for perhaps fifteen seconds, during which time* WALTER, *also known as* YOJIMBO, *shyly approaches, observes, and contemplates interrupting. At one point he turns away and begins to exit, only to have a change of heart. He impulsively breaks in on* RAUL's *work.)*

WALTER: Raul?

(RAUL *is startled, reflexively covers his writing pad.)*

WALTER: Oh, forgive me, you were working.

RAUL: Yes.

WALTER: I knew that, I could see, I recognize the signs, but I'm so selfish that I—I couldn't help myself.

(RAUL *just stares at him.*)

WALTER: A new play?

(*Indicating pad;* RAUL *nods.*)

WALTER: What's it about? Oh my God, did I just ask that? Did those words come out of this mouth? What is *wrong* with me today? Next I'll be soliciting your autograph and asking you where you get your ideas.

RAUL: It's all right.

WALTER: May I join you? I guess after a fashion I already have, haven't I, if a gross intrusion upon the creative process is tantamount to companionship.

(RAUL *motions him to sit and puts his pad away in a briefcase. But he does nothing to facilitate a conversation.*)

WALTER: Raul. I'm falling apart. Help me save me from myself.

RAUL: Two questions. How? And Why me?

WALTER: How? I need some simpatico. Why you? Because I can't go back in that room until you think better of me.

RAUL: Look, if you're worried about your emotions getting loose on you at the end of the session there...

WALTER: I am! I am worried about that. I'm terribly embarrassed and ashamed.

RAUL: Well, play past it. If it ain't Now, it's History. My brother used to say that.

WALTER: Used to?

RAUL: Yeah. *(Beat)* He's history.

WALTER: I'm sorry.

RAUL: Your real name is Walter, isn't it?

WALTER: Oh, what is real?

RAUL: Well, "Yojimbo" isn't.

WALTER: Merely my *nom de theatre*. You may refer to me by my colonial name.

RAUL: Walter. Are you one of these people who spend all their time being alternately terribly offensive and terribly apologetic?

WALTER: Yes. Yes. I am he. I am that.

RAUL: Then you just cancel yourself out, don't you?

WALTER: It's so true. I'm just a tentative construct, like everything else. A construct waiting to become history, like your brother. It's true. I am but a hemorrhoid upon the rectum of Nothingness.

(Despite himself, RAUL laughs, emboldening a confessional spirit in WALTER.)

WALTER: Do you know why I was rude to you this morning?

RAUL: Because you're attracted to me.

WALTER: I am nothing if not obvious.

RAUL: Same reason I used to snap Maria Olivares' bra strap in eighth grade.

WALTER: Are you repulsed?

RAUL: No, Walter. Neither am I about to impulsively abandon my wife and two children and plunge headlong into the madcap world of gay erotica.

WALTER: *(Mock disappointment)* Oh, poo. *(Beat)* You're who I always dream of meeting. You're just so very handsome and sensitive and intelligent—

RAUL: Where are you going with this, Walter?

WALTER: I'm...unmoored.

RAUL: I know.

WALTER: Yes, I'm sure you do. You and the others in that room. Do I give off some scent? A pheromone that signals Disorientation and Distress?

(RAUL shrugs, attempting neutrality.)

WALTER: I realized after a while, you know, as I plowed through all those plays? I realized I no longer have the remotest notion of what's good and what's bad.

RAUL: Ah. That's when you need a touchstone. Turn on a daytime T V talk show.

WALTER: Raul. I *am* a daytime talk show. *(Beat)* I'm an exhibitionistic freak, a little yellow curiosity piece.

RAUL: Why are you telling me this? I find it rather painful, and I'd prefer to avoid it if you'd let me.

WALTER: Think of me as the Ancient Mariner. You're the Wedding Guest.

RAUL: We have to go back, Walter.

WALTER: I'm not going back.

RAUL: Of course you are.

WALTER: I can't. I'm having a nervous breakdown.

RAUL: Well then, this panel is your lucky day. It requires you to function. It gives you a structure within which to behave. *(Silence)* What will you do if you don't return to our deliberations?

WALTER: I will surrender unconditionally to my basest self.

RAUL: Meaning?

WALTER: I will lock myself in my loft, unplug my phone, cry hysterically, swallow a bunch of pills but not quite enough to do the dread deed—basically just lie down in my own filth like some scrofulous dog until I become bored with myself. At which point I'll get up and throw a party. *(Beat)* Would you come?

RAUL: Probably not. I don't go to parties.

WALTER: No. You write. You write exquisitely. *(Beat)* I only pretended not to know you when we were introduced. I've seen every production you've had.

RAUL: You're fibbing.

WALTER: How can you tell?

RAUL: Nobody can find the theaters that do my work. Even when you know where it's happening, you've gotta be muy bravo to enter those neighborhoods after dark. And if you did, I'd have seen you and I'd have remembered you.

WALTER: DREAMS OF DEAD OCTOBERS at INTAR last April. FOUNTAINS OF JUANA MORALES in that loft off the Bowery a year ago. And the one about the blind puppeteer?

RAUL: IF WE SHOULD TURN OUR GLANCE.

WALTER: Yes, your first one. In the basement of some church over on Riverside.

(RAUL *regards him carefully, as if only now noticing him.*)

RAUL: Thank you.

WALTER: Obviously it is I who should thank you. For your art, for your vision, for your constant example of who I meant to be. *(Beat)* As for your not recognizing me...I'm a shape-shifter, master of a thousand visages. If you'd seen my act, you'd understand. But you haven't, have you?

RAUL: Seen your work? No. I don't go to the theater much.

WALTER: I'm relieved to hear it, actually. It's not the sort of thing you'd... respect. Even I don't, most of the time. *(Beat)* How does it happen, this abyss between our aspirations and our achievements? When I began writing, I felt I was plumbing depths, interiorities uncharted. Something about myself and my separation from this world. Something substantive and dreamlike at one and the same time. If I could just get it said, I would tell myself, they will be like the first syllables ever spoken, and they will be instantly comprehensible to all who hear them, and their sad lives will be transformed. *(Beat)* But by the time I got them onto the paper and into the minds of my hopelessly ill-equipped actors, by the time those syllables dribbled out of their mouths like half-masticated beef jerky, all my unique and precious emotions just sounded...silly. *(Beat)* I assured my friends who came that's how I meant them to sound. Silly. So we all shared our tittering laughter. *(Beat)* That's how those same friends react to *your* work, too. They will impose that reaction on anything presented to them, especially work of self-evident authenticity such as yours. They find no substance within themselves. So they savagely deny and refute its manifestation in others. *(Beat)* And so I make my ludicrous entrances and hope I will not be exposed by some naked exit such as you witnessed this morning. And all around me my friends just keep dying and dying while I prance and cavort in my disgusting performance pieces, and only rarely do I run into someone like you: an artist of vision. A man of substance. A dramatic poet born just for the Theater. What a mirror you hold up before me. *(Smiling bitterly)* Is it any wonder that I should hate you?

RAUL: Walter. There's so many people eager to hate a playwright. For playwrights to hate each other—isn't it redundant?

WALTER: Yes. But it's me. It's what I do. *(Beat)* Can I tell you a story?

RAUL: *(Glancing at his watch)* We have to get back, Walter.

WALTER: A short one? About a cowboy?

RAUL: Quickly.

WALTER: I always loved cowboys—samurai, gauchos, what you will. Except, unlike most of the other little boys, I didn't want to *be* one, I wanted to kiss one.

(To RAUL's discomforted look)

WALTER: Oh for God's sake, have mercy, will you? I am what I am and that's all that I am. Popeye. Anyway, one day it happened. I saw a cowboy, and I mean the best kind of cowboy—a *movie* cowboy. Glenn Ford. In the flesh. In Woodstock. He was tooling around in this nifty little red Corvette convertible. I recognized him immediately, and I was *so* in *love* with him! Oh! And then, maybe five minutes later, dear God, there he is, on foot, right across the street from me, just waiting for the red light to change. My heart was *pound*ing! I mean, as old as he must have been, he looked just... *scrump*tious! And our paths were going to cross. *Naturally.* Like it was made in Heaven. The light changed. He walked toward me. What could I *say*? What could I *do*? His entire filmography was scrolling behind my eyeballs, right down to when he played Superman's stepfather. *(He stops; his expression becomes crestfallen.)*

RAUL: Did you ask for his autograph?

WALTER: No. No, I didn't. I didn't thank him for all his wonderful performances. I didn't assure him that he would never ever be forgotten, no matter how lonely and neglected he must feel in his last years. I didn't even just smile and nod and murmur "Hello" in passing. I...

RAUL: Yes?

WALTER: I began to...*sneer* at him. I fixed him with my haughtiest expression of utter disdain and contempt. His eyes met mine as if to say, "Do I know you? Have I done you some harm? Something to merit this hatred you're projecting?" And then...he was gone. Infected for a moment not with the love I felt for him. But with my inexplicable *ugliness*.

(WALTER *begins to weep—not for effect, not theatrically. Rather quietly, openly. After a moment,* RAUL *awkwardly puts his arm around* WALTER's *shoulders.*)

RAUL: Walter. The best part of us...is terrified by the light of day.

(Blackout)

END OF ACT ONE

ACT TWO

(The following afternoon—a Friday, around three P M. Same conference room as Act I although props suggest disarray—coffee cups scattered haphazardly, jackets, purses, and other personal effects strewn about, files all over the table in no discernible order. The peer panel looks as if they have collectively thrown in the towel. They are slumped about the room, not talking to one another, not even looking at one another, motionless. The only property that is noticeably different is a moveable blackboard. Written large upon it in variously colored chalk are the names of the seven remaining plays still in contention for the three awards. They are written in reverse alphabetical order [at WALTER's insistence] as follows: Yoskowitz, Amy—NOT WITH A WHIMPER; Taylor, A C—SHUFFLIN' OFF TO TINSELTOWN; Sinclair, Remy—BLISTERS; Polanowski, Serge—SEBASTOPOL, or THE RAZORS; Novack, Julia—AULIS; Hardisty, Jonathon—GETTING IT DOWN; Beaubien, Alison—THE FORMER MISS EBONY AMERICA REGRETS. Hold on this tableau for about fifteen seconds)

LYNDON: There's never a *deus ex machina* when you need one.

RAUL: The curse of our godless age. We're all on our own.

(Silence; then:)

CHARLOTTE: There's always Penny.

(The panelists look at one another. It suddenly seems an excellent idea.)

CHARLOTTE: Room four-fifty-seven.

WALTER: *(Exits up right, calling out:)* Mom-meee...

X Y ZAMBEZI: She's going to think we're a pack of useless idiots.

RAUL: A six-pack of useless idiots. If we can count her.

LYNDON: Oh, what the hell. It's been about thirty-five years since anybody in this country agreed on anything. Why should we do any better?

CHARLOTTE: Please. Things are bad enough in here without you committing Sociology on us.

X Y ZAMBEZI: Three o'clock Friday. Is that possible?

RAUL: I was sure we'd have a consensus by this time *yesterday*.

X Y ZAMBEZI: I'm giving this another hour, and I'm outta here. If we're hung, we're hung. They can call a mistrial and throw the money back into the pot for next year.

CHARLOTTE: Not that bad an idea. A year from now Nigh-peck could give this to *six* people. *(Indicating blackboard)* Six would be a piece of cake.

RAUL: You all could walk away from this in good conscience? Really?

(He looks them over; they're uncomfortable.)

RAUL: When did it become so easy for you to abdicate your responsibility?

LYNDON: *(To* CHARLOTTE*)* What makes you think this year's money would still be here next year? Don't you know how the Legislature works? This would go back into the General Fund in the blink of an eye. Nigh-peck would instantly lose *all* credibility. Its political opponents would eradicate this budget line before their first cup of coffee cooled. Phfft!

CHARLOTTE: All right, all right. Can't a girl think out loud once in a while?

(Enter WALTER *with* PENNY.*)*

LYNDON: Penny! Save us from ourselves!

PENNY: Oh dear, you all look so—

CHARLOTTE: Defeated?

LYNDON: Wrung out?

WALTER: Stale as last week's bagels?

PENNY: *(Studying the blackboard)* Nil desperandum. *(Glancing at the panelists)* Motto on my family crest. It's Latin for "Chin Up" or something. Well. Down to the last seven. How hard can it be to eliminate four of them?

RAUL: Harder than diamonds.

WALTER: People, here's a suggestion: Try not to *care* so much. *(To* PENNY's *disapproving glance)* Well, it's not like they're Polish Jews and we're Oskar Schindler. *(To the panelists)* They're just indigent playwrights! And what are we talking about here—fifteen thousand dollars? What's fifteen thousand bucks *these* days?

X Y ZAMBEZI: For me? A year's worth of food and rent.

RAUL: Down payment on my first car ever. Braces for my little girl. Clothes. Books. A chance to actually *see* some plays instead of just reading reviews. An airplane ticket to see my parents for the first time in five years.

WALTER: Oh, just tear my tongue out, please! You're all right, of course. For half that amount, I'd sell the Chang family matriarch and throw in her Shih Tzu.

PENNY: O K , everybody calm down. There are ways to do this. Various methods. We just have to get methodical here—mathematical, in fact. Let's start by forgetting everything you've already said about these plays. *Tabula rasa*, as of now. First, let's congratulate ourselves on eliminating two hundred and ninety-nine candidates.

(She begins to applaud. The others look at her as if she's extremely odd.)

PENNY: No, I mean this quite literally. It's important for you to understand that you're doing *well*. This process is *working* thanks to your unselfish efforts. I am thanking you now *(As she continues to applaud)* and *you* will feel better if you thank yourselves and each other. Try it.

(A couple tentatively applaud—perhaps WALTER, then RAUL, then LYNDON.)

PENNY: *That's* it. Ladies?

(ZAMBEZI and CHARLOTTE join in, tepidly.)

PENNY: Very good. Now shake the hand of the person to your left.
Or closest to you, whichever. Come *on*!

(Panelists comply, awkwardly.)

CHARLOTTE: Don't make us do one of those end-of-service Christian hug things.

WALTER: Oh, I adore that moment! Are you kidding? That's the only reason I ever go to a church. *(Beat)* Not counting my friends' funerals.

PENNY: O K, any and all accumulated ill will which might have existed in this room between any of you three minutes ago is history. Agreed?

(Unenthusiastic nods, except for WALTER, who smiles at RAUL and says:)

WALTER: "If it ain't now, it's History."

(RAUL nods, smiles slightly.)

PENNY: My friends, thank you for coming. We have before us seven little plays—that's all, just seven. And we want to give money to the authors of three of them. Because we're generous and these playwrights need our help.

CHARLOTTE: Not all of them.

LYNDON: *Tabula rasa*, Charlotte.

PENNY: Now all our playwrights are very deserving, so how wrong can we go, really? Let me introduce them to you in...um, some kind of order?

RAUL: Reverse alphabetical.

LYNDON: Walter's idea.

WALTER: In honor of our very own X Y Zambezi. And every other poor soul perpetually stuck at the end of the alphabet.

PENNY: O K, first we have Amy Yoskowitz and NOT WITH A WHIMPER. Then A C Taylor with SHUFFLIN' OFF TO TINSELTOWN.... *(She's pointing these out on the blackboard as she goes.)* BLISTERS by Remy Sinclair, followed by—oh, this is a curious one by somebody named Serge Polanowski which seems to have *two* titles: SEBASTOPOL, or THE RAZORS. Perhaps an indecisive sort of playwright.

(Some chuckles from panelists)

PENNY: And here's AULIS by Julia Novack, and Jonathon Hardisty offers us something called GETTING IT DOWN. And finally Alison Beaubien—lovely name, like something out of Tennessee Williams—

(With a quick glance at LYNDON, who smiles)

PENNY: —and her effort is called THE FORMER MISS EBONY AMERICA REGRETS. Very creative titles, one and all.

(The panelists spontaneously and good-naturedly applaud PENNY.)

LYNDON: Well done!

PENNY: Thank you, thank you. My high school drama coach once said I could reduce an audience to tears just by reading the For Sale ads from the *Pennysaver*, and I guess this came close, yes?

(She has managed to defuse much of the animosity among the panelists.)

PENNY: Now can I assume that all seven of these plays have stymied you because they've each garnered all five of your votes?

PANELISTS: *(In unison and emphatically)* Nooo!

PENNY: Ooh...well—

RAUL: Four. On one ballot or another, all those got four votes.

LYNDON: Except TINSELTOWN.

PENNY: Less than four? Then why is it still on our list?

(An awkward silence ensues.)

X Y ZAMBEZI: I feel very strongly about that play.

PENNY: Oh.

X Y ZAMBEZI: I want a chance to make the case for it.

PENNY: Well. That's why we're all here, isn't it?

LYNDON: Yep. To pin the Blue Ribbon on our particular Sacred Cow.

CHARLOTTE: Or to gore somebody else's ox.

RAUL: *(A bit wryly)* Shouldn't we be here to collectively define our vision of the future of the Theater at its best? As embodied in the work of three of these playwrights?

PENNY: *Yes!* That's precisely why. As simple and as complex an agenda as that. Why is it so hard to stay focused on that objective?

WALTER: Because we are but frail and flawed human beings?

CHARLOTTE: Nobody ever called *me* "frail."

WALTER: How 'bout "flawed"?

CHARLOTTE: *(Laughing) That* I've heard. My whole life.

PENNY: Let's do a straw poll. Maybe you've already done this, but bring me up to speed. I'm going to ask you to name the *one* play you each feel most deserving of this grant. Not three. Just one. *(To* ZAMBEZI*)* You, I gather, would go for SHUFFLIN' OFF TO TINSELTOWN?

(ZAMBEZI *nods.* PENNY *makes a stroke next to the title on the blackboard.)*

PENNY: Anyone else have a clear first choice?

LYNDON: BLISTERS.

(PENNY *makes a mark after each title that's called out.)*

CHARLOTTE: AULIS.

RAUL: SEBASTOPOL.

PENNY: *(Smiling as she marks)* Or, THE RAZORS. Mr Chang?

WALTER: GETTING IT DOWN.

(PENNY *makes that final mark, then steps back and examines the board.)*

PENNY: Interesting. Five votes, five choices.

LYNDON: Does the problem begin to delineate itself?

PENNY: Quite. O K, let's try this. Reverse the process. Each of you pick the one play you would most readily strike off this list. Lyndon?

LYNDON: AULIS.

(PENNY *puts a horizontal "minus" sign next to each "least favorite" play.)*

CHARLOTTE: BLISTERS.

X Y ZAMBEZI: SEBASTOPOL.

RAUL: TINSELTOWN.

PENNY: And Mr Chang?

WALTER: Can I just whisper it in your ear and flee from the room?

(PENNY *smiles and waits.)*

WALTER: Oh, all right. TINSELTOWN.

PENNY: *(As she examines the board)* Yikes.

LYNDON: Precisely.

PENNY: What can we make of this?

CHARLOTTE: Chaos is come again.

RAUL: "There is no longer any Style. Only Styles." Friedrich Dürrenmatt.

PENNY: Interesting that nobody seems to have powerful positive or negative feelings towards either THE FORMER MISS EBONY AMERICA REGRETS or NOT WITH A WHIMPER. Is MISS EBONY anybody's *second* choice?

LYNDON: Mine.

PENNY: Third choice?

WALTER: Wait a minute, wait...I'm not yet that advanced in my thinking.

PENNY: It might be useful for everybody to quietly take a moment and rank *all* of these from Favorite to Least Favorite. Don't you think?

(*General murmurs of assent from all except* WALTER, *who groans...*)

WALTER: I'm just not a hierarchical sort of person. (*Nonetheless begins making his list, muttering:*) I'm a horizontal dude in a vertical universe.

PENNY: Everybody? (*Looks around*) Any more second or third place votes for MISS EBONY REGRETS?

WALTER: Me. Third. O K? You happy now?

LYNDON: No need to be getting spicy with Penny, Walter.

PENNY: That's all right, I know this is stressful.

CHARLOTTE: Walter, weren't you the one counseling us just now not to care so much?

WALTER: Leave me alone, I'm a sick man.

PENNY: Second place votes for Amy Yoskowitz's NOT WITH A WHIMPER? (*No response*) How 'out third place on that one?

(*Both* CHARLOTTE *and* ZAMBEZI *raise their hands.*)

PENNY: Hmmm. Tepid support. Whadaya think, can we eliminate either of those plays from consideration?

X Y ZAMBEZI: Dump EBONY.

RAUL: Premature. I don't think we should.

X Y ZAMBEZI: Premature? The weekend rush hour's starting up. How long you wanna dick around till it ain't premature?

PENNY: I have to confess, I'm getting a bit anxious. I have to pick up my little boy from day care no later than four-thirty. (*Hinting*) Does anybody see anything on the list we could eliminate?

RAUL & WALTER: TINSELTOWN.

LYNDON: Concur.

(Awkward silence as panelists either stare at ZAMBEZI *or, in the cases of* WALTER *and* CHARLOTTE, *try to avoid staring at her.)*

CHARLOTTE: Perhaps this might be the time for you to make your case for that play, Yvonne.

*(*WALTER *catches* RAUL's *eye and theatrically mouths "Yvonne?"* RAUL *smiles.)*

PENNY: Well, not to put Miss Zambezi on the spot...here's what I propose. The strongest advocate for each play should make his or her case to *me*— not to the other panelists. I shall be Ms. Everywoman, a stand-in for the curious taxpayer who might like to confront us at some point on how we're spending his money.

WALTER: You think those Yahoos give a stale fart about anything more creative than their own grocery lists?

PENNY: Many of our legislators are quite willing to pay more than lip-service to the notion of supporting culture. They just don't want to have to defend those higher impulses in the face of any more urine-soaked crucifixes.

LYNDON: And can you blame them?

WALTER: Yes, actually, I can.

PENNY: Please. No large policy issue questions right before I have to get to the Day Care Center. Ms Zambezi? Ready?

CHARLOTTE: I think each play should have a Devil's Advocate, too.

LYNDON: Why, for God's sake?

CHARLOTTE: Well, certainly not for God's sake. Call it a Check and Balance factor. Otherwise, we're in danger of giving fifteen grand to the best supporting rhetorician rather than to the best play.

PENNY: All right, with one caveat. Anybody have a watch with a second hand?

*(*RAUL *raises his hand.)*

PENNY: You're the timekeeper, Raul. Proponents get absolutely no more than two minutes to make their case. Devil's Advocate only one minute to refute it. One additional minute for comments from other panelists, if needed. Four minutes, tops, per play. Agreed?

(Panelists signify their assent.)

PENNY: Please remember, proponents, that I've not read one word of any of these scripts. Make the gist of them clear without bogging down in plot mechanics. Ms Zambezi?

(She nods.)

PENNY: Raul?

(He holds his hand up for a couple seconds, studying his watch, then points a finger at ZAMBEZI: *Go.)*

X Y ZAMBEZI: SHUFFLIN' OFF TO TINSELTOWN is set in Hollywood. Main antagonists are an African-American film director and an old-time African-American character actor who's auditioning for a supporting role in the director's new film. The director—secretly at first, then openly—despises the veteran actor because he made a career playing Uncle Tom roles back in the studio heyday. He uses the audition process—call-backs and interviews and what-not—to torture the old actor. The actor finally turns on him and makes his own case—that somebody had to open the doors for the likes of this hot-shot young director, and if it meant taking demeaning roles, well, those roles got white audiences used to seeing black faces on a movie screen, and they were paychecks that helped support black communities, and so on.

(She pauses, making sure PENNY's *with her so far. She is.)*

PENNY: Good. Go on.

X Y ZAMBEZI: O K, this is a little raw, the structure and all, because, well, I happen to know this is A C Taylor's first play. He's coming to it by way of acting. But we're here to reward *promise* as much as actual achievement as I understand it, right? To find new voices and make sure they have a chance to get heard? Well, here's your man. I can picture a black audience watching this play. I can hear them talking to the actors and to each other. I can hear them laughing and *thinking*, yeah, I can *hear* them *thinking*. About their identities and how they came to be shaped. I can feel them, and I know they will be moved, and you know what else? They will be *back*. To see another play. And man, brothers and sisters, if that's not what it's about, then I'm confused. Cause this guy's writing for why *I'm* writing, ya dig? It's about a search for Selfhood, the playwright's as emblematic of his people as a whole, *find*ing that Selfhood in the dialectics of the theatre, using the stage to expose institutionalized racism and then using it to show the souls of people pushing *past* that down shit into some kind of *real life*.

RAUL: Time.

PENNY: Thank you. Mr Taylor could not have better representation on this panel than you've provided. Counter-arguments, anyone?

LYNDON: I will reluctantly assume that responsibility.

RAUL: Ready?

(LYNDON *nods.*)

RAUL: Go.

LYNDON: This play is not "raw," as you suggest. Sushi is raw. This play is half-baked. Mr. Taylor has an intriguing premise, a potentially rich central conflict which, yes, could ideally expand to encompass Big Relevant Ideas. But it doesn't. He's not up to the task for one simple reason: He can't write. He thinks endless arguments piled on top of arguments add up to a play. They don't. He has no comprehension of not only structure, as you admit, but no clue as to rhythm, pace, or build. His characters are Plexiglas—thin, and you can see right through them. He fritters his good idea away very quickly into mere tedium. And I emphatically disagree that we are here to reward promise. We've already eliminated two-hundred-and-ninty-nine scripts that could make a case for promise. We're looking for scripts that *deliver*. This one aborts. I don't even know why we're still talking about it except that on an early ballot you got three other wishy-washy sympathy votes that the guilty parties desperately now want to take back.

RAUL: Time!

(*Strained silence as* ZAMBEZI *glares daggers at* LYNDON. PENNY *tries to defuse it.*)

PENNY: O K. Frank exchange. Frank exchange is good.

X Y ZAMBEZI: *(To* LYNDON*)* You. Are a racist.

(*Panelists, especially* PENNY *are aghast.* LYNDON *returns her stare, then sighs deeply, smiles, and responds mildly:*)

LYNDON: I'm dying to get up in a huff and make some hugely theatrical exit. But if I did, we'd no longer have a quorum, and three good people would be denied fifteen thousand dollars each. Your dirty little word is not worth that.

X Y ZAMBEZI: Then I'll leave.

(*And she begins to do so as the other panelists protest.*)

PENNY: No, you mustn't go, please...

WALTER: You're over-reacting here. Take a deep breath and re-focus, girl.

CHARLOTTE: Yvonne...

X Y ZAMBEZI: *(To* CHARLOTTE*)* Don't call me that! (*She completes her exit.*)

PENNY: She can't do this! This is the culmination of a whole year's work!

RAUL: Complete abdication of responsibility.

CHARLOTTE: Everybody chill. (*Goes after her*)

WALTER: *(To* LYNDON*)* You didn't have to be so harsh.

LYNDON: Oh please...everybody's been kissing her butt for the last two days, letting her cram that TINSELTOWN garbage down our throats, and why? Our mutual fear of precisely this: the Nuclear Bomb, dropping the Race Card, ka-BOOM, there it is. Well guess what? I'm still standing. I will not be morally blackmailed.

RAUL: Something's fishy. I smell a vested interest.

LYNDON: She knows this playwright, doesn't she? This Taylor guy?

RAUL: Sure sounds that way to me.

WALTER: I have a different theory. The ALL ABOUT EVE paradigm. *(Flips* LYNDON *a file)* Read up on Alison Beaubien.

PENNY: THE FORMER MISS EBONY AMERICA REGRETS?

WALTER: A much better play. Written by an African-American woman.

LYNDON: My second choice overall, my purported racism notwithstanding.

WALTER: Yvonne and Alison compete for the same producer.

LYNDON: *(Studying the file)* So I see.

PENNY: This job has made me lose a lot of respect for playwrights.

RAUL: Maybe you had too much respect to begin with. We're just people.

LYNDON: You know the irony is, this MISS EBONY script, it's practically the same idea as the TINSELTOWN thing she's in bed with.

RAUL: Right. Intergenerational black on black conflict, younger generation not honoring the sufferings of those who came before...

WALTER: There's a role in there that I was *born* to play. *(To* PENNY*)* The first ever African-American beauty queen is brought back to crown this year's winner of the same contest, and all the girls just basically ridicule her, the little sluts...

LYNDON: *That's* the show that would find that black audience she was rhapsodizing over....

WALTER: I am such a sucker for a tiara.

PENNY: I'm not paid enough for this aggravation! I've got to get to the day care!

RAUL: Is there any reason four panelists can't make the decision?

PENNY: The By-laws. Maybe I can make a call to see about some kind of emergency exemption or waiver...

(PENNY, *very agitated, heads for the door. She nearly bumps into* CHARLOTTE, *who is returning with a sullen-faced* ZAMBEZI *in tow.)*

CHARLOTTE: Shall we proceed?

(Everybody carefully returns to the table.)

PENNY: Who wishes to be the next proponent?

X Y ZAMBEZI: Before we continue. I would like to apologize. To the panel in general. *(To* LYNDON*)* To you specifically.

LYNDON: Thank you. Accepted, of course.

WALTER: This job's enough to make anyone pop a garter.

PENNY: *(To* CHARLOTTE *&* ZAMBEZI*)* In your, uh, absence, we had an informal discussion of THE FORMER MISS EBONY AMERICA REGRETS. It's my sense that all three of these gentlemen regard it as superior to SHUFFLIN' OFF TO TINSELTOWN. I know Lyndon is very enthusiastic toward it, Walter views it quite favorably, and Raul...?

RAUL: Can live with it.

PENNY: The floor's open to anything either of you might care to say about it at this time.

CHARLOTTE: A very respectable entry. I won't kid you, I like the fact that it's written by a woman—

WALTER: An African-American woman at that.

X Y ZAMBEZI: *(Sourly)* Two constituencies with one stone.

CHARLOTTE: If I may finish the thought? I love the fact that it's got about four great roles for African-American women, not one of them a stereotype. How many plays can say that? *(Beat)* I don't care whether we fund it or not, I'm going to do everything in my power to get it produced.

(Silence. Panelists wait expectantly on ZAMBEZI, *who is trying to overcome a reluctance about saying anything.)*

X Y ZAMBEZI: This play is slick, sentimental, and in my estimation, about twenty years out of date. The playwright's a dilettante who's been hanging around forever, and she ain't about to suddenly be going somewhere. But if ya'll are looking for a safe tokenism vote, jump in line.

(Another awkward silence, which WALTER *tries to un-curse with:)*

WALTER: Yes girl, but what do you *really* think?

(Small laughter; none from ZAMBEZI*)*

PENNY: May we have another proponent for one of the other finalists?

WALTER: Unaccustomed as I am to public speaking... *(Scattered chuckles)* ...I would like to put in my tuppence for Jonathon Hardisty's GETTING IT DOWN.

PENNY: Of course. Raul?

WALTER: *(To* RAUL*)* Don't you dare pressurize me with your pathetic little Timex! *(Beat)* I have an infallible internal clock attuned to my own peculiar diurnal rhythms. *(Takes a deep breath, and launches)* This is the AIDS play to end all AIDS plays. The straightest, most homophobic Chamber of Commerce suburbanite schmuck will weep buckets at this. Why? Because it takes the subject out of the realm of the panegyric and the bathetic— *(Breaking character)* Vocabulary points, people. Can you deny me? *(Some laughter from some panelists)* —and reduces this horrific pandemic down to one man's lonely face-off with death. This terminal man— *(Momentarily choked)* —rehearses his death, over and over, modifying and refining what he wishes to be his final actions, final gestures, final words. His only audience is his full-length mirror into which he plays the multiple roles of his mother, his high school drama teacher— *(To* PENNY*)* —you'd love that part— *(Back to business)* —the Archangel Gabriel, and many others, including, of course, the one true love of his life who nevertheless has walked out on him because he can't stomach this ultimate dissolution. *(A moment in which he composes himself)* It is the single most life-affirming play I've ever encountered. I've made no secret of the fact that I have a weakness for brave men and those who play them. Toshiro. Glenn Ford. But the hero of this play is the bravest hero of them all. To watch this man carefully water his favorite plant, *just so,* to listen to him formulate his benediction to his mother, searching desperately for some graceful, definitive closure even as his lungs are collapsing in on him, to see him selecting the garments he wants to be buried in, to hear the exquisite pain he feels at parting from his Burmese cat—

(ZAMBEZI *fails to suppress a snigger.* WALTER *is aghast, then outraged.*)

WALTER: Did you just *snicker* at me?

X Y ZAMBEZI: Sorry. *(She's not)* Allergy. Please, go on.

WALTER: I'm too stunned by your unconscionable insensitivity to continue.

PENNY: I'm pretty sure your time was about up anyway, Walter, thank you. *(Looking straight at* ZAMBEZI*)* Counter-argument, anyone?

X Y ZAMBEZI: This homophobic suburbanite you talking about whose gonna fall apart over this—how you planning on getting him into your gay theater to watch this thing? You gonna kidnap him? This shit is *ugly,* man, and you be asking people to part with their hard-earned for *this* down time? Ain't *no*body be there 'cept folks with AIDS and folks hoping they don't get it.

WALTER: Why are you turning on me? Because I didn't bet on your trick pony? That TINSELTOWN dreck? Amateur hour, girl, Ted Mack!

PENNY: O K, stop this, both of you.

WALTER: So what if GETTING IT DOWN plays mostly to gay audiences? You think TINSELTOWN's gonna cross over like THE WIZ? You write to black audiences, *period.* You take pride in that. *(To* CHARLOTTE*)* And *you* write for your dyke pals, *period.* So what? There is no "audience" anymore, only coteries.

LYNDON: And all you marginalized factions are so thrilled to at last be hearing the dulcet tones of your own marginalized voices, aren't you? P S: Nobody else is listening. While you were busy issuing manifestos about multiculturalism, the Theater died. There are no playwrights left— only vultures feeding on carrion.

PENNY: Can we please stay on task?

LYNDON: Is everybody happy? Isn't this a nice wake?

CHARLOTTE: Is this what they call the male menopause? Are you having a breakdown?

LYNDON: Pass the remote, I'm missing my favorite show. It's called "Kissing the Theater's Ass Goodbye."

RAUL: Lyndon.

LYNDON: *WHAT?*

(Stares confrontationally at RAUL, *who smiles and makes a "Calm down" gesture.* LYNDON *takes the hint.)*

LYNDON: Am I being cranky?

RAUL: Sometimes we have to act as if there *is* a God.

LYNDON: Or a Theater. Yes. All right. Carry on, then.

RAUL: Walter, there's an issue with GETTING IT DOWN not too dissimilar to the one Lyndon raised with AULIS. The Iphigenia play is an adaptation. This thing by Hardisty seems to me to be a performance piece, which, no offense, may be the real reason you're so intensely drawn toward it. Hardisty wrote this to be performed by Hardisty, and I'm sure he does it brilliantly. My question is, Could anyone else replicate that success? Would anyone else wish to try?

WALTER: Me! I'd be incandescent!

RAUL: Maybe. Maybe not. But at some point doesn't a play become so obsessively personal that for all practical purposes it ceases to be a play?

LYNDON: It's a fucking *monologue!* One plus one equals a play. One plus zero equals jerking off.

CHARLOTTE: Excuse me, but are we all from the same planet? GETTING IT DOWN is brilliant. I don't care if it's a performance piece. I don't care if it's by a gay for gays. It's a work of art by a genuine artist, and it has my enthusiastic support. *(To* RAUL*)* Now would you please explain to me what's so great about SEBASTOPOL, this pretentious piece of drivel you're flogging?

LYNDON: Now there's a pre-emptive strike if I've ever heard one.

RAUL: That's O K.

CHARLOTTE: Just tell me what it *means*.

X Y ZAMBEZI: Yeah, you got the Cliff's Notes on that thing?

RAUL: What's a waterfall "mean"? Or a Beethoven quartet?

CHARLOTTE: In other words, *you* don't know what it means.

LYNDON: What do *you* care about meaning? I thought you were the Robert Wilson groupie.

CHARLOTTE: No comparison.

WALTER: There is, actually. Maybe more so with Foreman. It's very imagistic.

RAUL: SEBASTOPOL means "Theater." It means, "This is not television." It means, "I am unsettled and a bit disoriented and now I feel myself becoming mysteriously frightened and I don't like this way of feeling." Do you see? Polanowski has a unique vision of the Theater. He not only has to find an audience for his play, he has to help them re-define the way they look at a stage before he can even make the thing do what it's supposed to do for them. Don't you realize how brave that is? How courageous?

X Y ZAMBEZI: How self-indulgent.

RAUL: There are three hundred and five plays in this contest that try to replicate some other play. There is only one play that seeks to revise our entire notion of what Theater can be, and that's SEBASTOPOL.

PENNY: Or, THE RAZORS.

CHARLOTTE: I'm sorry, but this is re-hashed Sixties avant-garde. All we're missing here is Ellen Stewart and her cowbell.

X Y ZAMBEZI: Did anyone in this room besides Raul actually get through this thing from beginning to end?

(LYNDON *and* WALTER *raise their hands.*)

WALTER: You have to see past the text itself to what he's trying to make happen on the stage. I grant you, it's a very difficult play to read. But it struck me as probably a very beautiful thing to *see*.

CHARLOTTE: O K. I liked the parts with the naked girls. Granted.

(LYNDON *sort of snorts;* PENNY *becomes very alert.*)

CHARLOTTE: C'mon. Isn't that the ultimate drawing card for Polanowski? Full frontal female nudity? Mix that in with his east European name and his textual opacity and you've got a made-to-order Snob Hit.

PENNY: *(Trying to hide her concern)* What...what happens after the women get naked?

CHARLOTTE: Different things. Sometimes actors smear them with pumpkin pie filling.

LYNDON: One of them plays the cello.

PENNY: While naked?

LYNDON: *Certainement.*

RAUL: You people are trivializing this. If that's your inclination, let's just move on to the next—what? Victim? That's what this is deteriorating into, isn't it? Set 'em up and knock 'em down?

LYNDON: He's right. This panel process has transformed us all into...

WALTER: *Critics!*

(He gets up and makes a choking, retching sound, reeling about the room before falling down and going into violent simulated convulsions. The other panelists laugh, except for ZAMBEZI, who allows herself a small smile. PENNY tries to restore order.)

PENNY: Excuse me, but *tempus fugits.* We still require nominating speeches for BLISTERS, AULIS, and NOT WITH A WHIMPER. Lyndon? Care to lead off?

LYNDON: Can I catch you up on the backstory here? I contend, and have contended from the start, that the best script we have perused is Remy Sinclair's BLISTERS. It has a voice that is at once literate and colloquial and resonant. It has a conscience, an element now apparently regarded as ludicrously passé or at least reactively humanistic. Miss Brill, while not challenging the merits of the script, has launched *ad hominem* attacks upon the playwright, dismissing him as too successful to be eligible for our funds.

PENNY: Too successful? But that's not intended as one of the criteria for either approval or rejection.

CHARLOTTE: Well perhaps it should be. The play's been produced already and it's received a couple other awards. O K, some people still like stuff about Southern Gothic degenerates, so good for them, but enough's enough. Remy Sinclair doesn't need us, and he should be ashamed for shoving his big fat snout into this trough.

PENNY: Oh dear.

LYNDON: Miss Brill, in her Sapphic wisdom—

CHARLOTTE: Watch it!

LYNDON: —prefers travesties upon Euripides as embodied in Miz Novack's AULIS, which features a castrating Iphigenia and a sort of perverse Julia Child-ish Clytemnestra.

CHARLOTTE: Are you having fun, Lyndon? This is just so shamelessly re*duc*tive.

LYNDON: Oh face it, will you? AULIS is a sophomoric radical lesbian wet dream.

CHARLOTTE: Let me ask you this, Mister: Would you have the guts to write a column in *The New York Times* featuring these over-ripe reactionary menopausal male bigotries you feel safe in spouting within these walls?

LYNDON: Refresh my memory—does *The Times* pay by the word?

PENNY: All right. I think I see the problem.

LYNDON: The problem? We haven't come to the problem. The problem is that AULIS is an adaptation. If it possessed none of the risible defects I've exposed, it would still be an adaptation.

PENNY: Yes?

CHARLOTTE: He hates adaptations. *(To* LYNDON*)* Would that include, say, Moliere's MISER? Taken from Plautus's THE POT OF GOLD, I believe.

RAUL: *(To* PENNY*)* This is known in some circles as a Mexican stand-off. I think it's safe to presume that these two will do their best to exercise a blanket veto over the other's choice. *(Beat)* Which, I must say, speaking candidly, pisses me off no end. Out of three-hundred-and-six entries, these two plays you're determined to block rank, in my estimation, second and third. And you two are prepared to see that neither one of them gets its just due?

(A brief, uncomfortable silence, broken by WALTER:*)*

WALTER: Isn't that what committees are for?

PENNY: Well, Walter, despite your good reverse alphabetical intentions, we seem to have left Amy Yoskowitz for last. Is there no one to speak for her? *(Silence)*

WALTER: May I speak *against* her?

PENNY: Oh, why not? I don't believe we've followed my proposed model for argumentation since TINSELTOWN. Why break the string?

WALTER: I don't get it. This NOT WITH A WHIMPER thing. Literally. I can't follow the action. And I'm not even sure of the tone or the intent. What's going on here? Am I the only stupid person in this room?

X Y ZAMBEZI: Rest easy, you're among peers.

WALTER: *(To* ZAMBEZI*)* Do you like it?

X Y ZAMBEZI: Yes, but I'm not sure why. At least, not sure enough to explain.

PENNY: Will somebody tell me what it's about?

CHARLOTTE: Paranoia. The American form of paranoia.

LYNDON: It seems to be set in the Fifties, but maybe not. It features husband and wife survivalists entertaining another couple in their underground bunker. One of them may be a cannibal.

PENNY: "*May* be a cannibal"?

LYNDON: Or maybe just an insurance salesman. *(Beat)* It's ambiguous.

WALTER: *Is* it.

RAUL: It's hysterically funny. At least I found it to be so. Anyone else?

(Both LYNDON *and* CHARLOTTE *nod agreement, then glance at each other in surprise.)*

RAUL: It's pretty accomplished, I think—surprisingly subtle, yet bizarre without losing coherence or credibility. Some extremely original language choices and an unpredictable but highly organic structural scheme.

WALTER: I don't know...maybe I'm just not Occidental enough.

RAUL: No affinity for the Absurd, Walter? You?

WALTER: You would think, wouldn't you?

PENNY: Might we have a potential compromise choice here?

LYNDON: *(To* CHARLOTTE*)* You know anything about this Amy Yoskowitz?

CHARLOTTE: No. *(Glancing at her file)* M F A in Playwriting from Indiana; couple things done on the fringe in Chicago. That's about it.

PENNY: Sounds like the kind of person we're here to discover, yes?

WALTER: Penny, I do believe you're exhibiting a certain favoritism here.

PENNY: My nerves are fraying. We have to decide. Now. *(Beat)* I have to go get Jacob! At the day care! What if I'm not there when he's ready?

LYNDON: *(To* CHARLOTTE*, smiling)* He's four. She's in love.

(CHARLOTTE *smiles back.*)

RAUL: Let's vote.

CHARLOTTE: How? Got a method?

RAUL: I suggest everybody re-examine their previous rankings, one through seven, in light of the arguments we've made. Submit them to Penny. First choice gets seven points, second gets six, and so on, down to your last choice, which would only get one point. Add 'em up. Top three get rich.

WALTER: For a poet, Raul, you have a surprisingly well-ordered brain.

PENNY: Everybody in agreement procedurally?

CHARLOTTE: I would prefer to list only our top three with the number one choice getting five points, number two getting three points, and number three getting one point.

(The panelists, and PENNY, *all look at her silently—and wearily.)*

CHARLOTTE: Penny, can't you compute it both ways? Same ballot, just a different way of counting? *(More silence. She relents.)* Forget it.

PENNY: O K, Panel. Descending order, top to bottom. Have at it.

(The panelists scribble away. Only WALTER *still seems torn with indecision.)*

WALTER: Never. Never. Never again.

PENNY: Before you hand in your ballots, will you please do Nigh-peck a favor? At the bottom of your sheet, list the names of a couple of your colleagues you think would make suitable Panelists for next year's awards.

CHARLOTTE: A light dawns. It comes to me. Flattery was not the appropriate response to learning of my selection to this panel. Who was on this thing last year?

PENNY: I'm not at liberty to say.

CHARLOTTE: *(To the others)* Don't you see? Are you putting down your best friends in the business?

WALTER: *(Laughing)* I just listed the little shit I most despise.

CHARLOTTE: Q E D. We here are the collective embodiment of the last panel's Enemies List.

(The panelists—except ZAMBEZI—*share a small laugh as* PENNY *demurs:)*

PENNY: Oh, I hardly think that...

CHARLOTTE: We've been punished.

WALTER: Anonymously.

PENNY: Ballots, everybody?

(They hand them in. Several stand up, stretch, move around, affecting disinterest in the outcome. ZAMBEZI *gathers her belongings and, disconcertingly to all, she exits without a word.)*

CHARLOTTE: Yvonne?

(No answer. She's gone. CHARLOTTE *turns to the others, shakes her head.)*

CHARLOTTE: Strange.

WALTER: A very angry person.

RAUL: I read it as really intense professional jealousy over Alison Beaubien.

CHARLOTTE: You've got it partly right. She doesn't just hate Beaubien....

LYNDON: *(It clicks.)* She loves A C Taylor.

CHARLOTTE: Bingo. Acie's her Saturday Night Man.

PENNY: That would explain this, then. *(Holding up a ballot)* Numbers One through Seven. SHUFFLIN' OFF TO TINSELTOWN, seven times.

WALTER: Oh, please...

RAUL: Invalid ballot. Toss it.

LYNDON: Absolutely.

CHARLOTTE: You have to, yes.

PENNY: Next year. Blind submissions, start to finish, or I quit.

CHARLOTTE: You think Yvonne wouldn't have recognized her boyfriend's script even without his name?

PENNY: *(As she continues to add results)* Of course she would've.

CHARLOTTE: Or Lyndon Remy Sinclair's?

LYNDON: *(To* CHARLOTTE, *without malice)* Or you the notorious Winnifred Tobler's?

PENNY: Tobler?

CHARLOTTE & LYNDON: SUCK MY SACRED PARTS.

CHARLOTTE: *(Still smiling)* Sorry about that.

LYNDON: For every system, a flaw. We must blunder along.

(PENNY *crosses to the blackboard and ceremoniously erases, in order, A C Taylor* SHUFFLIN' OFF TO TINSELTOWN; *Jonathon Hardisty* GETTING IT DOWN; *Remy Sinclair* BLISTERS; *and finally Julia Novack* AULIS. *As each name goes, the following lines are delivered at the appropriate time:)*

WALTER: And TINSELTOWN goes down.

CHARLOTTE: Lonely Saturday nights for Yvonne.

WALTER: *(As Hardisty is erased)* Poor Jonathon.

CHARLOTTE: You must've really deep-sixed that one, Lyndon.

LYNDON: Deep-fived it, as I recall.

WALTER: *(Not viciously)* Have you always been homophobic? Or did you just have an unpleasant encounter in Boy Scouts?

LYNDON: Walter, people who define themselves first and foremost in terms of their sexual preferences simply bore me to tears. Does that constitute a phobia?

CHARLOTTE: *(As Sinclair is erased)* Bye-bye BLISTERS. *(To* LYNDON*)* Do you think Remy even remembers he applied for this?

LYNDON: Probably not.

CHARLOTTE: *(As Novack is erased)* Et tu, Brute?

LYNDON: I gotta be me, Charlotte.

*(*RAUL *approaches the board, whistles.)*

RAUL: Wow. SEBASTOPOL and two long-shots.

WALTER: SEBASTOPOL and MISS EBONY. Oh goodie, I got two out of three.

LYNDON: Me too. Same ones you had, Walter.

CHARLOTTE: Am I the only one who put NOT WITH A WHIMPER in the top three?

PENNY: Amy Yoskowitz is a very lucky young lady. Several of you had her as your fourth choice, and nobody really blackballed her. She slips in.

CHARLOTTE: Good for her.

WALTER: Penny? Can I make the calls notifying the winners?

PENNY: Sure, Walter. Over my dead body.

WALTER: Spoilsport.

PENNY: Those calls are the only fun thing about my job. Think about that: the *only* fun thing. *(Glancing at her watch)* In fact, why deny myself any longer? I have just enough time to let them know. At least one of them. Who shall I call first? Serge Polanowski? Alison Beaubien? Or young Amy?

CHARLOTTE & WALTER: Amy.

PENNY: So shall it be. *(Encompassing the remaining panelists:)* Nigh-peck thanks you. The Theater thanks you. Goodbye, all. Enjoy your weekend.

(Quick hugs to all, ad-libbed good-byes, and PENNY *exits. The remaining panelists gather up their belongings.)*

WALTER: Well. That was intense. Are we all still friends?

CHARLOTTE: Walter. None of us ever *were* friends.

WALTER: Well...are we now?

CHARLOTTE: Sure, Walter. I'll be your friend.

(They exchange a constrained little hug.)

WALTER: *(Looking at* RAUL*)* Etes-vous?

(RAUL *smiles, holds his hand out to shake. To his momentary dismay,* WALTER *takes the hand and kisses it as if* RAUL *were a French grand-dame.)*

WALTER: You're a genius, and you're a dear. *(Turning on* LYNDON *with mostly mock petulance)* And you're a disgustingly straight old windbag, a bottomless pit of the worst kind of annoyance. *(Holds his hand out daintily)* Enchantez.

(LYNDON *magnanimously takes his hand.)*

LYNDON: Take care of yourself, Walter.

WALTER: I shall, as if my life depended on it. *(He flounces toward an exit, turning for what he hopes will be a "line.")* I think we all learned a lot about ourselves over the last couple days, don't you?

CHARLOTTE: We did?

RAUL: Like what, Walter?

WALTER: Oh, do I have to do all the work? Find your own insights! Toodle-oo! *(And he is gone.)*

LYNDON: *(After a moment)* Can there be anything more exhausting for all concerned than perpetual flamboyance?

(CHARLOTTE *is watching* RAUL *as he contemplates the three names left on the blackboard.)*

CHARLOTTE: Whadaya think, Raul? Did we advance our vision of Theater at its best? Isn't that how you put it?

(RAUL *doesn't answer at once. He gives the question close consideration before quietly concluding:)*

RAUL: We did well.

(LYNDON *stands before the board and offers his own assessment.)*

LYNDON: Polanowski. A self-absorbed visionary who hardly knows what planet he's on, let alone whether he's rich or poor, successful or ruined. When Penny tells him he's a winner, he'll take it as his rightful due and will probably neglect to so much as thank her.

RAUL: Correct. Ten minutes later he'll have forgotten the phone call.

CHARLOTTE: Alison Beaubien?

LYNDON: This train's been a long time pulling into the station for her. She's hung in there, kept working, kept getting better. She's suffered. This will seem like an angelic visitation. Answered prayers.

CHARLOTTE: Validation. Is there any better feeling?

RAUL: To feel so alone for so long. And then someone says, "We see you. *You.* Over there. You're good. Keep it up."

CHARLOTTE: You know the best moment for me of my first production? Calling up my mother after opening night. "I did it, Mom. I told you I could do it, and now I have. You can stop worrying for me. You can be happy for me."

(RAUL *is smiling and nodding as if to himself as he hears this.* LYNDON *is staring at Amy Yoskowitz's name. He taps it.*)

LYNDON: This one. Amy Yoskowitz. How old is she? You recall?

CHARLOTTE: Twenty-two.

(LYNDON *just shakes his head and gives out with a low whistle.*)

(*Lights up in a separate area isolating* PENNY *talking at the phone. She's very happy, thoroughly into the moment.*)

PENNY: Amy? Is this Amy Yoskowitz? Amy, this is Penny Pinchbeak from the New York Playwrights Endowment Council. We've concluded our deliberations on this year's NYPEC grants, and Amy, you're a winner. Yes. Oh yes, you are. I can vouch for it. *(Beat)* Are you O K, Amy?

LYNDON: *(Still referring to Amy)* This is the one I feel sorry for.

CHARLOTTE: Yep.

PENNY: *(Laughing)* Don't cry, Amy, don't cry.

RAUL: Sorry? She's twenty-two and she just won fifteen grand. Why sorry?

(LYNDON *and* CHARLOTTE *look at each other and smile. They head for the up right door.*)

LYNDON: Because we've just sealed her fate, Raul. Because now there's no turning back.

CHARLOTTE: We just made her a playwright.

(*They exit. After a moment* RAUL *crosses to the blackboard and, one by one, erases the names of the winning playwrights. He picks up his belongings, and then he too exits. Lights down and out on Panelists' Room.*)

(*Light on* PENNY *narrows to spot.*)

PENNY: Yes, it *is* wonderful! I'm so happy for you. My sincerest congratulations. Have you got a headshot? For publicity purposes? No? Well, this would be a good time to get one made. Send it along to us as soon as you can, will you? Thanks! And we'll be in touch about the press conference. Amy, Amy, don't thank me, I just work here. Thank your Muse. I have to run now. I have a little boy waiting for me. Congratulations! Enjoy your weekend! Bye-bye! (*She hangs up, seemingly nearly as thrilled as Amy. She*

grabs her purse, hugs it to her breast, and exclaims to the world at large:)
Oh, that's just *so* much *fun*!

(Blackout)

END OF PLAY

THE MISADVENTURES OF CYNTHIA M.

For my good friend Bob Hammel, the best sportswriter I ever read — and one of the best talkers!

All the best,
Dennis J. Reardon
May 11th '06
Bloomington

Note: THE MISADVENTURES OF CYNTHIA M. is basically a six-character play (four males, two females) supplemented by twenty cameo roles limited to one or two scenes. The cameos should, of course, be double or even triple cast at the discretion of the Company. Following the cast page I have included a SEQUENCE OF SCENES—visually somewhat daunting, perhaps, but hopefully a time-saver for directors and actors.

The genesis of this play concerned a young mother who dropped her child off at the sitter's, left to commit a felony, and returned to pick up her baby. The child was also present when she was subsequently arrested. Ergo, I need a child: NOAH. A doll can be used in ACT ONE. But in ACT TWO a "live" NOAH must appear briefly in three scenes—"Ruthie Babysits", "Bust", and "Wave to Mommy". He should be a boy no older than three... two-and-a-half would be ideal.

The only other casting issue has to do with CYNTHIA's height. It would be wonderful if CYNTHIA could be quite tall. This is a woman who could be a runway fashion model. If this is not achievable, cut NATHAN's line in "Jezebel" along with OTIS's rejoinder.

CHARACTERS & SETTING

CYNTHIA, NATHAN's *girlfriend*
DETECTIVE JOHNS
NATHAN, OTIS's *nephew,* CYNTHIA's *boyfriend,* NOAH's *father*
OTIS, NATHAN's *uncle,* RUTHIE's *husband*
PROFESSOR PERCIVAL ST JOHN, *a poet*
RUTHIE, OTIS's *wife*
DR JOHN THE ASTRONOMER
NURSE
JOHN, *a john*
DR JOHN E B GOODE THE EVALUATOR
BIG JOHN, *a different john*
NOAH, *toddler son of* CYNTHIA *and* NATHAN; *cared for by* RUTHIE
ANDREA MAYFIELD, *a bank teller*
two EVIDENCE TECHNICIANS
three ARMED MEN
DR JOANNA THE EVALUATOR
TIFFANY JOHNSON, *owner of an escort service*
JOHN JONS, *a TV talking head*
JOHN PROSECUTOR
JOHN Q PUBLIC, DEFENDER
JUDGE JOHANNES
JAIL MATRON
TIBETAN WOMAN

Time: In and around Now

Setting: a small Midwestern university town

The "sets" are extreme lights and props in their orientation—a unit set conducive to highly fluid, multiple time and place changes.

SEQUENCE OF SCENES

ACT ONE: BOY MEETS GIRL, ET CETERA

1. Interrogation (DETECTIVE JOHNS, CYNTHIA)
2. First Meeting: McDonald's (NATHAN, CYNTHIA)
3. Jezebel (OTIS, NATHAN)
4. Scorpio (CYNTHIA, NATHAN)
5. Nate and Cindy and the Deep Still Pool (NATHAN, CYNTHIA)
6. Nathan Has a Fear (OTIS, CYNTHIA, NATHAN)
7. Cynthia Conferences with Percival St John, Poetry Professor (CYNTHIA, ST JOHN)
8. Not Tonight, Honey (NATHAN, CYNTHIA)
9. Nate Consults Otis at 2 A M (OTIS, NATHAN)
10. Our Bodies, Our Selves (CYNTHIA)
11. Nate Consults Otis at 2 A M, Part Two (OTIS, NATHAN)
12. The Annunciation (NATHAN, CYNTHIA)
13. Cynthia and Ruthie Have a Heart-to-Heart (RUTHIE, CYNTHIA)
14. Cynthia Conferences with Dr John the Astronomer (CYNTHIA, DR JOHN THE ASTRONOMER)
15. Contractions (NURSE, CYNTHIA, DETECTIVE JOHNS)
16. Deliverance (RUTHIE, NATHAN, NURSE)
17. The Baby Is Sick (CYNTHIA, RUTHIE, OTIS)
18. Cynthia and Nate Eat Breakfast (CYNTHIA, NATHAN)
19. Cynthia Alone (CYNTHIA, THE JOHNS)
20. Cin's First House Call (JOHN, CYNTHIA)

ACT TWO: CAUSE AND EFFECT

21. Cynthia Is Evaluated, Part One (CYNTHIA, DR JOHN E B GOODE)
22. Nate Spills His Guts Over a Beer, Part One (NATHAN)
23. Cin's Thirty-First House Call (CYNTHIA, BIG JOHN)
24. Cynthia Is Evaluated, Part Two (CYNTHIA, DR JOHN E B GOODE)
25. It Could Happen (NATHAN, RUTHIE, OTIS, CYNTHIA)
26. Ruthie Babysits (CYNTHIA, RUTHIE, NOAH)
27. Withdrawal Symptoms (CYNTHIA, ANDREA MAYFIELD)
28. Let's Go Shopping (CYNTHIA, RUTHIE)
29. The Ship Comes In (NATHAN, CYNTHIA)
30. Otis and Ruthie Put It Together (OTIS, RUTHIE)
31. Otis Testifies (OTIS, RUTHIE, DETECTIVE JOHNS,

two EVIDENCE TECHNICIANS)
32. Business as Usual (DETECTIVE JOHNS, OTIS, RUTHIE)
33. Bust (RUTHIE, NOAH, CYNTHIA, OTIS, DETECTIVE JOHNS)
34. Knock, Knock. Who's There? (NATHAN, DETECTIVE JOHNS, *three* ARMED MEN)
35. "He's Badly Built and He Walks on Stilts" (DETECTIVE JOHNS, CYNTHIA)
36. Nate Spills His Guts Over a Beer, Part Two (NATHAN)
37. Cynthia Is Evaluated, Part Three (DR JOANNA, CYNTHIA)
38. Cin's Boss Gets On T V (TIFFANY JOHNSON, JOHN JONS)
39. Justice Rears Its Whorey Head, or, Prudence, Dear Juris (JOHN PROSECUTOR, JOHN Q PUBLIC DEFENDER)
40. Justice (JOHN PROSECUTOR, JOHN Q PUBLIC DEFENDER, JUDGE JOHANNES, CYNTHIA)
41. Verdict (JUDGE JOHANNES, JOHN Q PUBLIC DEFENDER, CYNTHIA)
42. "Wave to Mommy" (RUTHIE, CYNTHIA, NOAH)
43. Visitation (NATHAN, CYNTHIA, JAIL MATRON)

ACT THREE: BUT WAIT, THERE'S MORE

44. "Even If It Happened, It Didn't Happen" (NATHAN, CYNTHIA)
45. Tutorial: St John Critiques (ST JOHN, CYNTHIA)
46. Flossing (NATHAN, CYNTHIA)
47. The Astronaut's Nightmare (NATHAN, CYNTHIA)
48. Viviparous (ST JOHN, CYNTHIA)
49. Tibetan Mountain Climbing Woman Dream (CYNTHIA, ST JOHN, TIBETAN WOMAN)
50. Puke-Eaters (NATHAN, CYNTHIA)
51. St John's Stormy Monday (CYNTHIA, NATHAN, ST JOHN)
52. The Great Divide (CYNTHIA, NATHAN)
53. Black Hole (CYNTHIA, NATHAN, THE JOHNS, RUTHIE)

A NOTE ON INTERVALS AND AUDIENCE ATTENTION SPANS

I try never to write a three-act play. In the case of THE MISADVENTURES OF CYNTHIA M., I didn't know that's what I was doing until I had already done it. And now it's too late. Three acts, fifty-three scenes. Like it or lump it, that's what it is.

I will make one suggestion, humbly tendered. There should be a standard interval of about fifteen minutes between ACTS ONE and TWO. Between ACTS TWO and THREE may I suggest something akin to baseball's 7th inning stretch—a briefer interval of about five minutes.

I accept the challenge of keeping an audience fully engrossed beyond their customary span of attention. Some stories are just bigger than others, that's all.

This play is for my daughter Siobhan and for my Mary.

from "Eight Verses for Training the Mind," as quoted in *The Path to Tranquility* by Tenzin Gyatso:

When I see beings of wicked nature
overwhelmed by violent negative actions and sufferings,
I shall hold such rare ones dear,
As if I have found a precious treasure.

ACT ONE

INTERROGATION

(Lights up on CYNTHIA, *facing front, seated, and* DETECTIVE JOHNS, *standing, facing upstage. Except for chair, a bare stage.)*

DETECTIVE JOHNS: Why'd you do it?

CYNTHIA: What's it matter? *(Silence)* I don't like the "Why" question.

DETECTIVE JOHNS: Got a better one?

CYNTHIA: Why not?

(Blackout)

FIRST MEETING: (McDONALD'S)

(General note: All "sets" should be as minimalist and fluid as possible. In this case—)

(Lights up on CYNTHIA, *behind simple counter suggesting that she's working as a cashier/order taker. Elsewhere, a small table and a chair where* NATHAN *will take his food. Right now* NATHAN *is standing in front of her, having just placed his order. They both look very young, fifteen to eighteen.* CYNTHIA *is all business;* NATHAN *is infatuated.)*

CYNTHIA: Big Mac with cheese, small vanilla shake, no fries. Four twenty-one.

NATHAN: *(Handing her a five)* Man. You're cute.

CYNTHIA: Seventy-nine cents change. Next.

*(*NATHAN *looks around.)*

NATHAN: There ain't no next.

CYNTHIA: Just my luck.

NATHAN: Hey... *(Peering at her nametag)* Cynthia. My name's Nate.

(She just stares.)

NATHAN: You just started working here, didn't you? Where you from?

CYNTHIA: Look. You'll get me in trouble.

NATHAN: When you done?

CYNTHIA: Five hours from now. Bye.

(NATHAN *smiles, picks up his food, and moves off to the table to eat. But mostly he just sits and stares at her.*)

JEZEBEL

(*Lights remain up on* NATHAN, *fade on* CYNTHIA, *and up on a living room couch where a short, somewhat squatty older man is sitting. This is* OTIS, *Nate's uncle. He talks across the space to* NATHAN *as if they were in the same house.* CYNTHIA, *in the dimmer light now, continues to stand in the counter area, either "frozen" or slowly miming typical work movements.*)

OTIS: So where's she from?

NATHAN: Down around Jeffersonville. *(Beat)* She gotta be six feet tall. Most of it legs.

OTIS: Tall women laugh at me.

NATHAN: She got this perfect little nose, like she was maybe eight or nine, ya know? Eyes like...

OTIS: Like?

NATHAN: Like that Siamese cat you used to have.

OTIS: Remember that cat's name?

NATHAN: No.

OTIS: Jezebel. *(Beat)* Word to the wise.

NATHAN: I'm just saying it's the same color blue she's got in her eyes. You don't have to go saying nothing. You ain't never met her.

OTIS: Nate...

NATHAN: You always just, you know, take something beautiful and turn it into shit.

OTIS: That's not so.

NATHAN: I mean, just because your first wife turned into the She-Bitch from Hell on you—

OTIS: Nate, I'm just saying—

NATHAN: What're you just saying? All women are evil? What about Ruthie?

OTIS: What're you getting all pissy about?

NATHAN: I'm gonna marry this fucking girl!

(OTIS *laughs*)

NATHAN: I'm gonna!

OTIS: You ain't even been out with her!

NATHAN: It's a done deal! I got nothing to say about it.

(OTIS *stares incredulously at* NATHAN *for a couple moments, then gets up and exits. Lights out on couch area. Up brighter on counter area. Same on table area. Sound: Vacuum cleaner.*)

SCORPIO

CYNTHIA: Are you stalking me, or what?

NATHAN: Stalking?

CYNTHIA: You gonna follow me home? Peer through my windows with binoculars?

NATHAN: Hey, you got me all wrong.

CYNTHIA: You been sitting there staring at me now for the last five hours. You don't think that's kinda creepy?

NATHAN: It's been five hours? *(Beat)* You're right. That is kinda creepy. *(Beat)* I'm sorry.

CYNTHIA: How old are you?

NATHAN: Twenty-one.

CYNTHIA: Liar.

NATHAN: Whada*you* think?

CYNTHIA: Seventeen.

NATHAN: *Eigh*teen!

(She laughs a bit tersely.)

NATHAN: So what're you?

CYNTHIA: Same.

NATHAN: When's your birthday?

CYNTHIA: When's yours?

NATHAN: September twenty-third.

CYNTHIA: You know what that makes you?

NATHAN: Whadaya mean?

CYNTHIA: A Virgo. *(Beat)* A virgin. *(Beat)* You're a virgin.

NATHAN: You're not?

CYNTHIA: What would you guess?

NATHAN: Not.

CYNTHIA: Right. *(Beat)* I'm a Scorpio.

(Blackout)

NATHAN AND CYNTHIA AND THE DEEP STILL POOL

(Sound: Quietly gurgling creek. From off, voices of NATHAN *and* CYNTHIA*)*

CYNTHIA *(O S)* Nathan. Stop. Let's rest a bit.

NATHAN *(O S)* We're there, I promise. Just past this clearing. C'mon, Cindy.

*(*NATHAN *enters.)*

NATHAN: See?

*(*CYNTHIA *enters.)*

NATHAN: My secret pool.

*(*CYNTHIA *moves to the edge of the suggested pool; sits on a rock.* NATHAN *joins her.)*

NATHAN: I never showed anybody this place before.

CYNTHIA: It's real pretty, Nathan.

NATHAN: Quiet back in here. *(Beat)* Steadies my mind.

CYNTHIA: I don't know...it looks kinda snaky to me.

NATHAN: Never seen a one.

CYNTHIA: *(Beat)* Lonely.

NATHAN: Aw, not really. If you can get still enough, it's all around you, you know? Life? *(Beat)* Back there? Out there amongst humans? Now that's lonely. All the time I feel like a salmon swimming upstream. Fighting the current. Getting slammed under, down to the bottom of the river. *(Beat)* Drowning.

CYNTHIA: *(Beat)* Salmon don't drown. They got gills.

NATHAN: Yeah. Well. You know what I mean. *(Beat)* Doncha?

(She stares at him; then:)

CYNTHIA: I think boys is different than girls.

NATHAN: Can't dispute that.

CYNTHIA: I don't swim. I fly. In my dreams, I fly.

NATHAN: Like an angel.

CYNTHIA: No. Not like an angel. *(Beat)* In my dreams, it's always night. I see little lights below me. But they twist and flow and blur like I'm on some stomach-turning ride at the County Fair. *(Beat)* I been trying to think what flies like that. *(Beat)* You know what does?

(NATHAN *shakes his head "No."*)

CYNTHIA: Bat.

(Blackout)

NATHAN HAS A FEAR

(Lights up on props suggesting OTIS *and* RUTHIE's *living room—the couch seen in "Jezebel," maybe a chair, end table, lamp—bare bones and low end.* OTIS *walks into light: Direct address:)*

OTIS: We did our best to make her family. Just like we did Nate after his Daddy, uh, well, never mind about that. *(Thinks for a minute)* Sometimes she tried to fit in. Like when Ruthie gave her cooking lessons and stuff. I don't know. She just had this...way of carrying herself. We played this game once. What would you be if you were a, you know, a dog or something. She blurts out right off, "An afghan." *(Beat)* Me, I never heard of such a thing. I says, "We're talking dogs, not rugs." *(Beat)* Ah look, I got no quarrel with how she sees herself. She wants to be an Afghan, let her be a damn afghan. *(Beat)* Problem is, she makes everybody else feel like a mutt.

(Lights up cross-stage on NATHAN *and* CYNTHIA. *She's holding out a gift-wrapped present, and she's smiling.)*

CYNTHIA: Happy birthday, Otis.

NATHAN: Happy birthday, Ugly Uncle!

OTIS: Hey hey, whacha got here?

NATHAN: Open it and see! You ain't gonna believe this....

(OTIS *hefts the box.*)

OTIS: Too big to be a cigar box. *(Takes the gift-wrapping off to reveal a zippered, fabric-covered box. He stares at it cluelessly.)*

NATHAN: It's a cassette tape holder!

CYNTHIA: Well just *tell* him, why doncha?

NATHAN: Unzip it, look inside.

(OTIS *does so. He pulls out a single cassette.*)

OTIS: Who we got here?

(CYNTHIA *covers* NATHAN's *mouth before he can answer. She studies* OTIS *intently.*)

OTIS: Why, it looks to be Loretta Lynn and Hank Williams.

(CYNTHIA *smiles proudly.*)

NATHAN: Cindy drew it for ya!

OTIS: Really? You mean, like, traced it?

NATHAN: No! Hell, no! She just sat down and drew it right out!

CYNTHIA: Well, I...I was lookin' at a couple different album covers—

NATHAN: Well sure, yeah, but that don't count as *tra*cing.

OTIS: No, it don't. This is a doggone fine likeness, Cynthia.

CYNTHIA: Thank you.

NATHAN: Ain't she something? She got so many talents, man....

OTIS: She's full of surprises, no lie—

NATHAN: Hey, you know on my birthday? She gonna draw *me*! Right, honey?

CYNTHIA: Well, I...I said I'd take a stab at it, Nathan. *(To* OTIS*)* Never done nothing from life before.

NATHAN: She can do anything she sets her mind to. *(Hugs her)* Can't ya?

(She smiles, but pulls back.)

NATHAN: Tell him what you're doing this fall. Go on, just tell him.

(She shakes her head "No." She means it.)

NATHAN: She's going to the University!

CYNTHIA: You don't have to tell everybody about every private conversation we have.

NATHAN: Hell, he ain't "everybody"! This here's my Ugly Uncle Otis!

(He gives him a big hug as OTIS, *embarrassed, shoves him away.)*

OTIS: Back to school, huh?

CYNTHIA: It's no big deal. Just a couple courses.

OTIS: You mean, like correspondence courses?

NATHAN: *Hell*, no! She gonna be at a desk with an apple for that teacher come September three! College girl!

OTIS: So you gonna be quitting down at Walmart?

CYNTHIA: No, no, they'll work my hours around it. Can't quit. Are you kidding? *(Beat)* So, where's Ruthie?

OTIS: Helping out down at day care. So whacha gonna be studyin', ya don't mind me asking?

CYNTHIA: Uh, well...

NATHAN: Go ahead.

CYNTHIA: *(Shyly)* Introduction to Astronomy.

OTIS: No kidding?

NATHAN: And? *And?*

CYNTHIA: Poetry writing.

NATHAN: *(Triumphantly)* Poetry writing! Ain't that something!

CYNTHIA: Nathan, get a grip, will ya? *(To* OTIS*)* Can I make a sandwich or something?

OTIS: Help yourself.

(CYNTHIA *exits.* NATHAN *turns on* OTIS, *speaks confidentially but emphatically.*)

NATHAN: So *now* what you think of things, Otis? Huh?

OTIS: Like I say, she's full of surprises.

NATHAN: When you gonna start liking her? I mean, jeez o'Pete....

OTIS: Nate. It ain't up to me to like her. I ain't living with her.

NATHAN: Sometimes I get the feeling you wish you was.

OTIS: What?

NATHAN: If only just for a night.

OTIS: Get outta my house. Go on, get out. Take her with you.

NATHAN: Hey, Otis...

OTIS: I don't need that kind of filthiness under my roof!

NATHAN: Otis, Uncle, man, I'm sorry. Things just pop out of me sometimes, you know what I'm saying? I don't mean nothing by it.

OTIS: You forget sometimes I'm a Christian.

NATHAN: I know, Otis, jeez.

OTIS: Just cause I slip and occasionally use a vulgarity or something.

NATHAN: I just want you to love her like I do! Love her like a Christian. Can't you even do that? What she ever do to you, Otis? Why can't you stand to just let me be happy with her? I mean, it looks like jealousy sometimes,

Otis, that's all I'm saying—not like, you know, *sex*. More like you just flat out can't handle I'm *happy*.

OTIS: That so?

NATHAN: That's so.

OTIS: *(Takes a moment, thinks about it)* Well, then. I'm sorry. If it's like that, it's wrong.

(NATHAN *hugs him. This time with* CYNTHIA *absent,* OTIS *hugs him back.*)

OTIS: It's just I don't want you getting hurt real bad. Since your dad... you know.

NATHAN: I know.

OTIS: I'm the one's gotta look out for you.

NATHAN: Not no more, Otis. I mean, look at me. I got two feet. And I'm standing on 'em.

OTIS: Nathan. If she gave a hoot about you, she'd be wantin' ta marry.

NATHAN: That make you feel better? If we made it legal?

OTIS: *(After a moment)* No. I don't reckon it would.

NATHAN: I didn't think so.

OTIS: What I'm saying is, most girls, that's all you hear—marry me, marry me, marry me, till you do it just to shut 'em up.

NATHAN: Ain't it clear yet? She ain't like most girls. That's why I love her.

OTIS: O K, Nathan. I said my piece.

NATHAN: Take this school thing now, Otis. Don't that speak well of her?

OTIS: Well. Star gazing. Poem writing. Kinda weird, doncha think?

NATHAN: I'm telling you, it's what she's been missing, you know? I'm thinking it's a *good* thing. Something to keep her mind occupied. Keep her from all the time looking around, looking around... *(Silence)* Can you keep any secrets from Ruthie?

OTIS: No.

NATHAN: Damn.

OTIS: What can't you tell Ruthie?

NATHAN: I got a fear.

OTIS: *(Beat)* Might be I could keep something like that quiet.

NATHAN: *(Summons up his courage)* I got a fear. That I bore her.

(Long silence as lights dim out on NATHAN *and* OTIS*)*

CYNTHIA CONFERENCES WITH PERCIVAL ST JOHN, POETRY PROFESSOR

*(The Pulitzer Prize-winning poet is perusing poetry—*CYNTHIA's*, to be precise. She anxiously awaits his approval. At length he hands it back to her.)*

ST JOHN: And what, precisely, were you trying to convey with this, uh, poem?

CYNTHIA: Well, uh...you mean like what's the meaning? Or are you saying What's the feeling?

ST JOHN: Shouldn't they be the same?

CYNTHIA: Yes. *(Can't articulate an answer)* Doesn't it say anything to you?

ST JOHN: Oh, perhaps more than you would wish.

CYNTHIA: You don't like anything about it, do you?

ST JOHN: I didn't say that. I didn't even *think* that.

CYNTHIA: *(Relaxes slightly, then ventures:)* I was thinking about how you never really know anybody.

ST JOHN: Yes.

CYNTHIA: And since it's like that, why settle for just *one* self? Why not three? Or even fifteen or twenty?

ST JOHN: If there's no one self?

CYNTHIA: No, even if there is.

ST JOHN: *(Explaining her to herself)* Because even if the truth were there for all to see, no one would see it anyway except by accident since, in this world, "you never really know anybody."

CYNTHIA: Yes! You understand!

ST JOHN: Oh, I wouldn't go that far. *(He is staring intently at her.)*

CYNTHIA: Is there something wrong, Professor St John?

ST JOHN: Hmm?

CYNTHIA: You're uh...you're staring at me.

ST JOHN: Oh. Am I? I do beg your pardon. Let me understand something. You want some kind of private tutorial with me?

CYNTHIA: Well, I don't know what you'd call it for sure, but just something where I come into your office—you know, just me—and I show you some stuff and you tell me what you think. *(Beat)* Like now. Like this.

ST JOHN: Why don't you just take one of my classes?

CYNTHIA: Because I heard you make people read their stuff out loud. To everyone.

ST JOHN: And?

CYNTHIA: And talk about it?

ST JOHN: Well, yes. It's a Poetry Workshop. That's how I earn my check.

CYNTHIA: Right. And uh, that's fine, except, uh...

ST JOHN: Yes?

CYNTHIA: Well, they're all graduate students or something—

ST JOHN: Not all of them.

CYNTHIA: Or published and stuff, like they give *readings* and things. This is what I've heard, and I'm just...nobody. *(Beat)* Uh. You're staring at me again.

ST JOHN: Again? Well perhaps that's because you're not Nobody, Cynthia. You strike me as a Somebody. Yes, definitely a Somebody.

CYNTHIA: You don't understand. I just work at WalMarts. I don't even know why I'm here. I don't belong. You know it. I know it.

(He seems deep in thought.)

CYNTHIA: They told me you won a big prize, the Nobel Prize or something—

ST JOHN: Oh good god no. *(Beat)* You may be thinking of my Pulitzer.

CYNTHIA: Whatever. *(Beat)* Fact is, I've never been so scared of a man in my life as I am of you.

(Again, he seems to be drifting.)

CYNTHIA: Well, I'll be going now. *(She stands.)* Dumb idea. I get them sometimes. Sorry I wasted your time.

(Still he says nothing—hard to tell if he even hears her. At the door to his office she can go no further:)

CYNTHIA: Look. Do I have any talent? Yes or no?

ST JOHN: Hmm? Oh. No.

CYNTHIA: No?

ST JOHN: No. Not so far as I can tell, no.

CYNTHIA: God DAMN you!

(She takes a step toward him as if she would physically attack him. Then stops, covers her face, and just weeps. ST JOHN sighs...not the first time he's had this conversation, nor this reaction.)

ST JOHN: Please. Sit down. And shut the door, will you? Before they start muttering about revoking my tenure again?

(She sits, tries to compose herself.)

CYNTHIA: I'm sorry. I just didn't figure you to be so cruel. My fault.

ST JOHN: You're emotionally quite liberated, Cynthia.

CYNTHIA: I'm sorry.

ST JOHN: Please stop saying that. It turns a compliment into a defect.

CYNTHIA: A compliment? Did I miss a compliment somewhere?

ST JOHN: I complimented you on your emotional freedom. You're quite in touch with your feelings.

CYNTHIA: Look. I haven't heard anything since you told me my poetry sucks.

ST JOHN: *(Indicating her poems)* How long have you been expressing yourself this way?

CYNTHIA: Oh, what's the point?

ST JOHN: I want to know how serious you are about this.

CYNTHIA: *(Beat)* Since first grade.

(He gestures: "continue.")

CYNTHIA: Mr Miller. *(Beat)* He was a wonderful man, Mr Miller. *(Beat)* He taught me about rhyme.

ST JOHN: So I noticed.

CYNTHIA: He taught me how to make words do what I wanted them to.

ST JOHN: And what was that?

CYNTHIA: Sing.

ST JOHN: Uh huh.

(After a beat, she grabs her poems, shuffles through them, finds one, and shoves it under his nose.)

CYNTHIA: *That* one. That's my best one. What's wrong with that one?

ST JOHN: Look, Miss. You alarm me.

CYNTHIA: I do?

ST JOHN: Yes. I'm afraid you're going to attack me. You give off that feeling. You wouldn't do that, would you?

CYNTHIA: *(She has to think about it.)* I don't think so. *(Beat)* Please. Read my poem. Tell me about it. It hurts like hellfire, but I need you to tell me how to do it better.

(He scans it, then looks up at her.)

ST JOHN: I don't want to do this.

CYNTHIA: It's *that* bad? *(Almost crying)* Gol *dang*!

ST JOHN: Cynthia. If you would be good enough to get it together, I will pass along to you—absolutely free of charge—four words of wisdom.

(She calms.)

ST JOHN: Ready?

(She nods.)

ST JOHN: "Weepy Women Never Win."

(Beat)

CYNTHIA: Who said that?

ST JOHN: My mother. *(Beat)* The embodiment of that philosophy. *(Beat)* A terrifying creature. *(Beat)* All right. You said your poems are about...what?

CYNTHIA: Never really knowing.

ST JOHN: Right. The distance between what you're trying to say and what you're actually getting down on paper, well, it's a long long way to Tipperary, Cynthia.

CYNTHIA: What do you mean?

ST JOHN: Well. To the, uh, untrained eye, Cynthia, this poem is uh...pornographic.

CYNTHIA: *(Beat—not seeing a problem)* Yes?

ST JOHN: Precisely. That's the best part of it.

CYNTHIA: *(Almost shyly)* Thank you...

ST JOHN: As for the rest of it—

CYNTHIA: Uh-huh?

ST JOHN: It's like you never outgrew your Mr Miller's first grade poetry.

CYNTHIA: That's not good. Is it?

ST JOHN: Reading this poem is like listening to porn come out of the mouth of a little first-grade girl.

CYNTHIA: Uh-huh.

ST JOHN: This mixture of innocence and licentiousness, it's uh...disconcerting.

CYNTHIA: So...do you like it, or what?

ST JOHN: Well, I think perhaps this comes under the heading of Guilty Pleasures.

CYNTHIA: Look, are you just, you know...toying with me?

(He studies her; decides:)

ST JOHN: I'll let you sign up for one hour of credit. No more. Depending on how you progress, we'll talk.

CYNTHIA: And nobody's going to see it but you?

ST JOHN: No. Just me.

CYNTHIA: And we'll meet privately and talk about it?

ST JOHN: I'll see you for one half hour every other week. Bring new material with you each time.

(She is struggling to contain her joy, which is being tempered by one doubt.)

CYNTHIA: There's just one thing. *(She pulls up her top and exposes her breasts to him.)*

ST JOHN: Oh now Cynthia, don't go spoiling a good moment...

CYNTHIA: Do these have anything to do with your decision?

ST JOHN: Let me assure you, my dear, I come from a long line of thoroughly gay men.

CYNTHIA: *(Covering up)* Well I *thought* so. *(Beat)* I just had to be sure. *(She gives him a hug.)* Thank you so much.

ST JOHN: *(Disengaging)* Don't do that. Please. *(Checking his calendar)* I'll see you in two weeks.

CYNTHIA: Thank you, Professor St John. Thank you. I'll work really hard.

ST JOHN: Don't strain yourself.

(As she exits, pausing, almost meditatively, wistfully)

CYNTHIA: It's so strange, thinking about him now. After all these years.

ST JOHN: Who?

CYNTHIA: Mr Miller. My first-grade teacher. *(Beat; then, more to herself:)* Ole Johnny Miller.

(She exits. ST JOHN stares after her. Blackout)

NOT TONIGHT, HONEY

(Lights up but very dim. NATHAN *and* CYNTHIA *in bed. She's wearing a "Not Tonight Honey"-type nightgown, but* NATHAN *is being seductively persistent.* CYNTHIA *suddenly and emphatically removes his hand from her anatomy.)*

CYNTHIA: You just don't understand "subtle," do you?

NATHAN: *(Meekly)* I was being subtle.

CYNTHIA: You don't know how to *read* things, Nathan. I mean, you court rejection.

NATHAN: But...you're my...girlfriend.

*(*CYNTHIA *hops out of bed, flips on a table lamp, and models a heavy nightgown.)*

CYNTHIA: Look what I'm wearing. Does this turn you on? Huh? Thirty-five yards of flannel?

NATHAN: I just figured you must have a cold or something.

CYNTHIA: *("Modeling" it)* You know what they call this, Nathan?
(She contorts it until she can read the label.) "The Great Wall of Cynthia."

NATHAN: C'mon, Cin, don't be like this....

CYNTHIA: Now I want to get back into bed. I want to roll over on my side—away from you—and I want to forget you're in this bed with me. *(She crawls into bed as described.)* And if I get real lucky, I'll be long gone before you start snoring. *(Fluffs her pillows violently, then plunks her head down)* Adios, muchacho.

*(*NATHAN *stares up at the ceiling for awhile. Suddenly he sits bolt upright, throws the covers back. There's a chair by their bed. He gets up and sprawls in it, clad in his underwear. She violently pulls the blankets back over her, keeping her back to him, intent on ignoring him. When he can speak, he sounds muted, almost hoarse.)*

NATHAN: You make me feel so bad. *(Silence)* This is the only thing I live for.

(She rolls over, props up on her elbow, and regards him.)

CYNTHIA: What is? Sex with me?

NATHAN: *Being* with you.

CYNTHIA: "Being with me." *(Beat)* Weren't you just in my bed? I mean, you weren't off in Sheboygan someplace, were you? *(Beat)* So... "being with me" is bullshit, right? What you're trying to say, Nathan, is "Fucking me." "Fucking me" is the only thing you live for. Right?

NATHAN: That's part of being with you. *(Silence)* Yes. *(Beat)* Fucking you is the only thing I live for.

CYNTHIA: Well, thank you. Now we're getting somewhere. Get back into bed.

(He does. She takes off her nightgown.)

CYNTHIA: Get it on.

NATHAN: What?

CYNTHIA: Fuck me.

NATHAN: Cin...

CYNTHIA: We aims to please here at the Mustang Ranch.

(NATHAN, slowly this time, gets out of bed and sits in his chair.)

NATHAN: Since I met you...my head is full of snakes. And my heart, my heart, is full of worms.

CYNTHIA: *(Without missing a beat, ad-libbing a country western tune)* "Head fulla snakes, heart fulla worms..." All you need's a steel guitar. *(Smiles, sort of)* Little Nate and the Heartbreak Ridge Boys.

NATHAN: *(Stares at her with new eyes)* Good Lord, you're cruel.

CYNTHIA: This? This is "cranky."

(Pounds her pillow a couple more times, and settles in, her back to NATHAN, as lights dim to blackout)

NATHAN CONSULTS OTIS AT 2 A M

(Lights up isolating OTIS. As he speaks, light fills to include NATHAN. OTIS is very serious throughout this duologue, as if he were fulfilling a sacred trust to advise and counsel NATHAN.)

OTIS: You know, talking to you like you are now, Nate, well...it's hard not to slip back into the language of the secular.

NATHAN: Say whacha gotta say, Otis.

OTIS: You're pussywhipped.

NATHAN: Jeez, Unc, don't dress it up for me, huh?

OTIS: I ask that He forgive me my vulgarism. I just don't know the Christian word for that.

(A short silence as NATHAN self-examines his recent history and his conscience)

NATHAN: You're right. You're right as rain.

(OTIS does not gloat; he commiserates, perhaps even patting Nate's hand.)

OTIS: Nate, you have just taken the first and hardest step towards a cure: You admit your disease.

NATHAN: Look at me. I'm a mess. Two in the morning, I'm pulling you out of bed, maybe scaring Ruthie—

OTIS: Ruthie don't scare easy, specially not with me here.

NATHAN: I cry a lot, Otis. Does that surprise you?

(OTIS *is a bit taken aback.*)

OTIS: Nothing wrong with that, Nate. Just pains me that you're hurting.

NATHAN: You warned me. You warned me from the git-go.

OTIS: I got an instinct for predators. That's all.

NATHAN: Well...I appreciate you not saying "I told you so."

(OTIS *disparagingly waves it off.*)

NATHAN: No. No. You got a right. You seen it coming. You warned me like a friend and like good kin, and it was too late already. *(He shakes his head, marveling.)* You know how long it took?

OTIS: What?

NATHAN: Till she turned me into a dog in heat? About thirty seconds. Long enough to tell me what I owed her. *(Remembering their first meeting)* That fast food joint. Big Mac with cheese, small vanilla shake, no fries. Cost me four twenty-one.

OTIS: Yeah. That plus your balls.

NATHAN: Yep.

OTIS: She never *stops* telling you what you owe her, Nathan. No sir...you got the kinda woman makes you pay for a long, long time.

NATHAN: What am I going to do, Otis?

OTIS: My opinion? No hard feelings?

(NATHAN *indicates he should continue.*)

OTIS: Dump the bitch. Hit the road. See ya shopping some day. Gone. *(Beat)* I mean, where's the problem? You weren't stupid enough to marry her...Nathan...you didn't elope or nothing for god's sakes, did ya?

NATHAN: No, Otis. We're still just engaged or something, I don't know...

OTIS: Well, there you go...right?

(NATHAN *looks at* OTIS *like he wants to cry. Crossfade to* CYNTHIA.)

OUR BODIES, OUR SELVES

(CYNTHIA *takes a home pregnancy test. It is positive.*)

CYNTHIA: No. No. I've done this wrong. (*She reads the directions again, frantically. No doubt: She's pregnant... She seems to get an adverse physical reaction to this—faintness, clammy skin, nausea, all the while murmuring weakly to herself...*) I can't...I can't. Oh God don't make this happen oh God... (*She is lying on the floor. Distraught, despondent...but not yet angry. It sounds like she's saying....*) I'm not...this old...I'm not....

(*Lights dim on* CYNTHIA, *but not out. Lights back up on continuation of* NATHAN *and* OTIS *scene.*)

NATHAN CONSULTS OTIS AT 2 A M, PART TWO

NATHAN: She wants to abort it.

OTIS: You ain't gonna let her?

NATHAN: It appears I don't have much say in it.

OTIS: That's your child as much as hers! Don't you forget it!

NATHAN: (*Exhausted*) Otis? Could you do me a big favor? Could you please not yell at me? Yelling's the one thing I'm getting enough of.

(*Lights dim on* NATHAN/OTIS *area as lights brighten on the prostrate* CYNTHIA. NATHAN *turns from* OTIS, *who recedes to O S.* NATHAN *gets into the moment of first finding* CYNTHIA *on their bathroom floor.*)

THE ANNUNCIATION

NATHAN: *Cindy!* (*He rushes to help her.*) What's happened? Are you hurt?

(*At first, as if dazed or drunk, she doesn't respond to him...but then she starts slapping at him, lashing out, following him as he retreats, bewildered.*)

CYNTHIA: You sunuvabitch, you stupid hick-ass son of a bitch! I hate you, I just fucking *hate* you!

NATHAN: What's wrong? Why are you—?

CYNTHIA: You got me PREGnant you dumb shit! I *told* you this was going to happen!

NATHAN: What about your pills? I don't...?

CYNTHIA: Vag infection! Antibiotics! Pills no good! Any of this coming back to you?

(Every time he tries to embrace her or soothe her, she bats him away.)

NATHAN: Cynthia, honey, you gotta calm down.

CYNTHIA: This is what I get for giving in to your goddamn whining....

NATHAN: Why does it have to be a bad thing? I...I *want* to be a daddy.

(A sort of scream escapes from CYNTHIA.)

NATHAN: Maybe this is just God's way of telling us it's time to get married.

CYNTHIA: I'M TOO YOUNG TO BE SADDLED WITH A BABY, DIPSHIT!

(He backs off from her.)

NATHAN: I don't like you calling me that.

CYNTHIA: You're not sup*posed* to like it! *(She paces, chewing her nails.)* All right. All right. Just gotta deal with it...

NATHAN: That's right, get our heads around it, you know...

CYNTHIA: I know a place, a clinic out past State Line—Christ where are we gonna get the money for this—?

NATHAN: Well, don't you girls, you know, throw baby showers and stuff? I mean, isn't the idea everybody pitches in and gets you cribs and clothes and all?

(She stares at him slack-jawed.)

CYNTHIA: My God. You are just dumber than pure white lead.

NATHAN: *(Lost)* No?

CYNTHIA: I am *not* having this *baby*!

(A long silence. He stares at her but she's oblivious to him, pacing.)

NATHAN: I think we gotta talk about this. Maybe not tonight. But soon.

CYNTHIA: No talk. *(Beat)* No. Talk.

NATHAN: Cynthia. It's my baby, too.

CYNTHIA: Your baby? It's your baby?

NATHAN: It's ours.

CYNTHIA: The fuck it is. *(Beat)* You gonna walk around the rest of the year looking like you swallowed a watermelon? You gonna try to squeeze this cannonball out a hole about as big as your dick? *Your* baby...

NATHAN: You're so...vulgar.

CYNTHIA: Having babies is vulgar! Blood and water and piss and shit! *LIFE* is vulgar! We're fucking *animals*!

(After a silence, NATHAN *starts putting on a jacket.)*

CYNTHIA: Where you going?

NATHAN: Gonna go see Otis.

CYNTHIA: It's two in the morning.

(He is undeterred.)

CYNTHIA: Go ahead! Line 'em all up against me! Won't matter! You think I give a shit whether Ruthie and Otis think I'm Princess Di? They've hated me from first sight!

NATHAN: Why don't you try and get some sleep?

CYNTHIA: Otis. Your role model.

NATHAN: No need to be putting him down.

CYNTHIA: And Ruthie! You think I'm *her*? You think I'm ever gonna be?

NATHAN: You could do a lot worse. *(Beat)* You could be you.

(He exits. Blackout)

CYNTHIA AND RUTHIE HAVE A HEART-TO-HEART

(Lights up on a kitchen table in OTIS *and* RUTHIE's *house.* CYNTHIA *and* RUTHIE *are seated, staring at each other. Coffee cups and danish indicate it's morning. A five-count, then:)*

CYNTHIA: You hate me.

RUTHIE: No.

CYNTHIA: You don't like me.

RUTHIE: We're different.

CYNTHIA: Amen to that.

RUTHIE: You look down on me.

CYNTHIA: No I don't.

RUTHIE: You look down on everyone. *(Beat)* Why?

CYNTHIA: Like you say. I'm different.

RUTHIE: Special.

CYNTHIA: Yes.

RUTHIE: The rest of us, we're all white trash. *(Beat)* If we are, you are.

CYNTHIA: *(Calmly)* No I'm not. I'm something. But I'm not that. *(Beat)* Neither are you, Ruthie. But no one but me will ever know.

RUTHIE: You're killing Nate. Every time he comes by here, it's like you've taken another chunk out of him.

CYNTHIA: I know. I can't help it.

RUTHIE: If you can do that to him, what will you do to this baby?

CYNTHIA: Then why don't you want me to abort?

RUTHIE: We've been through that. *(Pause)*

CYNTHIA: I feel invaded. Like there's a parasite using my blood. Know what I mean?

RUTHIE: No.

CYNTHIA: That's because you can't get pregnant. *(Beat)* You want to and can't. I don't want to and did. *(Beat)* It's like God's got nothing better to do than fuck with us.

RUTHIE: *(After a beat)* Maybe your life came into being just so this child could come into the world.

CYNTHIA: Hey. Do I look like the Virgin Mary to you? *(Beat)* Ruthie. You know I wasn't meant to be a mother. Help me.

RUTHIE: I'm trying. I told you. I'll help you find a home for it.

CYNTHIA: Will you take him?

RUTHIE: No. Not with you in the picture. Baby's got to go away. Someplace you can't find him.

CYNTHIA: Nate won't let that happen. As soon as he sees him—

RUTHIE: He won't see him. Not if you have it over in St Joe's. They'll take care of all the adoption arrangements.

CYNTHIA: I'll see it. What happens then?

RUTHIE: You'll cry when they separate you. And then you'll stop. Sooner or later, you'll stop.

CYNTHIA: *(Beat)* How much will they pay me?

RUTHIE: What?

CYNTHIA: For the baby? How much?

RUTHIE: That's an evil question.

CYNTHIA: A healthy white baby? Ruthie? You think maybe money will change hands? Somewhere along the line? *(Beat)* Why should Saint Joe's get it all? Are they the ones puking up their guts every morning? Are they the ones gonna have their innards ripped out delivering this thing? You bet their not-for-profit tax-exempt assholes they're not.

RUTHIE: You're a real piece of work, Cynthia.

CYNTHIA: Yeah? Well. Maybe I'm the one shoulda been aborted, huh Ruthie?

(RUTHIE *can only stare at her. She looks very tired.* CYNTHIA *is now admiring her own hands. After a while:*)

CYNTHIA: Do you like my hands?

RUTHIE: What?

CYNTHIA: I think they're my best feature.

RUTHIE: Why shouldn't they be nice? They've never done a day's work.

CYNTHIA: I used to play the piano. Just so I could watch my fingers move. *(Beat)* Scuttling over the keys like roaches looking for a dark corner. *(Beat)* A man told me once, he said, "You have the hands of a surgeon." *(Beat)* I was jerking him off at the time.

RUTHIE: Stop!

CYNTHIA: Most women don't have a clue how to do that, you know?

RUTHIE: Stop talking about this!

CYNTHIA: Even the most experienced women. They just grab a guy's dick and start yanking on it. Like it's a cow's udder and they're milking.

RUTHIE: God, you disgust me. *(She gets up and agitatedly starts clearing the table.)*

CYNTHIA: Why is that, Ruthie? Because I like penises?

RUTHIE: You're a born slut.

CYNTHIA: I've thought about that. I don't think so. I don't really like men very much. I don't like them to touch me.

RUTHIE: You're dirty. Dirty mouth, dirty mind...

CYNTHIA: I just like dick. You know, just to play with. Like a bath toy. Sometimes it's like they're not even attached to a guy, like he's not even there. It's just this ugly, sorta interesting thing stuck on him. I like to make it do things.

RUTHIE: Would you please leave my house? Before you make me vomit?

CYNTHIA: You're throwing me out? Why? Jeez o'Pete, it's just words, you know.

RUTHIE: I feel so sorry for Nate.

CYNTHIA: Yeah, me too, sometimes. But you know what? He told me once, he said every guy in his plant envies him. Cause at the end of the day, he gets to come home and sleep with me. Isn't that sweet? *(Beat)* He was crying when he said that...He cries a lot. You wouldn't know it to look at him, would you? Just a big ole baby.

RUTHIE: The day he met you, his life was trashed. Just that fast.

CYNTHIA: *(Back to admiring her hands)* If I was a guy, I'll bet I could have been a brain surgeon.

RUTHIE: You really have to leave now. I have shopping to do.

CYNTHIA: Can I go with you?

RUTHIE: Oh...why? Why, Cynthia? Aren't you done upsetting me for today?

CYNTHIA: I don't have any girl friends. You come closest.

RUTHIE: Can't you see? How uncomfortable you make me?

CYNTHIA: You think I'll improve?

RUTHIE: What?

CYNTHIA: If I hang around you? *(Beat)* I mean, do you think people get better? Or are you just stuck with what you are?

RUTHIE: You want to get better?

CYNTHIA: In theory.

RUTHIE: Come to my church. Church can make people better.

CYNTHIA: You think? I doubt it. Just another kind of club. I'm in, you're not, so fuck you. *(Beat)* Only one thing makes people better. Love.

RUTHIE: And what would you know about that?

CYNTHIA: Not very much, Ruthie. Not too goddamn much. *(Beat)* That's why I've got to do it.

RUTHIE: What?

CYNTHIA: Have this baby. And keep it. Be a mother for it.

RUTHIE: *(Slowly shaking her head "No")* Cynthia...

CYNTHIA: I want to be a better person, Ruthie. I do.

RUTHIE: What if it makes you a worse person?

CYNTHIA: I'm counting on hormones. You know what I mean? Aren't there things in breast milk that gentle you up?

RUTHIE: I got a bad feeling about this, Cynthia. Some women are just born short of patience. You're one of them.

CYNTHIA: Well, it's like I'm always saying, you know?

RUTHIE: "You'll try anything once."

CYNTHIA: That's me all over.

RUTHIE: We're not talking about eating raw oysters or skydiving here, Cynthia. We're talking about a life.

CYNTHIA: Two lives—three, if you count Nate's. *(Beat)* I got nothing going for me, Ruthie. I can't see the hand in front of my face right now. I'm bumping into walls, know what I mean? Maybe if my life is just going to be one big shit-pile, maybe I can make another life that does better. *(Beat)* Besides, it's like my mom used to say: Every cat should have at least one litter.

(She smiles. RUTHIE doesn't. Blackout)

CYNTHIA CONFERENCES WITH DR JOHN THE ASTRONOMER

(Enter DR JOHN THE ASTRONOMER—sort of frazzled, rushed. CYNTHIA's on his heels, respectful but determined. He is tossing off comments to unseen people he is passing in the hall.)

DR JOHN AST: Yes, uh, Miss Carlinsky—Tuesday, three-thirty—right? Very good. Oh, uh, Jeremy, did you see Peters? He catch up with you? I dunno, something about that goddamn faculty meeting. O K. *(He turns briefly to CYNTHIA as he ostensibly opens his office door.)* I'm sorry, your name was...?

CYNTHIA: Cynthia.

DR JOHN AST: Yes. Come in, please, have a seat...

(They enter office space—area lighting and two plain, functional chairs. And maybe a desk. She sits as he quickly consults his roster/grade book.)

DR JOHN AST: Ah, ah yes, Cynthia Masters, yes? Here we are. *(Beat)* Hmm. Ah...did you not do the reading prior to taking this exam?

CYNTHIA: Well, I did and I didn't.

(He waits.)

CYNTHIA: It was very much like I imagine reading a foreign language. Would be.

DR JOHN AST: I'm sorry.

CYNTHIA: Thank you. It's just not what I thought it would be like, astronomy.

DR JOHN AST: No?

CYNTHIA: There's a lot of math involved.

DR JOHN AST: Uh-huh. Well. Yes, that's true.

CYNTHIA: I just wanted to learn about the stars. How far away they are. How bright. How hot.

DR JOHN AST: Uh-huh. Well—

CYNTHIA: I want to be an astronaut. *(Beat)* I want to help find life on other worlds.

(Beat. DR JOHN AST is increasingly uneasy, on edge.)

CYNTHIA: I'm sure it's out there. Aren't you?

DR JOHN AST: Well, uh, in some form...it's a virtual certainty.

CYNTHIA: *(As if some point has been proven)* There! You see?

(Beat—he doesn't.)

CYNTHIA: So what's God got to do with anything?

DR JOHN AST: What exactly did you want to see me about?

CYNTHIA: It's just things floating around randomly in some Planet Soup till it gets hot enough to boil and all come together. *(Pause)* Everything's chemical. Just like people. When the chemistry's right, you make a baby.

(He waits.)

CYNTHIA: Can I re-take the last test?

DR JOHN AST: No.

CYNTHIA: Well see, I have mitigating circumstances.

DR JOHN AST: I'm sure.

CYNTHIA: I was sick when I took it.

DR JOHN AST: Uh-*huh*.

CYNTHIA: I could barely sit up straight. I can't believe I didn't puke outright.

DR JOHN AST: That's unfortunate, but I'm afraid I can't help you.

CYNTHIA: Morning sickness, O K? I'm pregnant.

DR JOHN AST: Oh. Oh. Well. Uh, you'd never know.

CYNTHIA: What do you mean, Professor John?

DR JOHN AST: Well, you're...not showing.

CYNTHIA: Excuse me? *(Silence)* Why are you looking down there? That's kind of personal, don't you think?

DR JOHN AST: Well, I...perhaps. I'm sorry.

CYNTHIA: When you get right down to it, telling a pregnant woman she doesn't look pregnant is about as rude as asking if a lady's pregnant when she's not. You know? When she's just fat?

DR JOHN AST: I have to prepare for my next class, Miss...uh, Mrs....uh....

(She doesn't budge.)

CYNTHIA: So you're not going to help me. You're just going to comment on my appearance and not help me at all.

DR JOHN AST: Let me understand this. You want to re-take the same test.

CYNTHIA: No. I want to take, like, a make-up exam. Different questions. Questions where you don't have to be good at math.

DR JOHN AST: I see. Well, that's novel.

CYNTHIA: Thank you.

DR JOHN AST: Why don't you just drop the course?

CYNTHIA: Because I believe that a quitter never wins, and a winner never quits. *(Beat)* I'm a winner, Dr John.

DR JOHN AST: Oh, I'm sure. Look. I'll just scrub the last test for you. Not factor it into your overall grade. That's the best I can do.

CYNTHIA: Well, that's a step in the right direction, I guess.

DR JOHN AST: A step?

CYNTHIA: Well, the next test is probably going to have math on it, too, isn't it? Maybe even harder?

DR JOHN AST: Did you have math in high school?

CYNTHIA: I didn't notice. *(Beat)* You know what? Math is a goddamn fraud. You think I can't live my life without it? It's only any use to overeducated people like you who can't function out there in the real world.

DR JOHN AST: *(Beat)* I think you should leave.

CYNTHIA: Well, shoot. That just kinda popped out. Are you taking it personal?

DR JOHN AST: Should I not?

CYNTHIA: It's like my mom used to put it: "I meant what I said, but I didn't mean to say it."

DR JOHN AST: As of this moment, I have erased the results of your last test. Perhaps you'd be good enough to leave before I change my mind?

(She smiles, moves toward edge of Office Space, stops:)

CYNTHIA: I think your lectures are very. Stimulating. *(Silence)* No doubt about it. You're my favorite professor. Bye-bye!

(She exits. DR JOHN THE ASTRONOMER looks like hell. He finds some stomach calmers and pops several into his mouth. He stares after her. Blackout)

CONTRACTIONS

(Out of the blackout...very bright hospital delivery room lighting. DETECTIVE JOHNS *is eating Chinese food out of little boxes. He would seem to be in his barren office space from INTERROGATION at top of show. Except:* CYNTHIA *is wheeled into the light on a gurney, and there she is left. She is in labor. It's not going well. She is in pain. She focuses on breathing but also shouts expletives, groans, etc.* DETECTIVE JOHNS *is oblivious to her condition. Comports himself with the offhanded casualness of a cop several hours into an interrogation. He speaks only in the silences between* CYNTHIA*'s labor outcries.)*

DETECTIVE JOHNS: Seen any good movies lately? *(Munches sloppily between queries)* Me, I love a good movie. Amazing what they can do with 'em these days, ain't it? *(Holds up ticket stub)* You went to the early show that Thursday...don't know this one. Who's in it? *(Expletives deleted)* Ever want to be a movie star, Cynthia? Huh? Do girls still dream of that? *(Beat)* Dream of fame. Get their names in all the papers? T V interviews? Good-looking boyfriends. Hot tubs. You dream like that, Cynthia? Is that why you did it? So you could get caught?

*(*DETECTIVE JOHNS *casually throws away the now-emptied carton of food and saunters out of the light and offstage amidst a flurry of labor pain expletives. Quick blackout)*

DELIVERANCE

(Lights up on NATHAN, *sitting in a chair in a hospital waiting room, head in hands, wearing a maternity-room gown.* RUTHIE *enters with a* NURSE *who is holding a heavily-blanketed newborn [doll].)*

RUTHIE: You have a son, Nate. *(He inspects the infant* NOAH.*)*

NATHAN: I thought he'd be uglier.

*(*RUTHIE *smiles.)*

NATHAN: How's Cindy?

NURSE: Sedated.

NATHAN: Was she...?

NURSE: It was difficult. She'll have to stay here for awhile.

NATHAN: Hello, Noah. *(To* RUTHIE*)* He's grabbing my finger. He's gonna be strong.

NURSE: Say "Bye-bye, Noah."

(NURSE *exits with the "baby."* NATHAN *is suffused with hope.*)

NATHAN: Everything's gonna be O K, Ruthie. I'm just getting that message so clear right now.

(RUTHIE *smiles but does not endorse.*)

NATHAN: She got something to occupy herself. This changes everything. She don't need to be all the time focusing on me and the trailer and being miserable. *(Beat—feels her doubts)* You'll see. You'll see.

(Fade to blackout)

THE BABY IS SICK

(In blackout. Sound: car arriving and doorbell/baby crying. Lights up as RUTHIE *flips on a switch or lamp, moves very quickly to* OTIS/RUTHIE *entrance area.* RUTHIE *yanks open the door to see* CYNTHIA *with a blanketed eight month-old Noah (doll). She thrusts her burden upon* RUTHIE *as if once and for all washing her hands of the problem.)*

CYNTHIA: Take him! Take him before I throw him against the wall!

RUTHIE: You settle down! *(She quickly retreats protectively with the child, checking it out, soothing it.)*

CYNTHIA: I can't stand it!

(Enter OTIS, *blearily.)*

OTIS: What the hell's going on out here?

CYNTHIA: He won't shut up! Hours! Hours!

OTIS: *(To* RUTHIE*)* Noah sick?

RUTHIE: Fevered.

CYNTHIA: What are you supposed to do?

RUTHIE: *(To* CYNTHIA*)* You take his temp? (RUTHIE *exits to O S bathroom, baby in arms, before* CYNTHIA *can answer.)*

CYNTHIA: He wouldn't stop squirming and kicking. I couldn't put it in. *(She's quickly puffing on a smoke and pacing.)*

OTIS: I keep telling you, Cynthia, get one of those ear thermometers.

CYNTHIA: What, do I look like one of them fucking H M Os to you?

OTIS: Don't use that language in my house.

CYNTHIA: I'm agitated!

OTIS: Yeah. I wish you two would quit dropping in on us at one, two in the morning.

CYNTHIA: Where else am I gonna go?

OTIS: Where's Nate?

CYNTHIA: Pulling more overtime.

(RUTHIE *comes charging out, already pulling on her coat. To* OTIS:)

RUTHIE: Call Dr MacKenzie. Tell him to meet me in the E R. *(To* CYNTHIA*)* I'm taking your car—I need the baby seat. *(To* OTIS, *who's at the phone)* Follow in yours.

CYNTHIA: I'll drive—

RUTHIE: The hell you will. Gimme your keys.

(CYNTHIA *does.*)

OTIS: What'll I tell Doc?

RUTHIE: A hundred five point eight. Convulsions. *(She's gone.)*

(*Sound of car pulling away.* OTIS, *on a cordless phone, edges out of his light. Focus on* CYNTHIA *alone, smoking, chomping her gum, pacing.*)

OTIS: *(O S)* Doc? Sorry to bother you at this hour. Wife's bringing in my nephew Nate's baby boy. Real high fever, convulsing. Can you meet her at the E R? *(Beat)* What? Oh, Otis. Ruthie and Otis. Sorry. Yeah. Thanks. Thanks.

(OTIS *re-enters area with* CYNTHIA. *He's hurriedly dressing, finding warmer clothes and glaring at her whenever possible, which she finally acknowledges.*)

CYNTHIA: *What?*

OTIS: Did you hurt him, Cindy?

CYNTHIA: You would think that about me, wouldn't you? Prick.

OTIS: *Not* in *my house!*

(*She stares, unafraid.*)

OTIS: You make me sick. You're lucky I gotta get outta here.

CYNTHIA: "Judge Not Lest Ye Be Judged!"

OTIS: That may be so. That may be so. *(Beat)* But if they find anything wrong with that little baby boy, you're in big trouble, Cynthia.

CYNTHIA: Don't be threatening me, Otis. You can't hardly tie your shoelaces without Ruthie.

OTIS: You know what? I hope they do find something. *(He exits.)*

CYNTHIA: *(Yells after him)* You little Frog Man! You Wart!

(Sound of car starting up, driving away)

CYNTHIA: *My life is not over!!!*

(Blackout)

CYNTHIA AND NATHAN EAT BREAKFAST

(She is engrossed in the newspaper, front section; he in the back section, sports. They break away from this only long enough for Danish, coffee, etc. She's getting off from a shift at WalMart; he's heading out for a shift on the line.)

CYNTHIA: *(After a few moments)* The Dalai Lama's coming to town.

NATHAN: *(Unimpressed)* Not again.

(She puts her paper down and contemplates him.)

CYNTHIA: That is not an appropriate response.

NATHAN: Well shit, he was just here three years ago.

CYNTHIA: *(Getting steamed)* Maybe that's because...his *big brother LIVES HERE????*

NATHAN: Hey. Don't yell at me at this hour.

(She slaps the newspaper up between them.)

NATHAN: Jeez. *(Beat)* Where were you the last time he was here?

CYNTHIA: In a house with wall-to-wall carpeting and four bathrooms and decks all around it!

NATHAN: *(After a beat)* You really know how to send a guy off to work feeling good about himself, doncha darlin?

CYNTHIA: *(Fingers the front of her uniform)* Hey. See this? It ain't like I'm sitting around sucking down Milk Duds and doing my nails, is it stud?

(He just sits back and stares, once again amazed by her ability to wound. She backs off a bit.)

CYNTHIA: I'm sorry, Nate.

NATHAN: Wow, you got a tongue on you....

CYNTHIA: Look. I just got off work. I'm tired. I'm tired, but I was still trying to make some conversation with you. And you crapped all over it.

NATHAN: Is that what happened? Is that what I did?

CYNTHIA: From where I'm sitting, yeah.

NATHAN: Then I'm sorry.

CYNTHIA: O K.

(He approaches her. They kiss. It arouses him. It doesn't her. She effortlessly repels his advances.)

CYNTHIA: O K, Big Guy. Save it for after work.

NATHAN: That's just it, ain't it? It's never "After Work."

CYNTHIA: I know. You think I like it?

NATHAN: I don't know. How much you suffering? You suffering as much as me?

CYNTHIA: *(With poorly concealed sarcasm)* Oohh, I think so.

NATHAN: *(Dead serious now)* Yeah. Probably so. *(Beat)* I'm nineteen years old.

CYNTHIA: I know.... *(Silence. Then softly:)* Goodbye.

(NATHAN exits. She gets up and appears to watch him leave as if through the window of their trailer. Sound: car starting up, driving away. Lights dim on breakfast nook area. Soft focus up on their bedroom area: the bed, a chair, a mirror.)

CYNTHIA ALONE

(CYNTHIA walks toward their bedroom. She is grieving—that is, her posture suggests that, since no sound is coming from her. She wanders around the limited space with her hands out, groping as if she were in a cave, or a box, or a cell. She creeps onto the bed as if every muscle aches. And now we can hear something: sobbing. Out of it, in the midst of it...)

CYNTHIA: Twenty...Nathan...I'm twenty.... *(After awhile, fearful of falling asleep in her work clothes, she drags herself up, stares at herself in the mirror, doesn't like it.)* Who's that hag? Nathan? Is that my mom? *(In a sudden rage, she throws a pillow—or something else soft—at the mirror.)* I will *not*. Get old for you! *(She angrily takes off her clothes and gets under the sheets. She tries to sleep, but she's too wound up, too agitated.)*

(Lights change. The JOHNS assemble to watch. At first, as they materialize from the perimeter of the lighted Cynthia area, they are so quiet and unobtrusive that they could be drapes in the recesses of some Sun King boudoir. They stay at some remove from her bed and observe her almost religiously. They may upon closer inspection be seen to be costumed in character—all the JOHNS of the play—but with a heightened formality. Oddly funereal. At no time in any way does CYNTHIA acknowledge their presence. In her frustration over sleeplessness, CYNTHIA irritably grabs a tabloid newspaper from under the bed, leafs through it restlessly, absently. Something in it catches her eye. She thinks about it. She gets out of bed and looks at herself in the mirror. She poses. From a drawer under the mirror, she rummages around and pulls out some sexy underwear. She tries these things on, one after another, striking

model's odd posturings. Sound/music cue? Omit if not an instrumental or otherwise non-vocal cue—no songs. Perhaps "found sounds" like the amplified tick of a clock or the purring of a cat. Sensuous but not overpowering, real but distorted. CYNTHIA *is aroused, touching herself, sighing. She crawls back into the bed, back under the sheets. She masturbates successfully. The* JOHNS *must not react at all to this. They remain for all the world nothing more than curtains providing her with privacy, security, warmth, as if she were nestled within the regal world of four-posters. As she recovers, the* JOHNS *all fade from view, receding almost imperceptibly from the light, dissipated energies. Lights change, "realer" now. Sound cue out)*

(CYNTHIA *is calmer now, but still restlessly bored. She remembers the newspaper, finds the item of interest. She decides.* CYNTHIA *pulls an old-fashioned princess phone out from under her bed. Pink, of course. She dials.)*

CYNTHIA: Hello? Is this Party Girl Modeling? Huh? Well, I got this number from the paper...oh. What is it, Busy Beavers? Really? Well it doesn't *sound* like the same company. Yeah? Well... what do I have to do? I mean, you know, if I wanted to work for you? *(She listens. She listens some more. Occasionally ad-libs neutral "uh-huh" -type responses. Businesslike. Not shocked or titillated.)* And all this is legal? *(Beat)* Uh-huh. Well, like, what would I make? For doing that? *(She laughs)* Yeah. Yeah, I *would* like an interview. My name? *(Beat)* Cin. That's C...I...N. Like in Cinnamon. Thanks. *(Beat)* O K, Tuesday, two o'clock. Yeah, I know where you are. Yeah. O K. Bye.

(She hangs up. She lies back in bed. She stares up at her ceiling. Lights fade on her to blackout.)

CYNTHIA'S FIRST HOUSE CALL

(Out of the blackout, sound cue: music. Some Latin lounge lizard organ instrumental like Esquivel's version of "Speak Low." Re-dress the bed so that it becomes the queen-size in the condo of JOHN, CYNTHIA'*s date for the evening. Props add to look of* JOHN'*s reasonably tasteful but obviously bachelor digs.* JOHN *is heard offstage, fumbling with keys, coats, and nerves.)*

JOHN: *(O S)* Well here—here we are. I don't mind the climb, do you? Good for the glutes, right? *(He laughs with a hideous self-consciousness and enters—a pleasant-enough man, perhaps middle-aged, well-dressed, trying hard to be worldly without being smarmy, failing pretty much all around. He is pitifully polite.)* Always live on the top floor. Principle of mine. Never want anybody on top of me. *(Beat)* Well, almost never. *(An embarrassed and embarrassing smirk)*

(CYNTHIA *enters. She is dressed beautifully with an understated elegance so different from what we've seen of her that she's a bit hard to recognize initially. She sizes things up in an instant: probably safe. She relaxes a bit.)*

JOHN: Make yourself comfortable.

(CYNTHIA *sits on edge of bed.*)

JOHN: Uh. Can I...can I get you something to drink?

CYNTHIA: Coke'd be good.

JOHN: *(His mind racing)* Coke? Coca-cola?

CYNTHIA: Whatever. Something fizzy. You got any Perrier?

JOHN: Can do. I think. Let me check.

(*He exits. She uses his absence to quickly check out the room—if there are drawers, she noiselessly opens and shuts them, either to look for money or to discover anything weird or dangerous. She's back demurely on the bed as he re-enters with a glass of sparkling water for her.*)

JOHN: Just call me Johnny-on-the-Spot. One sparkling water for the Lady.

CYNTHIA: Thanks.

(*He pulls up a chair, faces her from a discreet distance. An awkward silence ensues.* JOHN *smiles but seems not to know how to speak.*)

CYNTHIA: So. What's your pleasure?

JOHN: I beg your pardon?

CYNTHIA: What do you like to do for fun, John? I mean, besides play miniature golf?

JOHN: You didn't mind that, did you? I thought it was, you know, kind of fun and...and...spontaneous. *(Silence)* It's regarded as one of the most innovatively-designed miniature golf courses in this part of the state, actually, and well, it's practically right across the highway from Busy— from where you work, so...

CYNTHIA: I was a bit over-dressed, John.

JOHN: Oh. Yeah. I noticed your shoes were...well, on the rolling parts of the...holes.

CYNTHIA: I'm still a bit over-dressed, John.

JOHN: Uh-huh. Well. What am I supposed to do right here?

CYNTHIA: What do you feel like doing?

JOHN: Well, uh...can I ask you a question?

CYNTHIA: Shoot.

JOHN: How do I know you're not a cop?

CYNTHIA: Good question, John. *(Beat)* Wanna see my badge? *(She flashes him and laughs.)* Come over here and sit on the bed with me.

(He does.)

CYNTHIA: Now relax, will you? You're making me jumpy.

JOHN: Sorry. First time I uh...ever had an escort.

CYNTHIA: That's O K. This is the first time I've ever made a house call.

JOHN: Really?

CYNTHIA: I'll believe you if you'll believe me. *(Smiles)* Look. Do you want to see a Fashion Show? I brought some extra lingerie.

(It sounds like a good idea to JOHN.)

CYNTHIA: The modeling fee is sixty dollars for the first half hour.

JOHN: O K.

CYNTHIA: In advance, John.

JOHN: Oh. Sure.

(He fumbles around, finds some cash. She pockets it.)

CYNTHIA: That-a-boy. Aren't you hot? Get out of some of those clothes, honey. That's what I intend to do.

(CYNTHIA exits. With some reluctance, he strips down to his very ordinary-looking underwear and crawls under the sheets. She re-enters wearing whatever local community standards allow. She poses, part self-mockery, part self-proud. Slowly a huge smile forms over JOHN.)

JOHN: Oh my god...

CYNTHIA: You like?

JOHN: It's...very elegant.

CYNTHIA: Thank you.

JOHN: Uh...Cin, is it O K? They said I could take pictures?

CYNTHIA: Sure. Photographic modeling fee is five dollars per picture.

JOHN: O K. *(As he finds his camera)*

CYNTHIA: For ten dollars a shot we'll develop them for you.

JOHN: Really?

CYNTHIA: No, John.

(As he snaps a couple pictures)

CYNTHIA: Can we lose that cheesy music?

JOHN: *(A bit hurt, but hiding it)* The music? Oh, yeah, I guess.

(Sound: Kill Latin lounge music in synch with JOHN turning off amp.)

CYNTHIA: Oof. Like Ricky Ricardo on Lithium. *(Beat)* You can turn on the T V if you like.

JOHN: The T V?

CYNTHIA: Yeah. That thing over there in the corner.

JOHN: Uh, well—sure, why not?

CYNTHIA: Turn it to Jay Leno.

JOHN: O K.

(Sound: Loop of Leno's talk show, not fully audible or recognizable.)

CYNTHIA: Be right back. *(She exits.)*

(Leno loop plays on. JOHN gets increasingly engrossed in it—chuckling, laughing. CYNTHIA re-enters wearing different lingerie, striking a different pose, working.)

CYNTHIA: Ta-dah!

(JOHN seems less impressed this time, clearly distracted by the T V.)

JOHN: Pretty.

CYNTHIA: Who's he got on?

JOHN: Kids. You know, little inventor kids. Things they made up.

(CYNTHIA is instantly absorbed in it.)

CYNTHIA: Aww, they're so cute. *(She crawls into bed with him.)* Jay is so good with kids.

JOHN: *(Pretty much glued to the T V)* I don't think he has any of his own, do you?

CYNTHIA: That's pretty much the way it goes, don't you think?

JOHN: Huh?

CYNTHIA: Them that should, don't. Them that shouldn't, do.

JOHN: Uh...

CYNTHIA: Look at that little girl...*(Caught up unexpectedly and intensely)* Look at that little girl. That little, little, thing...*(She begins to weep.)*

JOHN: Hey, what's wrong? Are you all right?

(CYNTHIA gets it under control but is still visibly upset. She leans into him and hugs him. He's confused, trying to figure out if the embrace is sexual. Decides, correctly, that it isn't. He gently consoles her. When she's comforted, she leans back in bed, not touching. They watch T V for a while, laughing at the same time. Lights dim. He reaches out and touches her hand. She takes his in hers. They watch T V. Lights out. T V out last. Blackout)

END OF ACT ONE

ACT TWO

CYNTHIA IS EVALUATED: (PART ONE)

(CYNTHIA *enters, looks around, sits in one of two chairs facing each other about five feet apart. At her quietly stylish best, impeccably groomed. She sizes up the place. Takes out a cigarette, lights up. Enter* DR JOHN E B GOODE, THE EVALUATOR— *to be known typographically as* DR JOHN E. *He's a rather portly guy about sixty, sixty-two. Suit. Notepad.*)

DR JOHN E: Cynthia?

CYNTHIA: Yes.

DR JOHN E: Dr Goode. *(He offers his hand.)* Dr John E B Goode, the evaluator?

(She tries not to, but she laughs.)

DR JOHN E: Uh...why are you laughing?

CYNTHIA: *(Waving him off, getting it under control)* Sorry...sorry.

DR JOHN E: *(Noticing the cigarette)* Could you put that out, please?

(She doesn't move. She doesn't speak. She evaluates him. Then takes a long, deliberate drag, exhales at leisure, finds an ashtray, delicately stubs it out, leans back in her chair and smiles, not warmly)

DR JOHN E: I've been retained to make a report on what it was you were feeling at the time of the, um, alleged felony. *(Beat)* Do you understand?

CYNTHIA: You'd like me to suck your cock, wouldn't you?

(He jumps up indignantly; then, as if extricating his leg from a snare, imposes composure upon himself. Takes his seat, stares at her coolly)

DR JOHN E: Perhaps there is something you don't understand here, Miss uh... *(Glancing into his file)*

CYNTHIA: Call me Cynthia.

DR JOHN E: Yes Miss...—Cynthia. You're not under oath here, but— *(Pats the far side of his chair, a spot she can't see)* —you are being taped.

CYNTHIA: You got that on tape? *(Again, she laughs.)*

DR JOHN E: Actually, no. I haven't activated it yet.

CYNTHIA: Shoot. Want me to do another take?

DR JOHN E: *(Stares at her for a while)* I see you have a sense of humor. That's good. I like a good joke now and again. *(Beat)* But sometimes humor betrays our ignorance of context. So, before I turn on this cassette, let me explain your situation. O K?

(She stares impassively.)

DR JOHN E: If you care about your ability to go shopping again anytime within the next decade—do you understand what I'm saying?—if you care about where you're going to be living for the next ten years or so, and with whom, then right now, right here, you are looking at the most powerful man in your life. *(A substantial pause)* Now I'm going to turn this tape on, and when I do so, I expect you to submit to this evaluation with a better spirit of cooperation. Do you understand?

CYNTHIA: Why do you keep asking me if I understand? Do you think I'm stupid?

(DR JOHN E begins talking for the record.)

DR JOHN E: Taping nine-thirty A M. July twelfth, case number— *(Consults notes)* 47CO59832RB07129. *(Beat)* Cynthia, I want you to take your mind back to that Thursday morning last month—

CYNTHIA: Are you allowed to do this? You know, tape me like this? Shouldn't my Public Defender be here?

(Pause. Then...)

DR JOHN E: Are you angry with me, Cynthia?

(Silence. She has a small smile on her face, but she is glaring at him.)

DR JOHN E: You seem to be staring angrily at me this moment, Cynthia, would that be accurate? *(Silence)* Cynthia? *(Silence)* Subject refuses to be responsive to the simplest questions—

CYNTHIA: Turn it off. If you would be so kind.

DR JOHN E: All right. For a moment. *(Does something, or appears to do something, in the arm of the chair shielded from her view)* It's off.

CYNTHIA: How do I know?

DR JOHN E: You don't. *(Beat)* You don't even know for sure if it exists. *(Beat)* That's just how it is. Your position is not favorable. And you're making it less so with each passing minute.

CYNTHIA: *(Exaggeratedly smarmy)* Uh-huh, and which position do you regard as most favorable, Doctor John E B Goode?

DR JOHN E: Not the one you're assuming, Cynthia. Not the one that guarantees the next time you see your toddler, your two-year-old, your... *(Consults notes)*

CYNTHIA: *(Begins to unwrap chewing gum)* Noah.

DR JOHN E: Yes. He'll be in seventh grade. Your two-year-old Noah will be twelve, Cynthia.

(Beat—she pops the gum in.)

DR JOHN E: That's avoidable. I can almost promise you that. *(Beat—quintessentially reasonable)* Cynthia. All it takes. Is an Attitude Adjustment.

(She seems to be re-evaluating him in some fashion, perhaps appreciatively?)

CYNTHIA: You're pretty good at this, you know?

(He says nothing, betrays nothing.)

CYNTHIA: You forget one thing. *(Beat)* Not all of us think like Breeders.

DR JOHN E: *(Confused)* You mean...what, exactly?

CYNTHIA: Some of us should never have been Breeders. Should never have happened. *(Beat)* Like, for instance...your momma.

(Blackout)

NATHAN SPILLS HIS GUTS OVER A BEER: (PART ONE)

(Small table. Pitcher of beer. Two mugs. NATHAN *sits in one chair. The audience sits in the other. In* NATHAN's *world, this is not a direct address, this is him talking to* OTIS *or a friend from work at the local pub.)*

NATHAN: I got people laughing at me. I got people feeling sorry for me. I don't know which one hurts worse. *(Beat)* I heard a story once—I don't know if it's true, I can't even see how it could be. This guy lives with this woman a long time. Maybe twenty years. Something like that. And he loved her the whole time like it was the day he first met her. And then one day somebody tells him, "You know, your wife ain't a woman, she's a man." *(Beat)* "You didn't figure that out? Ya dumb shit?" *(Beat)* O K. Now I know how he feels. He feels really bad. He feels like God played a real dirty joke on him and then told the whole world. *(Beat)* Because the thing is, see, he still loves her. Even when he finds out his wife's a man, he still loves her. She's still his wife. It can't be helped. It's a done deal. *(Beat)* He's just so screwed. Coming and going.

(Blackout)

CYNTHIA'S THIRTY-FIRST HOUSE CALL

(A hotel room. BIG JOHN is stretched out on a bed in his underwear. Knock on door is heard.)

BIG JOHN: Yeah? Who is it?

CYNTHIA: *(O S)* Your date.

(BIG JOHN gets up, opens door, looks both ways out in corridor.)

BIG JOHN: C'mon in honey.

(She does.)

BIG JOHN: What's your name?

CYNTHIA: Cin. Short for Cinnamon.

BIG JOHN: Cute. Get your clothes off.

CYNTHIA: Did they, uh, explain our policies?

BIG JOHN: *(Amused, but not very)* And what would they be, sugar?

CYNTHIA: What are you looking for?

BIG JOHN: What are you offering?

CYNTHIA: Lingerie modeling, sixty dollars for half an hour, no touching. Nude modeling, a hundred dollars a half-hour, no touching. Nude massages, no genital contact, a hundred and fifty per half hour. Pay in advance.

BIG JOHN: That's it?

CYNTHIA: That's it.

BIG JOHN: How much to fuck you?

CYNTHIA: This is a modeling and massage service. We're not hookers.

(BIG JOHN laughs. She doesn't.)

CYNTHIA: They should have explained this to you when you called. Sorry you had the wrong idea.

(She starts to go. He blocks the door and locks it.)

BIG JOHN: Quit fucking around and get those clothes off.

CYNTHIA: I don't like the way you talk.

BIG JOHN: Jesus Christ, how long you been doing this?

CYNTHIA: I don't like you at all. *(She tries to unlock the door.)*

BIG JOHN: *(Grabbing her)* Hey! You're really starting to piss me off. You don't wanna do that.

CYNTHIA: Get your hands off me.

BIG JOHN: Who the fuck you talking to, huh? *(He slaps her—not brutally hard, but enough to really scare her.)* Huh? Who the fuck you think I am? Some little college jerk-off?

CYNTHIA: I'm warning you! I got back-up out in the car!

BIG JOHN: *(Laughing)* I love it! A Two-fer! Send her in! *(He starts tearing her clothes off.)*

CYNTHIA: Stop it! Stop it, you fucking pig! I'll have cops all over your ass, you hear me?

BIG JOHN: *(Still laughing, grabs his wallet, flips it open to reveal a badge)* What's that look like to you, you stupid fucking bitch!? Zat look like some motherfucking student I D card to you?

CYNTHIA: You're a cop?

BIG JOHN: And you're a whore. And this one's on the house, you got it? We understand each other? *(Slaps her again)* Get to work, bitch.

(CYNTHIA *begins to take her clothes off. She hasn't gotten far when lights up in opposite area on* DR JOHN E. *She turns in his direction. Lights fade out on* BIG JOHN.)

CYNTHIA IS EVALUATED: (PART TWO)

(Lights up on DR JOHN E *and the same two chairs as "Part One". He is seated in the "taping chair.")*

DR JOHN E: Were you close to your father, Cynthia?

(She moves smoothly to the available chair, gets comfortable before answering.)

CYNTHIA: How much do they pay you for this? *(Beat)* Is it by the case? *(She seems genuinely interested.)* Or by the hour? Yearly retainer?

DR JOHN E: You are still being recorded.

CYNTHIA: *(Trying to see the machine in the arm of the chair)* You gotta be almost out of tape. *(Beat)* How long we gonna be in here for? What do I have to say to you to bring this to a speedy conclusion?

DR JOHN E: They're going to be looking for mitigating circumstances. Do you know what they are?

CYNTHIA: My father abused me.

DR JOHN E: Sexually?

CYNTHIA: My husband doesn't understand me.

DR JOHN E: So you *are* married?

CYNTHIA: I'm on drugs. Have been for years.

(DR JOHN E *begins to feel she may be putting him on.*)

CYNTHIA: I'm a nymphomaniac. I can't get enough of your hot hot stuff. *(Beat)* I trade sex for dope. *(Beat)* My cat got run over. *(Beat)* Am I mitigated yet?

(A "signal" in the taping chair—a small light? sound of a tone?—indicates his tape is indeed spent. With a slight smile he goes through the process of changing the cassette, fumbling it in his surreptitious haste. She seizes the occasion.)

CYNTHIA: There *are* no fucking mitigating circumstances! I did it because I did it!

DR JOHN E: *(Nervously fumbling tapes)* One moment, here, till I, just a second—

CYNTHIA: You're a fucking charlatan! You're a Gun For Hire at two grand per day, am I close? Is that why you're dragging me through this goddamn quicksand at one inch per hour? Because Time Is Money???

(She scans his walls as his tape exchange becomes comically inept.)

CYNTHIA: Where are your fucking diplomas? Whachado, take a correspondence course? Huh? The Colonel Klink School of Interrogation? *Who's paying you? Who are you? You fucking FRAUD!! You WHORE!!*

DR JOHN E: *(To recorder, at last up and running)* Tape three continuing, July Twelfth—

CYNTHIA: *(Instantly only mildly distraught and in a restrained, dignified way)* And then after my mother died of ovarian cancer... *("breaking down" for the tape)* Must you torment me with these questions, Dr John? It's been hours now, I've told you everything I could tell you about what made me what I am. For the love of God, Dr John—!

DR JOHN E: End of session.

(Turns tape off. He glares at her in silence. She returns his stare for a moment, then elaborately produces a cigarette and prepares to light it in front of him. Stops. Thoughtfully offers him one. He doesn't budge. Blackout)

IT COULD HAPPEN

(At lights up, NATHAN, RUTHIE, and OTIS are sitting in a kind of thoughtful silence—a pause in the middle of an intense conversation.)

OTIS: Jim's a horse's ass. You can't let guys like that get to you.

NATHAN: It ain't just him. Thanks, Otis, but you know it ain't just him. *(Pause)* Nope. Where there's smoke, there's fire. Sometimes it just ain't no more complicated than that.

RUTHIE: When would she have time to be doing this, Nate? I mean, with the shift work at WalMarts, I just don't see how—?

NATHAN: *(On "WalMarts")* That's just it. They been cutting way back on her hours.

RUTHIE: And her college classes?

NATHAN: Aw hell, that whole thing's bogus. She gets these ideas, you know? They blow over.

RUTHIE: She's not following up on that?

NATHAN: I think she dropped the astronomy thing. She goes and meets with that fag poetry professor once in a while. God only knows what *they* do when they're alone. *(He rubs his temple as if a sudden pain has struck him.)*

OTIS: Nate? You all right?

NATHAN: You know, Ruthie...you do something that irritates me.

OTIS: And what would that be, Nate, if I'm a party to this conversation?

RUTHIE: You're not. *(To NATHAN)* Yes?

NATHAN: You keep asking me questions you know the answer to. Like a lawyer. Or a cop.

OTIS: Now look, there's no call to be using that kind of language in this house.

RUTHIE: Otis. You got no dog in this fight.

NATHAN: And you know why you do that, Ruthie? You do it to find out what I know. *(Beat)* You sit there all day, all neat and submissive and invisible, and all the time you're just thinking, thinking, thinking. So when you get around to talking, see, it's gotten all twisted up and complicated for you. And so you just can never say what you're really thinking. *(Beat)* Women tire me out, Ruthie. *(Beat)* You know so much more than you say. *(Beat)* You cover up for her. Don't you?

OTIS: Don't get me riled up, boy. You know what I'm like.

RUTHIE: Do you want me to ask you to leave the room?

OTIS: No need. No need a'tall, Mother. *(He exits, sort of, a bit wounded, and still hovering.)*

RUTHIE: Nathan. Just because we're women don't mean we're girlfriends. *(Beat)* You know how I feel about you and Cynthia. I never made no bones about it. I fear for you, son, and the fact you can't make a clear once and for all break from this woman is for me one of Life's Great Mysteries. *(Beat)* The more I think about it, the more I don't want to think about it.

NATHAN: So you can't tell me nothing about this pager thing she's walking around with? Nothing she swore you to secrecy never to tell?

RUTHIE: This girl don't work like that.

NATHAN: No. She don't. *(Beat)* Think back on what you tole me, coupla weeks ago? How she'll be sitting around here, shooting the breeze with you, and that pager'll go off, and what she say again? When that happens?

RUTHIE: Just "I gotta go to the bank" or "I gotta pick up some milk."

NATHAN: Yeah, that. Ruthie..."bank"? "Milk"? You giving this any thought? And then she bugs out of here for a coupla hours? Right? And when she comes back?

RUTHIE: Money.

NATHAN: Fifties? Fifties, was it, she was flashing? Peeling off fifties for you babysitting? Just happier than a hog in wallow?

(Silence. Broken at last by a solemn and thoughtful OTIS, who hasn't missed a word.)

OTIS: Sounds to me like you may have Trouble in Paradise.

(NATHAN starts to say something sarcastic to OTIS, but refrains.)

OTIS: *But.* But. It's one thing to say maybe she's got something on the side. It's a whole other thing to buy into what those hillbillies at work...well, what they're saying.

NATHAN: "Saying"? Publishing? Broadcasting? Televising? That piece-a-shit Jim guy is telling the whole fucking plant that Tony *bought* her, man!

OTIS: Well you wanna talk Born Liars? Huh? Start with them two. And he didn't say he "bought" her. *(Beat; very embarrassed to say this in front of RUTHIE)* Just said something about her showing him her panties or something.

NATHAN: Ooh...is *that* all? Well then I got no fucking problem, do I? *Shit!*

RUTHIE: You noticed any change in spending habits? She buyin' a lotta stuff?

NATHAN: No. Not really.

RUTHIE: Well. That's a good sign. Isn't it?

NATHAN: I'm telling you. I'm fucked, man. I'm sorry, Ruthie, but that's the word for how I'm feeling.

(Sound: car engine, then out)

OTIS: She's here. *(Beat)* Everybody act normal.

RUTHIE: *(After a beat)* Unless...

NATHAN: Unless what?

RUTHIE: Unless you think it's time to hash this out with her. Just get it on the table?

(Silence as NATHAN *considers this possibility. Before he can decide, enter* CYNTHIA. *She too is silent, contemplative, vaguely troubled, and way too self-absorbed to notice the similar mood in the others. She sits. Maybe a five-count before* RUTHIE *ventures:)*

RUTHIE: Hello, Cynthia.

(She looks over at them. She seems stunned, almost as if in a waking dream.)

CYNTHIA: I just met the Dalai Lama.

(The others glance at one another. Is this a joke? A lie? A fantasy? CYNTHIA *thinks about elaborating for them, then just shakes her head, and crosses offstage, out to kitchen.* NATHAN, RUTHIE, *and* OTIS *can only stare at each other as lights dim to blackout.)*

(Production note: All the events depicted in ACT THREE occur between the end of this scene and the beginning of the next, "Ruthie Babysits".)

RUTHIE BABYSITS

*(*CYNTHIA *enters* OTIS *and* RUTHIE's. *She carries Noah in one arm and a plastic bag in the other.* RUTHIE *is ironing.)*

CYNTHIA: Hi, Ruthie! Need you to watch Noah for me for a while.

RUTHIE: Sure. Hello, Noah. How's the big boy today?

*(*RUTHIE *holds him and plays with him as* CYNTHIA *exits to a room offstage. They continue to converse as* CYNTHIA, *who entered wearing shorts and a T-shirt, changes into the clothes in the plastic bag.)*

CYNTHIA: *(O S)* I gotta run some errands, you know? Take maybe an hour?

RUTHIE: Has he eaten today? *(To Noah)* Is oo hungry?

CYNTHIA: *(O S)* Not much. Coupla crackers. He's been real fussy. I think he's teething.

RUTHIE: *(Feeling his gums)* Oo got a sore toothie?

CYNTHIA: *(O S)* You got any sunglasses I can borrow?

RUTHIE: Look on my bureau.

(Lights up on a functional, ordinary-looking dresser.)

RUTHIE: Oh yeah, I can feel it. Right upper gum. Almost breaking through. Poor baby.

(Enter CYNTHIA in bureau area. She's pulled blue jeans on over her shorts and added a loose-fitting, unbuttoned cotton long-sleeved shirt over her T-shirt. It is clear from the staging: RUTHIE can't see her. CYNTHIA is all business. She pulls open a dresser drawer. She knows exactly what she's looking for and finds it immediately: OTIS's shiny nickel-plated snub-nosed .38. We get a good look at it as she swiftly and expertly checks to see if it's loaded. It is. She jams it into the waist of her jeans. She puts on her baseball cap and makes sure her shirt covers the pistol. She grabs RUTHIE's sunglasses off the dresser, puts them on. She takes a deep breath to compose herself.)

(She exits the bureau spot, enters RUTHIE's spot. Lights out on dresser/bureau area.)

RUTHIE: Why'd you put on jeans? Too hot for them today.

CYNTHIA: Sick of dirty old men staring at my legs. See you soon.

RUTHIE: Where you going?

CYNTHIA: Gotta pay my phone bill. They cut us off again, the bastards. You need anything?

RUTHIE: Maybe a quart of milk if it's no trouble.

CYNTHIA: You got it. Bye-bye, Noah. You be a good boy.

RUTHIE: Say "Bye-bye, Mommy, bye-bye."

(CYNTHIA exits.)

RUTHIE: "Bye-bye, Mommy."

(Blackout)

WITHDRAWAL SYMPTOMS

(Lights up on ANDREA MAYFIELD, a bank teller fronted by her customer service counter. Enter CYNTHIA, dressed as at the end of "Ruthie Babysits". She looks around. She seems calm. ANDREA smiles at her. CYNTHIA is carrying the same plastic bag she used to carry her jeans and shirt into OTIS and RUTHIE's.)

ANDREA: Whenever you're ready.

(CYNTHIA *walks up, puts the plastic bag in front of the teller, and pulls the .38 from her waistband—all very calmly. She speaks casually.*)

CYNTHIA: Don't make any noise. No sudden movements. Fill that bag with all your cash.

(ANDREA *seems momentarily paralyzed, stares open-mouthed at* CYNTHIA *as if waiting to be told it's all a joke. No change in* CYNTHIA'*s voice as she says:*)

CYNTHIA: This is a thirty-eight. It's real and it's loaded and I'm pointing it at your heart. Fill the bag.

(ANDREA *does so.*)

CYNTHIA: Take two steps back from the counter and keep your hands where I can see them.

(*Again,* ANDREA *complies.* CYNTHIA *casually exits, gun now pointed at the floor, mostly obscured by her leg, keeping her eyes on* ANDREA *all the while.* ANDREA *remains motionless. Thunder-struck. Terrified. Blackout*)

LET'S GO SHOPPING

(CYNTHIA *enters* RUTHIE'*s space.*)

CYNTHIA: Ruthie? I'm back!

(*Enter* RUTHIE)

CYNTHIA: How's Noah?

RUTHIE: He's too fussy to nap. The teething pains. Did you remember the milk?

CYNTHIA: Oh shit. Slipped my mind. Lemme just change into my shorts and I'll go get it. (*She exits, but we hear her O S.*)

RUTHIE: Don't bother. You're here, I'll just run out for it.

CYNTHIA: (*O S*) Hello, Noah. Do you wanna go for a ride?

RUTHIE: Nate called from work. He wanted to remind you to talk to the lady at the phone company.

(*Lights up on dresser/bureau area.* CYNTHIA *carefully but quickly replaces* OTIS'*s .38 and exits out of light. Lights out on bureau area. All cues very quick, precisely executed, to seem a bit like old-fashioned "scene of crime" police photographer flash cameras popping.*)

CYNTHIA: (*O S*) Say what?

RUTHIE: Nate's hoping you can work out something with the gal at the phone company.

CYNTHIA: *(O S)* Oh yeah, no problem. You seen Noah's Squishy-Guy?

RUTHIE: It's not in the crib?

CYNTHIA: *(O S)* Oh yeah, got it.

(CYNTHIA *re-enters* RUTHIE's *area. She's wearing her shorts and a T-shirt again.*)

RUTHIE: Jeez, how many times a day do you change outfits?

(CYNTHIA *pulls out a wad of cash. She peels off a couple fifties and hands them to* RUTHIE.)

CYNTHIA: This oughta catch me up with you, right?

RUTHIE: *(Actually a bit frightened)* Lord, Cindy. What'ja do, rob a bank?

(CYNTHIA *reacts.*)

RUTHIE: No kidding, girl. Where'd you get that wad?

CYNTHIA: Daddy's bailing us out again—wired me some cash this morning. That's where I've been. C'mon, let's go shopping.

RUTHIE: I really shouldn't. I got stuff to do.

CYNTHIA: Oh, live a little, Ruthie. When's the last time you were out of the house?

RUTHIE: What about Noah?

CYNTHIA: He'll conk out in the car.

(RUTHIE *holds up her two fifties.*)

RUTHIE: You just gave me these. You wantin' me to blow it before Otis even sees it?

CYNTHIA: What he don't know can't hurt him.

(*She laughs.* RUTHIE *smiles but seems doubtful.*)

CYNTHIA: Hey. Keep the money, Ruthie. Lemme treat you to something.

RUTHIE: What, you mean like an ice cream cone?

CYNTHIA: *Ice* cream? You been pinching pennies too long, Ruthie. When's the last time Otis bought you a dress? Huh? When's the last time you had your hair done?

RUTHIE: Oh Cindy, I couldn't...

CYNTHIA: Then *you* pick. *(Beat)* Let me do something good for you.

RUTHIE: Cindy, you worry me. You're so irresponsible. Your dad sent you this to get you out of hock.

(CYNTHIA *takes* RUTHIE's *hand, which rather startles* RUTHIE.)

CYNTHIA: Do you know that Noah loves you?

RUTHIE: Well, yes, him and me's good buddies.

CYNTHIA: He loves you more than he loves me.

RUTHIE: Oh, that's not so!

CYNTHIA: Yes it is. And you know it. And I don't have a problem with it. You're more of a mother to him than I am. He *should* love you more.

RUTHIE: Cynthia, is something wrong? I never heard you talk like this.

CYNTHIA: That's because you've never seen me in a good mood. I'm just such a bitch. *(She wanted it to be a joke, but it nearly makes her cry for a moment.)* I want to make it up to you, Ruthie. You been so good to me.

RUTHIE: We are what we are. You don't owe me nothing.

CYNTHIA: Ruthie. If something happened to me, you know, something bad—

RUTHIE: Girl. What are you talking about? Are you in trouble?

CYNTHIA: Say I was in like a car wreck or something. Would you look after Noah?

RUTHIE: You know I would.

CYNTHIA: And Otis? He'd be O K with that?

RUTHIE: Otis would give his life for Noah.

(This is too much for CYNTHIA. She hugs the disconcerted RUTHIE.)

CYNTHIA: I'm so bad. I'm so bad.

RUTHIE: Cindy...Cindy...

CYNTHIA: I keep trying to be somebody. But I just don't know who.

(RUTHIE holds her until CYNTHIA pulls away, wipes her face on the hem of her T-shirt, forces a smile and says:)

CYNTHIA: Let's go shopping.

(Blackout)

THE SHIP COMES IN

(CYNTHIA is seated at her kitchen table. She's studying travel brochures. Plastic bags containing goods from various discount stores are strewn around. Enter NATHAN, home from work, and it's been a bad day at the office.)

NATHAN: Hi.

CYNTHIA: Hi.

(NATHAN *exits to kitchen O S, returns with a beer. Sits where he can see her, but not too near her. He finds the sports section, starts reading.*)

NATHAN: You talk to the lady at the phone company?

CYNTHIA: Yeah. It's taken care of.

NATHAN: You work out a payment plan?

CYNTHIA: We're even. All hooked up again.

NATHAN: You paid it off? In full?

CYNTHIA: Yes sir. That's an affirmative.

NATHAN: How?

CYNTHIA: I robbed a bank.

NATHAN: He laughed. Pretend it happened.

(*He stares at her. She returns it. Neither is smiling. She tosses him a couple of the bags on the floor.*)

CYNTHIA: Happy birthday.

NATHAN: That's next month.

CYNTHIA: Take it while you can get it.

(*He inspects the contents: couple pairs of blue jeans, some underwear, socks, a few casual shirts.*)

CYNTHIA: I was gonna get you some new work boots, but I figured you oughta be there to try 'em on....

NATHAN: What the fuck's goin' on, Cindy?

CYNTHIA: I think the words you're groping for are "Thank you."

NATHAN: You adding shoplifting to your rap sheet?

CYNTHIA: *And* you're very welcome.

NATHAN: I'm asking you, point-fucking-blank, where you got all this money.

CYNTHIA: And I told you: I robbed a bank.

(*They stare at each other like it's draw poker.*)

CYNTHIA: When's the last time you believed anything I told you?

NATHAN: When's the last time you told the truth?

CYNTHIA: About two seconds ago. You're such a shithead. I try to do something nice for you and you do your usual number—just crap all over me.

(NATHAN *checks out the kitchen table.*)

NATHAN: Travel brochures? Virgin Islands? Hawaii?

CYNTHIA: I need a vacation. I don't care whether you come or not. Fact is, you're such a mope, I'd have more fun by myself.

NATHAN: Yeah. I'll bet you would.

CYNTHIA: What is that, some kind of trope or something? You got something on your mind, Nathan, you just go right ahead and spit it out.

NATHAN: I been hearing things. At work. Things that make me get into fights. Things about you. Things I never believed for a second until now. *(Beat)*

CYNTHIA: I'm all ears.

NATHAN: *(Beat)* I'm too ashamed to go on.

CYNTHIA: Then why'd you bring it up? You're like a little girl saying I've got a secret but *I'm* not going to tell *you.*

NATHAN: *(Beat)* Some guys are saying you work for an escort service.

CYNTHIA: What's an escort service?

NATHAN: You know. Don't you?

CYNTHIA: You mean like...no. What? Like a dating thing? Personals, like Lonely Hearts, uh...?

NATHAN: *(Studies her, then)* Never mind.

CYNTHIA: No, like those eight-hundred numbers you see on T V? Those things where you make a video so you can try and get a boyfriend?

NATHAN: Look, just forget it, O K?

CYNTHIA: *(She goes to him.)* I got a boyfriend already. Remember? *(Kisses him)* You know what's going down, don't you baby? You told me yourself, those wall-eyed bastards are all jealous of you. They say mean things cause they wanna sleep where you do. They finally getting to you, huh?

NATHAN: A little, I guess.

CYNTHIA: Just laugh in their faces and send em home to their three-hundred-pound pork pies.

(NATHAN *laughs, now hugely relieved.*)

NATHAN: O K. So truth now, where'd you get the money?

CYNTHIA: Daddy.

NATHAN: Aw jeez, you hit him up again? I can't look him in the face as it is.

CYNTHIA: He's not doing it for you, he's doing it for me. It's like giving me my inheritance when I need it. This way he gets the satisfaction of seeing how much he's helping out. I mean, what's the point of giving it away when you're dead, you know?

NATHAN: It's my job to take care of you, not his.

CYNTHIA: You do, honey. You take care of me the best way there is.

(*She kisses him passionately. He reciprocates. Lights dim on their embraces till blackout.*)

OTIS AND RUTHIE PUT IT TOGETHER

(OTIS *is in his easy chair, reading the paper.* RUTHIE *is sewing a button on his shirt.*)

OTIS: Did you see this? Somebody knocked off the branch bank up the street.

RUTHIE: There's been a rash of that lately.

OTIS: This ain't your usual Perpetrator. Some girl.

(RUTHIE *perks up.*)

OTIS: "...described her as tall, blonde, very attractive, about twenty years old."

(RUTHIE *puts down her sewing.*)

RUTHIE: When?

OTIS: Little before noon yesterday.

RUTHIE: Did they catch her?

OTIS: Not yet. Shouldn't be long, though. They got her picture off the surveillance camera.

RUTHIE: Lemme see.

(OTIS *shows her.*)

OTIS: Can't make out her face too well.

(RUTHIE *looks ill.*)

OTIS: Ruthie? You O K?

(RUTHIE *exits hurriedly.*)

OTIS: Are you sick, Mother?

(RUTHIE *re-enters. She's holding* CYNTHIA's *blue jeans, long-sleeved shirt, and baseball cap.*)

RUTHIE: Cynthia left these here yesterday.

OTIS: So?

RUTHIE: Otis. Look at the picture. The clothes she's wearing...

OTIS: Yeah? Everybody wears those clothes.

RUTHIE: Does everybody wear those sunglasses?

OTIS: *(Peering closely at photo)* Man, they look just like yours.

(RUTHIE *opens the pocket of the long-sleeved shirt. She pulls out her sunglasses.*)

RUTHIE: Cynthia borrowed 'em yesterday when she ran off to do her errands. *(Points to photo)* You're looking at one of her errands. It's her, Otis.

OTIS: Oh no...

RUTHIE: She came back around noon with a wad of cash. Changed out of these clothes.

OTIS: Oh Lord...

RUTHIE: Otis. I noticed this morning, your thirty-eight. It was in the right drawer, but it wasn't facing the way it always is.

OTIS: Oh God. Oh God. Please tell me she didn't use my gun... *(He holds his head in his hands for a moment. A thought strikes him, and he jumps up, galvanized.)* SHE TOOK YOU SHOPPING! She knocked off the bank and came back here and took you shopping! In her *getaway* car! That *bitch*! That stupid fucking *bitch*!

RUTHIE: Otis...

OTIS: I'm sorry. I'm upset. She coulda got you *killed*! *(He grabs for a phone, starts to dial.)* What's that number? The F B I number the paper's got?

RUTHIE: Otis. Otis, let's talk a minute.

OTIS: Talk? It's *her*.

RUTHIE: Well...can we be sure?

OTIS: What are you *talk*ing about? Of *course* it's her! You said so yourself!

RUTHIE: Maybe that's not for us to say.

OTIS: Are you out of your mind? Think for a second here. She used my thirty-eight to commit a crime prosecutable by the F B I. Do you understand? I'm at risk here. Just like you were yesterday. This woman is nuts. *Nuts*. And she doesn't care who goes down with her.

RUTHIE: That's what I'm saying.

OTIS: *What?*

RUTHIE: Nathan. And Noah.

(OTIS *takes her point.*)

RUTHIE: This is family, Otis. *(Pause)* What'll become of them? Let the police do their job, that's all I'm saying. What will be, will be. But I just can't... I can't have it on my conscience that I....

OTIS: We've got to.

RUTHIE: It's...too sad.

OTIS: She's robbing banks, Ruthie. What the hell else is she capable of doing? She don't like me. Never has. She's used my gun in a felony already. Be easier for her next time to use it again. For what? Huh, Ruthie? To settle a score, maybe?

RUTHIE: I'm in a nightmare. One minute I'm sitting here sewing. The next minute...this can't be happening, Otis.

OTIS: I gotta make this call, Ruthie.

(RUTHIE *starts crying quietly.* OTIS *tries to comfort her.*)

OTIS: Nathan and Noah, she's no good to them anyway. You know that. Maybe this is God's way of freeing them up. Maybe with her out of the picture something good can happen for them. And they still got us. They'll always have us.

(OTIS *hugs her, but she gives no assent to this.* OTIS, *newspaper in hand for reference, makes the call. Fade to blackout*)

OTIS TESTIFIES

(*An excited and angry* OTIS *is seated at a table in his house—when he's not jumping up and pacing about—with* DETECTIVE JOHNS, *giving testimony.* RUTHIE *sits quietly listening. Two* EVIDENCE TECHNICIANS *work the room, dusting the .38 and the sunglasses for fingerprints, then bagging and sealing them. Clothes used in the crime are collected, along with the plastic bag. A camcorder periodically records some of this process.*)

OTIS: She took her shopping! She robs a bank, comes back here, picks up her kid and *my wife*! And drives to K-Mart or WalMart or some god-forsaken place! In the getaway car from a bank robbery! Every trooper in the state looking for it! Do you understand? Can you get your mind around that?

DETECTIVE JOHNS: It's easier to get this down on tape if you try to remain seated, sir.

OTIS: You ever see *Bonnie and Clyde*? You remember how that ends?

DETECTIVE JOHNS: Uh...Warren Beatty gets it?

OTIS: It ends with about thirty-seven thousand bullet holes riddling the getaway car! And my wife's in it!

RUTHIE: I'm O K, Otis.

OTIS: I'm talking! I'm talking here, Ruthie! O K? *(Beat)* When it's your turn to talk, the Detective here will tell you, O K?

(RUTHIE *is used to this, but* DETECTIVE JOHNS *looks away from them till—)*

OTIS: The bitch! The evil bitch! I want you to throw the key away, you hear, Detective Johns? I want her to rot in there! What she's done to my nephew and to that little boy of theirs and to my *wife*!

RUTHIE: I'm just fine, Otis.

OTIS: Didn't I tell you to hold your peace? Didn't I just?

DET JOHNS: Uh, her...your nephew?

OTIS: Nathan. Nate. The poor bastard.

DET JOHNS: I know he's kin, but uh...

OTIS: But what?

DET JOHNS: Well. We have to explore the possibility that, uh....

(Pause. It lengthens. Finally, OTIS *gets it.)*

OTIS: No. No way. Not a chance. You can't be thinking that...

DET JOHNS: Your nephew lives with her. Say they have money problems. Say they talk about how to get out of the hole...

OTIS: No! Nathan is the most honest kid on the face of the planet.

DET JOHNS: So...

OTIS: He knew *nothing*.

DET JOHNS: Not even that she worked for an escort service?

(He notices that RUTHIE *and* OTIS *exchange a glance.)*

DET JOHNS: You knew about this?

OTIS: *(Embarrassed)* We'd heard rumors.

DET JOHNS: She was a Busy Beaver. *(Chuckling to himself as he consults his notes)* Busy Beaver...you gotta like small businesses with a sense of humor about themselves, you know? Ah, here it is. Yeah. Cynthia—or "Cin," as she calls herself, Masters. *(Beat)* She had seventy calls in April.

OTIS & RUTHIE: *(Equally appalled) Seventy?*

DET JOHNS: Dates, yes. *(Pause)* Makes you wonder where your nephew thought she was going all the time. *(Pause)* Makes you wonder if they didn't arrive at some kind of uh...understanding.

OTIS: There's a word for what you're calling my nephew. It's an ugly word, Detective.

DET JOHNS: Look. The point is this. If he knew about the one, we have to wonder if he knew about the other.

OTIS: So if he's a pimp, he could also be a...what?

DET JOHNS: Oh, buncha things...co-conspirator. Accomplice. Accessory before or after the fact. Buncha things dragging big numbers behind them.

OTIS: You're barking up the wrong tree here.

DET JOHNS: M'am? You share that opinion?

(RUTHIE *looks at* OTIS *for permission.*)

OTIS: Tell him.

RUTHIE: Nathan never knew nothing about Cynthia. Not from day one.

DET JOHNS: Not a man to ask many questions?

RUTHIE: A boy. A boy who works a hard job and comes home to a woman who doesn't talk. He ain't stupid, and he ain't in on nothing. *(Pause)* He hurts a lot. Mostly, he keeps it to himself.

DET JOHNS: I see. Well. I hope he's a good father.

RUTHIE: He tries.

DET JOHNS: He's young enough to start over. Maybe he'll catch a break next time around. *(Pause)* Tough dose for that little one, though.

RUTHIE: Noah's got us.

DET JOHNS: Lucky boy. *(Pause)* Got any ideas why she pulled this?

OTIS: Tell him what she's always saying, Ruthie. Go on. Tell him.

RUTHIE: "I'll try anything once." It's like, her motto.

OTIS: She means it.

DET JOHNS: You think she knew what she was doing?

OTIS: Damn straight I do.

DET JOHNS: M'am?

RUTHIE: *(Thinking about it)* She's in the moment.

OTIS: What?

RUTHIE: She's here. She's now. Whatever she thinks she is, that's who she is. Last month she thought she was a brain surgeon.

OTIS: A very superior bitch. Nothing but attitude.

DET JOHNS: And Thursday she was a bank robber?

RUTHIE: She just keeps making herself up. Like she has no yesterday. No past.

DET JOHNS: Yeah. Hmm. Not much of a future, either.

(Blackout)

BUSINESS AS USUAL

(Lights up on the same principals as "Otis Testifies" above. Different room in same house. Time has passed. DETECTIVE JOHNS *is discreetly, almost shyly, talking into his wrist.)*

DET JOHNS: Copy. We're good to go here. Honk me up when they hit the bypass. Over.

*(*DET JOHNS *looks over to* OTIS *and* RUTHIE. *They are sick with apprehension.)*

DET JOHNS: O K. The most important thing is to be very business-as-usual. I know that's going to be tough. You're probably a little tense, a little on edge, hey, who wouldn't be? But if you value the life of that little boy—what's his name?

RUTHIE & OTIS: Noah.

DET JOHNS: Right. You *must* get the child safely from her and out of the way before we move in, do you understand? Act like it's any other morning. Babysitting. Period. Got it?

RUTHIE: Should I take Noah? Or Otis?

OTIS: I'll do it.

DET JOHNS: Is that your routine?

RUTHIE: Normally it's me.

DET JOHNS: Then you greet her.

OTIS: Sir, I...

DET JOHNS: What, Otis?

OTIS: I want my wife as far away from this as she can get.

DET JOHNS: I understand, but—

(Sound: low-level static or something subtle and brief that DET JOHNS *could notice.)*

DET JOHNS: A moment. *(He moves off discreetly to talk into his wrist.)*

*(*OTIS *seizes the moment to confer tensely with* RUTHIE.*)*

OTIS: Stand over there where she can see you. Over by the ironing board. Be ironing so she can see why you're not at the door.

RUTHIE: She'll *never* hand him to you—it'll tip her off.

OTIS: *Listen.* Anything could happen. Physical stuff. Maybe guns.

RUTHIE: Noah won't go to you.

OTIS: Get me that toy he likes, that whachama call it—

RUTHIE: The plush thing...

OTIS: Yeah, yeah, the squishy thing, he'll go for that.

(DET JOHNS *approaches them.*)

DET JOHNS: All right. Little glitch here, folks, nothing major, just a pain, you know...(*To* OTIS) Your nephew isn't driving. Just her and the kid. (*To* RUTHIE) Would have been more...elegant, you know? If we could have intercepted them both in the same Ops? (*Shrugs*) Life lacks structure. That's why we need art. (*Claps his hands: to business*) O K. You folks understand what's gonna happen here?

OTIS: She pulls in the driveway, walks to the door. Hands the baby to me—

DET JOHNS: No. To your wife.

OTIS: Please.

DET JOHNS: Will she buy it, M'am? Your husband taking the child?

RUTHIE: He'll have Noah's favorite toy. That should be enough.

DET JOHNS: Be ready to assist him if there's any hesitation on her part. As soon as they separate, our cars will block your driveway. I'll be positioned on the landing near the door. (*Pause*) Any questions, folks?

RUTHIE: Are you going to hurt her?

DET JOHNS: We don't believe she's armed. Should be perfectly routine.

RUTHIE: And Noah? Does he have to see this?

DET JOHNS: We'll try to avoid that. Just get him into another room as smoothly as you can without alarming him or tipping her. Can you do that?

RUTHIE: I'll do my best.

(*Silence. They look at one another.*)

DET JOHNS: I'm sorry.

RUTHIE: Thank you.

(*Fade to blackout*)

BUST

(It is a few minutes after BUSINESS AS USUAL above. In blackout, sound: car approaching, then engine off. RUTHIE and OTIS's entranceway, at least for this scene, needs to include a rigid wall section, something solid enough to support a body pressed up against it. Can be cleared after this scene if so advised. Lights up on RUTHIE at ironing board in view of entrance to apartment. OTIS is in front of her, looking toward entrance, tenaciously clutching a plush toy, a fixed and forced smile on his face. DETECTIVE JOHNS is concealed from the entrance but visible to us. He is holding handcuffs. He has a small, holstered revolver. RUTHIE makes the sign of the cross and then begins ironing. CYNTHIA approaches, carrying a two year-old NOAH. She stops when she sees OTIS rather than RUTHIE. And OTIS is a bit too friendly.)

OTIS: Morning Cynthia! Hi there, Noah, how you doing you big ole boy? C'mon in, buddy, I got your Squishy-Guy here...

(Displaying the toy for him. Even if he happens to reach for it, CYNTHIA doesn't budge.)

CYNTHIA: Ruthie?

RUTHIE: C'mon in, I'm just finishing up some ironing.

(CYNTHIA doesn't move.)

RUTHIE: Hey there, Noah. Do you want some juice?

(Seen by us but obviously not by CYNTHIA, DETECTIVE JOHNS motions RUTHIE to come get the child. She approaches. Very tentatively, CYNTHIA enters, clearly sensing something is not right. RUTHIE keeps up her patter as she takes toy from OTIS and hands it to NOAH, taking him from CYNTHIA and removing him from immediate vicinity.)

RUTHIE: You got your favorite shirt on today, don't you Noah? You look so handsome in that. You want some Cheerios?

OTIS: Come on in and have some coffee, Cindy.

CYNTHIA: No, I...why are you acting so weird, Otis? *(She starts to spook, backing off.)*

OTIS: Can't I be feeling good?

CYNTHIA: I gotta go.

(DETECTIVE JOHNS moves in quickly from her blind side and efficiently but not brutally clasps her wrists behind her and forces her up against the entranceway wall structure.)

DETECTIVE JOHNS: Don't move, Cynthia. Just be still.

(He claps the cuffs on her. We can see her face in profile, pressed up against the wall. She does not resist, seems almost resigned, murmuring...)

CYNTHIA: Oh God...

(OTIS *is frozen; speechless.*)

DET JOHNS: *(To his wrist-com)* Go. Go. Go.

(Sound: cars, screeching to a stop. No sirens)

CYNTHIA: Noah...

DET JOHNS: You're under arrest, Cynthia. Stay calm. Move with me. Outside. This way, young lady.

CYNTHIA: Noah...

(OTIS *is shaken.* RUTHIE *is now visible on the periphery, now without* NOAH.)

OTIS: He's O K, Cynthia. He's O K.

CYNTHIA: Noah...

(She is quickly led off by DET JOHNS. RUTHIE *covers her face.* OTIS *tries to console her. Blackout)*

KNOCK, KNOCK. WHO'S THERE?

(From the blackout of "Bust" comes a muffled but violent kind of sound: wood pounding on metal, rattling glass. Lights up, dim on a startled NATHAN *in his bed. He's actually laying more or less on top of it, sort of half-in, half-out of his work clothes from the plant. So he's fallen asleep before he could undress, and now he's not sure if he's awake or dreaming.)*

DETECTIVE JOHNS: *(O S)* Take the muthafucker *down*!

(Sounds intensify. NATHAN *is fishing around for some kind of weapon.)*

NATHAN: Who are you? Get the fuck outta here! I gotta gun!

(Three ARMED MEN *leap onto his bed and violently subdue him as he screams and struggles. He's cuffed, and things calm somewhat.* DETECTIVE JOHNS *presents himself to* NATHAN. *He shows* NATHAN *a paper.)*

DETECTIVE JOHNS: Search Warrant, Nathaniel. Read it while you're getting dressed.

*(*NATHAN *actually tries to read the document despite being cuffed and bewildered.* ARMED MAN #1 *calls out:)*

ARMED MAN #1: Hey Detective Johns? You got a keen nose for this here sort of thing. You smell any of that Wacky Weed in here? Cause I think I do.

NATHAN: You're cops?

DET JOHNS: Let's not belabor the obvious, Nathan.

ARMED MAN #2: *(Teasingly)* What's this what's this? Detective Johns, the lady in this magazine, she ain't wearing no undies...Not a stitch. Looks pretty horny-porny to me, sir. Course, you gotta better eye for this sort of thing than I do...

(ARMED MAN #3 *is saying nothing. He is brusquely assisting* NATHAN *in getting dressed.* NATHAN *catches a glimpse of the warrant.*)

NATHAN: What're you looking for? "Adhesive tape"? Did that say "adhesive tape"? You can arrest me for possession of *that*?

(*Suddenly, just because he can no longer help himself,* ARMED MAN #3 *turns* NATHAN *around to face him, and smashes him in the nose.*)

NATHAN: OOOWWWW!!! Mother-*fuck!* Whacha do that for?

ARMED MAN #3: *(To* DET JOHNS*)* Sorry, Boss.

DET JOHNS: That's all right. I love your spontaneity. *(Beat)* Why do you think we're here, Nate?

NATHAN: I'm guessing one of those wall-eyed assholes at my plant set me up for something. I dunno. I got no clue. *(Another glimpse at the warrant)* "Women's underwear"? What the...what the fuck *are* you doing here?

(*The two* ARMED MEN *break into a spontaneous grade schoolish rhythmic rebuke of* NATHAN, *each alternating the phrases:*)

ARMED MEN #1 & #2: Nathan said a Potty-Mouth Word, Nathan said the Naughty-F-Word. We're gonna tell on Nathan, Nathan's gonna get in trouble, trouble trouble trouble...

NATHAN: Is this about Cynthia?

(*Everybody gets very quiet.*)

NATHAN: It is, isn't it. Oh god. I don't wanna know.

(*They let him slump to the edge of his bed.* ARMED MEN #1 & #2, *with mock delicacy and over-discretion, go back to work, picking through Nate's stuff. After a while* ARMED MAN #1 *softly takes up another grade school chant.* ARMED MAN #2 *quickly joins in.*)

ARMED MAN #1: I see London...

ARMED MAN #2: I see France...

(*The* TWO ARMED MEN *whip around on* NATHAN, *each holding a pair of* CYNTHIA's *more provocative panties.*)

ARMED MEN #1 & #2: I see Cindy's underpants!

(ARMED MAN #3 *laughingly holds the angry* NATHAN *under control.* DETECTIVE JOHNS *turns away from this scene and walks decisively towards... Harsh lights up fast on a seated* CYNTHIA *in the interrogation area. Lights out fast on* NATHAN *and the three* ARMED MEN.*)*

"HE'S BADLY BUILT AND HE WALKS ON STILTS"

DETECTIVE JOHNS: *(Looming over her chair)* Why'd you do it?

CYNTHIA: The question doesn't interest me that much.

DET JOHNS: You do know why you did it, though. Don't you Cynthia? That much we can presume to be true? *(Beat)* Or no?

CYNTHIA: You got more experience with this sort of thing than I got. You tell me. Why do people usually rob banks?

DET JOHNS: Lot of different reasons, Cynthia, most of them boring. My most recent client hit the Elletsville Bank because he had to get to Florida in time for the fishing season. *(Beat)* So what hair did you have up *your* ass? *(Beat)* Huh? Cynthia? *(Silence)* You got a habit, Cynthia?

CYNTHIA: Get me a lawyer.

DET JOHNS: Are you a hooker, Cynthia? Excuse me— *(To something O S)* —are we running, Bob? Groovy. *(Back to* CYNTHIA*)* Sorry, where were we? Oh yes: Are you a hooker, Cynthia?

(She is meeting his gaze, but clamming up.)

DET JOHNS: We talked to your boss. What's her name? Tiffany? *(As if remembering)* Yeah, that's it. "Tiffany." *(Beat)* Ontogeny recapitulates phylogeny, huh? *(He chuckles to himself)* Don't know what the fuck it means, Cynthia. Just one of those things I like to say every once in a while. You know, like "viviparous." *(Smiles, genially)* Makes me feel educated. Good feeling. But you know all about that. Don't you? Cynthia? I mean, you being a college girl and all that? Right? I mean, when you wasn't hooking? *(Smacks his head, as if finally putting together the obvious)* Trolling Grounds! I get it! You could kinda advertise your services in person, right there on campus. *(Marveling)* Kids today...they are so into Marketing Skills, you know?

CYNTHIA: I'm not talking if you're taping. Not without a lawyer present.

DET JOHNS: Anyway, Tiffany says you had seventy calls in April alone. *(Grins)* They don't call you Busy Beavers for nothing, huh? *(Shrugs)* Sorry. Just another one of those things I like to say. Difference is, I know what this one means.

CYNTHIA: Is this legal? What you're doing?

DET JOHNS: Moreso than what you've been up to, Boopsie.

CYNTHIA: I think I got some rights being violated here.

DET JOHNS: Seventy times what, a hundred and fifty? Two hundred? Plus tips? Do the math with me. *(A moment)* What you come up with? I get somewhere between ten grand and fifteen grand, yes? For April? *(Pause, chuckling)* Didn't they let you keep none of it? You chump. I mean, I'm sorry, but you live in a fucking trailer, you drive a 1990 piece-of-shit Geo. Come *on*. What the fuck you doing with all that money, Cynthia?

CYNTHIA: I subscribe to a lot of magazines.

DET JOHNS: What a drag. You're gonna be needin lots of Change of Address cards.

CYNTHIA: Why's it so cold in here?

DET JOHNS: You got a lousy four grand out of that teller.

CYNTHIA: It's like a meat locker.

DET JOHNS: We recovered eighteen hundred. You blew twenty-two hundred in five days. On what?

CYNTHIA: I had to pay my phone bill.

DET JOHNS: I think you're using. And I think you're pushing. *(Beat)* I'll tell you something, honey pie, I don't give a shit about this bank. They got insurance. And they don't even offer Free Checking, so screw em sideways. *(Pause)* But if I find out you're helping pump that pig-trough Drano into some kid's veins…if that's what you're into, Cynthia… I'm gonna fuck you over so bad you'll never see the light of day again. Are you hearing me? *(Silence)*

CYNTHIA: You need a hobby. *(Beat)* You oughta take up golf or something.

DET JOHNS: The one thing you got a lot of. Clothes. You're a real fashion plate, sugar. I noticed you don't have a lot of orange, though. No jumpsuits. *(Beat)* We can fill that need for you, Cynthia. We got you covered for about the next twenty years.

CYNTHIA: Are you gonna get me a fucking lawyer or not?

DET JOHNS: *(Backing off with mock reassurance)* Sure, honey. We gotcha Public Defender fresh outta Community College. He would have been here a few minutes ago, but they tell me he's hung up waiting for the ink to dry on his diploma.

CYNTHIA: I'm freezing! Get me a goddamn jacket or something!

DET JOHNS: Give me some names, Cynthia.

CYNTHIA: What the fuck you talking about?

DET JOHNS: Suppliers. Dealers. Help us out here.

CYNTHIA: Now who's trolling?

DET JOHNS: I don't think you realize how much you have going for you right now. You don't have to go to the Barricades just yet. Step back. Take a look. *(Beat)* You're a bright girl. Taking college classes, working your way through school thanks to Walmart, I like it, don't you? Working mother trying to better herself? I think that could play. O K, so you got a few problems. We can work with you, Cynthia. *(Beat)* Just give us some names.

CYNTHIA: *(Showing her arms)* These look like junkie arms to you? Do they?

DET JOHNS: O K, so you shove it up your nose, c'mon, c'mon...

CYNTHIA: You like names? You want names? I got some names for you. How bout John Solomon? You like that name? Lovelock? John Lovelock? You recognize these names? I got the name of every goddamn prosecutor in this town, right in my Big Black Book. You want Judges? Pick one. I know them all. I date them, O K? They're our best customers. They don't tip worth shit, but they're steady business. I know half your fucking police force, Detective. You want their names, too? John. They're all named *John*.

(DET JOHNS *contemplates her anew.*)

CYNTHIA: Now get me a lawyer. And get off my ass.

(Blackout)

NATHAN SPILLS HIS GUTS OVER A BEER: (PART TWO)

NATHAN: I knew this guy, he used to say, "Ignorance is bliss." It didn't much register with me for a while cause I didn't, uh... I wasn't sure about the last word. Finally I says to him, "What the fuck are you talking about?" And he says, "What you don't know can't hurt you." And I said, "Well, why the fuck didn't you just say so?" *(Beat)* So that's what it means. Ignorance doesn't hurt you. Ignorance is bliss. *(Beat)* Finding out you're ignorant is what hurts.

(Blackout)

CYNTHIA IS EVALUATED: (PART THREE)

(CYNTHIA *is seated, awaiting yet another evaluation by yet another evaluator. A casually elegant woman in her forties enters:* DR JOANNA THE EVALUATOR. *We gather this is not the first time the two women have had a session.* CYNTHIA *is far more comfortable and hence more responsive to her than to either* DR JOANNA's *male predecessor or the detective.*)

DR JOANNA: Good morning, Cynthia.

(CYNTHIA *nods.*)

DR JOANNA: I'm hoping this will be our last session. I'm sure you are, too.

(CYNTHIA *is noncommittal.*)

DR JOANNA: The truth is, the Judge is leaning hard on me for my evaluation report. I'll probably have to file one based on whatever I've got so far regardless of the outcome of today's interview. So this may be your last chance to help yourself.

(*Pause.* CYNTHIA *nods again.*)

DR JOANNA: I'd like to re-visit the morning of the robbery. As I understand it, you left Noah off with the sitter and went directly to the bank five blocks away. You sat in the parking lot watching the entrance, waiting for the customers to leave. You sat there for how long?

CYNTHIA: About an hour.

DR JOANNA: Uh-huh. (*Pause*) Were you nervous?

CYNTHIA: No.

DR JOANNA: No anxiety?

CYNTHIA: None.

DR JOANNA: Didn't worry about the guard?

CYNTHIA: I knew there wasn't one. Little nowhere branch bank. Three tellers and a potted plant.

DR JOANNA: No fear of consequences? Arrest, prosecution, jail—all the things you're looking at now?

CYNTHIA: Nothing.

DR JOANNA: You thought you'd get away with it? Clean?

CYNTHIA: I thought about Hawaii.

DR JOANNA: Excuse me?

CYNTHIA: When I wasn't counting customers in and customers out. I thought about beaches. White sand. Hot on my feet. Breakers off-shore, out on a reef. Me in a bikini. A purple one. Laying on a yellow and black beach towel. Alone. No one for miles. Waves whooshing up to my feet, making little sucking noises. Trying to suck me out with them, just not reaching me, giving up, whispering back into the blue, trying again, giving up, wanting to touch me, stretching out for me, giving up. (*Silence*) I wanna be a mermaid.

(*Fade to blackout*)

CYNTHIA'S BOSS GETS ON T V

(Lights up on W J O N-T V reporter JOHN JONS *getting set to interview* CYNTHIA's *boss at Busy Beavers,* TIFFANY JOHNSON.)

TIFFANY: I'm a little nervous.

JOHN JONS: Really? Hm. I haven't felt that way in a long time. O K, counting down. *(He's on, and so is his persona.)* Thanks, Janet. Efforts to interview Cynthia Masters, alleged perpetrator of Thursday's daring daylight bank robbery, have been impeded by her uncooperative court-appointed public defender. But standing here with me now is her employer of the past few months, Tiffany Johnson, owner of Busy Beavers Escort Service. Tiffany, what can you tell us about Cynthia?

TIFFANY: She was a model employee. Never broke no rules of any kind.

JOHN JONS: So this bank robbery comes as a surprise to you?

TIFFANY: It sure does, John. Very un-Cynthia-like.

JOHN JONS: What drove her to this desperate act? Was it her starving born-out-of-wedlock infant son?

TIFFANY: I'm stumped, John. She was our most popular girl. She made a ton of money the last couple months.

JOHN JONS: So you're perplexed and upset?

TIFFANY: Yes, I am, John. I mean, if she needed money that bad for something or something, she should have said. I'd have found a way.

JOHN JONS: This can't be good for the reputation of Busy Beavers.

TIFFANY: No way, John. Lots of people think we're just a bunch of hookers anyway. That's not what we're about at all.

JOHN JONS: So you're more of a...?

TIFFANY: That's right, John. More of a dating service kind of thing. Strictly up and up. We don't hire criminals or the play-for-pay type.

JOHN JONS: I see.

TIFFANY: Think Geisha Girls.

JOHN JONS: So if Cynthia can somehow beat this rap, you'd take her back?

TIFFANY: In a heartbeat, John. She's quality.

JOHN JONS: *(To camera, ending interview)* So Janet, the mystery deepens. Just who is Cynthia Masters? College girl? Cold-blooded Bonnie Bank Robber?

Or just another troubled Party Girl? *(Beat)* John Jons, W J O N-T V. *(Hold a moment, then drop persona)* Thanks, uh—

TIFFANY: Tiffany.

JOHN JONS: Yeah.

TIFFANY: This gonna be on at six?

JOHN JONS: It will if those assholes know what's good for 'em. *(Starts to exit)* Oh, uh...you got a business card?

(Blackout)

JUSTICE REARS ITS WHOREY HEAD, OR, PRUDENCE, DEAR JURIS

(Two impeccably-dressed lawyers are negotiating. They are JOHN PROSECUTOR *and* JOHN Q PUBLIC, DEFENDER.*)*

JOHN PROSECUTOR: Why should I cut you anything? The bitch walks into a bank, sticks a .38 up the nose of a teller—who is *still* to this *day* shitting her pants—says... *(Consults his notes and quotes)* "This is a thirty-eight. It's real and it's loaded, and I'm pointing it at your heart. Fill the bag." *(Looks up)* Cute, huh? A real pixie-doll.

JOHN Q PUBLIC, DEFENDER: We all have our moments.

JOHN PROS: We got a match on clothes. We got a confession. We got a fucking videotape. What the fuck have you got?

*(*JOHN Q *holds up a rather hefty black notebook.)*

JOHN Q PUBLIC, DEFENDER: We got the Busy Beaver client list.

JOHN PROS: *(Unhappy)* Ah, fuck...

(Blackout)

JUSTICE

(Lights up on JUDGE JOHANNES, *a sober and self-possessed magistrate, but not above a little levity now and again. For instance, right now everybody is sharing a good laugh. It is a "Counsels to the Bench" moment and the* JUDGE *is joined by* JOHN PROSECUTOR *and* JOHN Q PUBLIC DEFENDER. *Lights up slightly apart in a dock area of the court on* CYNTHIA, *confused and concerned-looking but absolutely gorgeous. She seems to know this is her last chance to wear nice clothes for awhile. She is trying to be calm around the fact that her* PUBLIC DEFENDER *is so friendly with the* PROSECUTOR. *And is the* JUDGE *laughing a good sign? In other words,*

she's scared to death. Suddenly, they all look over at her at the same time, all smiling, nodding...for all the world as if they were checking her out. Then they all look back at each other and chuckle quietly. Blackout)

VERDICT

(Lights up on the same set-up, essentially, as "Justice," except that JOHN PROSECUTOR *is nowhere to be seen and* JOHN Q PUBLIC DEFENDER, *is now seated alongside the still-exquisitely-dressed* CYNTHIA. JUDGE JOHANNES *looms over them from behind his podium. He seems a kindly enough man who performs his job with no particular animus nor joy.)*

JUDGE JOHANNES: *(Examining papers)* Defense and Prosecution having concurred on the pre-trial disposition of case number 47CO59832RB07129, State v. Cynthia Masters, and there being no further issues before this Court—is that correct, Counselor? *(Beat)* Let the record show so entered without dispute. Will the Defendant please rise and approach the Bench?

(CYNTHIA *does so.)*

JUDGE JOHANNES: Cynthia Masters, having waived a Jury of your Peers, you have received a Bench adjudication in which you now stand convicted of Armed Robbery, a Class A felony. It is my duty now to pass sentence upon you. Do you understand?

CYNTHIA: Yes, your Honor.

JUDGE JOHANNES: I have carefully reviewed the medical and psychological evaluations ordered by this Court, and I regret to say that I am insufficiently guided by the conflicting conclusions arrived at by the good doctors. I seem to be very much left to my own devices in this matter. *(Beat; he smiles.)* But that's why they pay me, isn't it?

(She is uncertain how she is supposed to respond to that.)

JUDGE JOHANNES: Cynthia Masters. You went into a bank and pointed a lethal weapon at the body of a bank teller named Andrea Mayfield, and you took four thousand dollars that belonged to other people. At no point, right up until this present moment, have you given anyone any explanation as to why you did what you did. Nor have you ever expressed the slightest remorse for your actions. Finally, and most disturbingly, I lack any persuasive evidence that you are not capable of some similar breach of the law in the future. *(He takes a long drink of water.)* I have taken into consideration that you have no prior offenses of any kind. And I am personally greatly distressed that you are the mother of a small child who must to some considerable extent bear upon himself the consequences of your rash and precipitous actions. *(Beat)* This will be your last opportunity to plead mercy before the passing of this sentence. If you have anything to say on your own behalf, this would be the time to do it.

(CYNTHIA *seems pretty out of it, almost as if drugged from the exhaustion of the court experience. After a time spent thinking, she looks up at* JUDGE *and speaks to him in a very soft voice.*)

CYNTHIA: I don't know why I do what I do. *(Pause)* I don't know who I am. *(Pause)* I don't know why I'm alive.

(*The* JUDGE *is not unmoved. Neither is he swayed.*)

JUDGE JOHANNES: You will now have time to think about these things. Cynthia Masters, I am compelled by law and by my conscience to remand you to the Women's House of Detention for the next twenty years of your life. *(He bangs the gavel, stands, and exits.)*

(A SHERIFF'S DEPUTY *approaches* CYNTHIA *from behind, carrying handcuffs. She can barely keep on her feet. Her lawyer, the* JOHN Q PUBLIC DEFENDER, *is elated.*)

JOHN Q PUBLIC, DEFENDER: He says twenty. He means ten. With good behavior, you're out in five. *(He holds his hand up as if he is waiting for her to "high five" him. She is completely dazed. The* SHERIFF's DEPUTY *cuffs her. She looks out quickly over the audience as if looking for a face. She doesn't see it. Blackout)*

"WAVE TO MOMMY"

(*Lights up on a site that suggests an urban sidewalk.* RUTHIE *and* NOAH. RUTHIE *is looking up, way up, and pointing at something out of our view.*)

RUTHIE: There's Mommy. See? Way up there? Wave to Mommy.

(NOAH *either does or doesn't.* RUTHIE *looks up and either waves with him, or waves for him. Lights out on them but crossfade to* CYNTHIA *in a different space meant to be her cell.* CYNTHIA *wears a prison orange jumpsuit. She is looking down, far down, at* RUTHIE *and* NOAH. *If possible, lights should suggest that* CYNTHIA *is waving down at them from behind bars or reinforced glass.*)

CYNTHIA: O K. O K. It's O K.

(*She is smiling. She is weeping. Blackout*)

VISITATION

(NATHAN *and* CYNTHIA *in the dayroom of the Women's Detention Facility. It's pretty stark, despite the occasional pitiful decorative effort made as a vague acknowledgment that often children are visitors, too.* NATHAN *and* CYNTHIA *sit in silence. She's in her orange jumpsuit and wears no make-up and her hair is neglected. And still she looks beautiful. Also, abysmally depressed. As for* NATHAN, *his protracted silence is that of a man long since out of conversational gambits. Clearly, this is not his first visitation, perhaps not less than his forty-first. Finally, as a last resource, he offers:)*

NATHAN: You wanna play some cards? *(Silence)*

CYNTHIA: She coulda brought him, you know.

*(*NATHAN *shrugs.)*

CYNTHIA: If he's afraid to come.

*(*NATHAN *looks away.)*

CYNTHIA: The bitch.

NATHAN: C'mon...

CYNTHIA: *(After some thought, flatly)* She's stealing him from me. *(Beat)* Ruthie's Revenge.

(He stares at her, chewing his gum; then looks away again. Can't hold it in any longer:)

NATHAN: Kinda late to be getting all motherly now, ain't it?

(She stares at him: the end is now.)

CYNTHIA: Get the fuck outta here.

*(*NATHAN *instantly gathers up his things.)*

CYNTHIA: And don't come back.

*(*NATHAN *stops; looks at her.)*

NATHAN: You mean that? *(Beat)* You mean that, Cindy? Cause I guarantee you, I can think of things I'd rather be doing than baby-sitting your sorry ass.

(Enter a JAIL MATRON. CYNTHIA *instantly turns to go with her.)*

NATHAN: Cindy. Cynthia. Cin...

(She looks back at him.)

NATHAN: I'm sorry. *(Beat)* I'm so fucking sorry. About the whole fucking mess.

MATRON: Sir, I'm gonna have to ask you to watch your mouth.

NATHAN: I'm sorry.

(CYNTHIA *doesn't acknowledge his emotion in any way—just turns to leave.* NATHAN *calls after her.*)

NATHAN: Are *you* sorry? Cynthia? *(Very, very upset)* Are you sorry about any fucking thing?

(She turns back to look at him. She is interested in this question. She thinks hard about it. Finally she thinks she knows, and she tells him:)

CYNTHIA: I'm sorry I didn't get to testify.

(She turns, and she exits. Blackout)

END OF ACT TWO

ACT THREE

"EVEN IF IT HAPPENED, IT DIDN'T HAPPEN"

(The events of this act occur between the Dalai Lama moment and the bank job. Lights up in the middle of a fight.)

NATHAN: You embarrass me! You embarrass me in public, you embarrass me in private, you embarrass me in front of my friends, and you embarrass me in front of Ruthie and Otis!

(CYNTHIA is working hard, apparently, at unwrapping a piece of gum.)

NATHAN: You will say anything to anyone at any time!

CYNTHIA: *(Pops the gum in)* Yep.

(He glares at her, having run out of indictments. She stares back at him, silently, impassively. Defeated, he makes a dismissive gesture and turns his back on her. She chews her gum. Suddenly, behind his back, she unleashes a mute tirade, mouthing savage, silent words. Meanwhile, NATHAN has thought of more things to say. When he turns back to her, she instantly reverts to her impassive/indifferent mode.)

NATHAN: It's simple, Cynthia: Otis and Ruthie are *Chris*tians. They don't want to hear all this bullshit about the Dalai Lama.

CYNTHIA: It was the Dalai Lama I bumped into on Fountain Square. If I bump into Jesus Christ next week, I'll tell Otis and Ruthie all about *that*.

NATHAN: Here's the thing. Nobody believes you. They think you're a nut job. I ain't saying you're a liar exactly. I'm just saying you suffer from an over-active imagination.

(She throws the newspaper at him.)

CYNTHIA: Here! Try reading the part they wrap the fucking sports section in! In fact, you don't even have to be able to *read*, Einstein. There's a pretty full-color pitch-ur on the front page.

(Reluctantly, petulantly, he looks.)

CYNTHIA: Fountain Square. Buncha little guys wearing red and yellow sarong thingies? Huh? One wearing glasses and smiling?

NATHAN: *(Quietly, conceding)* Dalai Lama.

CYNTHIA: Snapped him coming out of W J O N after taping an interview.

NATHAN: So what?

CYNTHIA: *(Points to something in picture)* Who's this? Background here, who's this? You seen that dress before? You think there's two dresses like that in *this* town?

(He's lost and he knows it.)

NATHAN: Look. I'm telling you. As far as Ruthie and Otis is concerned, even if it happened, *it didn't happen*. You get me?

(CYNTHIA *gets it.*)

CYNTHIA: Oh. Oh yeah. Loud and clear, pardner.

NATHAN: It's not like I don't, you know, not that I'm not interested, in these things that, come out of your mouth...

CYNTHIA: Loud and clear.

NATHAN: But you don't have to go blabbing all that to whoever!

(Silence. A gulf too wide)

NATHAN: Look. Nuff said, O K?

CYNTHIA: More than enough, Nathan.

NATHAN: Move on. Life's Rich Pageant, right?

CYNTHIA: Indeed. *(Beat)* That's fascinating, though. What you said?

NATHAN: Yeah? About...?

CYNTHIA: Even if it happened, it didn't happen. *(Pause)* You see, I often feel that. More often than not, in fact. And increasingly so.

NATHAN: Well...good. Listen, I been meaning to ask you, uh...this poetry thing, is that still, you know, on-going?

CYNTHIA: On-going. Yes.

NATHAN: So uh, you're still having meetings with this uh.

CYNTHIA: Poet. Say it, Nathan. Just spit it out. Yes. Professor St John.

NATHAN: So, I should budget this as...?

CYNTHIA: On-going. I feel we are on-going, Nathan. Can you feel it?

NATHAN: Would you talk straight with me just once! *(Beat)* Quit tormenting me with these faggy little head games. *(Beat)* All I'm asking is, are you taking another semester of this or not? I gotta start laying aside the money for it now if you are.

(She abruptly moves to put a jacket on and heads for an exit.)

NATHAN: What's up with you? Where you off to, so lickety-split?

CYNTHIA: Someplace not so real. *(Beat)* Maybe Tibet.

(He intercepts her before she can exit.)

NATHAN: Where do you go when you leave this house? Huh?

(He has her by the arm.)

CYNTHIA: Oh, why should it matter, Nathan? Even if it happens, it doesn't happen.

NATHAN: Don't start with me on this Buddhist shit.

CYNTHIA: *You're* the one that said it! Asshole!

NATHAN: It's your fucking Flavor of the Month. You got more pretensions than my dog's got fleas, arrogant bitch...acting like you know everything about everything when really you don't know nothing about nothing.

(She stares at him, then quietly:)

CYNTHIA: You're so sad.

(NATHAN absorbs it for a moment. Suddenly he draws back his fist as if to slug her. He holds the pose. She never flinches. Actually, she sneers.)

CYNTHIA: Oh, go ahead. That would make another cute picture for the paper. You wearing an orange jumpsuit, being led away in manacles....

(He lowers his fist, turns his back, tries to walk away from her; can't.)

NATHAN: When did it get like this?

CYNTHIA: What?

NATHAN: Us.

(Silence. Hold. Then a gradual crossfade as she gets into the next moment:)

TUTORIAL: ST JOHN CRITIQUES

(ST JOHN is nearing the end of CYNTHIA's latest batch of poems. He is serious about it. He finishes. He thinks about them. CYNTHIA is dying the anxiety of the condemned.)

ST JOHN: *(Using the French pronunciation)* This has a striking air of *reportage* about it.

(She has no clue.)

ST JOHN: It's almost as if you were there. As if it really happened.

CYNTHIA: Well...yeah.

ST JOHN: And yet strangely surreal, as befitting this dream, this dream of life.

CYNTHIA: *(A bit confused)* It's not a dream.

ST JOHN: You're saying you met the Dalai Lama on the sidewalk downtown?

CYNTHIA: Uh-huh. Right outside the Princess Theater.

ST JOHN: This is not a trope?

(She thinks she knows this one.)

ST JOHN: An image?

CYNTHIA: This is not a metaphor.

ST JOHN: Still. Something you made up. Or wish could happen? Or perhaps something you fear might happen? Something from out of your head instead of from in front of your eyes. Yes?

CYNTHIA: Why does everybody have such a problem with this? *(Beat)* It's a small town, you know? He gets around. *(A thought occurs to her.)* It seems impossible only because it's me. Isn't that right? It's not that the Dalai Lama bumped into someone. It's that he bumped into such an insignificant piece of shit as me. Isn't it?

ST JOHN: If that helps you, sure. *(Beat—renewed interest)* This poem seeks to convey that experience? What it's like to meet—accidentally coincidentally bump into on the street—a world leader?

CYNTHIA: Right.

ST JOHN: Then it fails totally.

CYNTHIA: *Totally?*

ST JOHN: Well, there are no absolutes, but...

CYNTHIA: Do you have to be such a prick about it?

ST JOHN: We've come a long way in achieving frankness, Cynthia, haven't we? *(Beat)* Perhaps too far.

(She stands to go.)

CYNTHIA: This is the third time I've taken off work to learn something from you. You've taught me nothing. All you do is make me feel bad.

ST JOHN: Did you see him before he saw you?

CYNTHIA: *(After a moment)* No.

ST JOHN: He saw you first?

CYNTHIA: Why is this important?

ST JOHN: You see, it's questions like that that make me feel like an idiot for having taken you on.

(CYNTHIA, *with* ST JOHN's *guidance, re-captures her experience, though this is a gradual process that sneaks up on her unawares.*)

CYNTHIA: I was staring at his poster in Howard's Book Store. I turned to walk on, and he was staring back at me.

ST JOHN: How close?

CYNTHIA: From me to you.

ST JOHN: His expression?

CYNTHIA: He was smiling. He had these little gold, round little glasses on. He was looking right through me...at me.

ST JOHN: Did you turn away?

CYNTHIA: I couldn't.

ST JOHN: Why not?

CYNTHIA: I was too happy. I started laughing. And then he laughed. He pointed to his poster in the window of the book store and then he pointed to me and then himself and then he....

ST JOHN: What?

CYNTHIA: Made a circle in the air. He made a circle in the air above his head. And he turned himself completely around under it...

ST JOHN: He...?

CYNTHIA: Like a little dance. He, like, almost like pirouetted. Then he looked at me again. And smiled. And put his hands together. And bowed. He bowed to me. And then he was gone.

(CYNTHIA *falls into a deep silence. Somewhere out of this,* CYNTHIA *must begin to weep. Like grieving. Very deep, very cleansing.* ST JOHN *is not in the least upset about this. In fact, he starts to smile appreciatively, happily. He hands her some tissues when she seems to need them. She composes herself.*)

CYNTHIA: Thank you.

(*He laughs. He gets up and pulls down a book off his shelf.*)

ST JOHN: When's your birthday?

CYNTHIA: November thirteenth. Scorpio.

ST JOHN: (*Scanning pages in the book*) This can be kind of fun sometimes. (*Finds the page*) "November thirteenth: The illusion of the permanent self secretes a danger that lies in wait for all of us: I want this, I want that. You might end up killing someone, as we all know well."

(*He smiles and hands her the book. She studies the title, and then looks at the author photo on the back.*)

CYNTHIA: That's him. That there's just how he looks.

(With some difficulty, she makes herself try to hand it back. He waves it off.)

ST JOHN: From me to you.

(She reacts. He's getting a bit embarrassed.)

ST JOHN: Till next time, then?

(Lights up on NATHAN. *His back is still to* CYNTHIA *as if he hasn't moved since the end of "It Didn't Happen."* ST JOHN *steps discreetly out of the light on his office area. Light* CYNTHIA.*)*

FLOSSING

*(*CYNTHIA *re-assumes her blocking from the beginning of ACT THREE's "Even If It Happened, It Didn't Happen." She is now engaged in some banal, studiously bored business. Like flossing)*

NATHAN: Where do you come by this? This superior attitude? By what right? What have you ever done?

CYNTHIA: Done not fit in. Takes more work than you'd think.

NATHAN: Would it kill you to let people like you?

CYNTHIA: Well now Nathan, oddly enough I've often thought about that. And I keep banging up against this one question: *(Beat)* What for?

NATHAN: Because it's our *home*!

CYNTHIA: Maybe yours, Roscoe. Not mine. I got plans.

NATHAN: Wake up! Wake up, you ditzy bitch!

(She flosses on.)

NATHAN: People like us don't got *plans*. If we're very fucking lucky, people like us got *jobs*!

(Silence. Floss on. After some time, NATHAN *imposes calm upon himself, and asks very quietly:)*

NATHAN: Am I in them?

CYNTHIA: In what?

NATHAN: Your plans.

CYNTHIA: Do you want to be?

NATHAN: Sometimes. *(Beat)* Most of the time. *(Silence)* Because. I love you, Cindy. *(Silence)* You know that, don't you?

(Silence as she continues to floss. Blackout)

THE ASTRONAUT'S NIGHTMARE

(The one moment in the show where fairly sophisticated visuals would be greatly appreciated. In some fashion project: The familiar image of space-walking astronauts, two of them. Serene. Slides or footage focus/isolate on one astronaut who: recedes. Diminishes. Vanishes. From that blackout: a man screams. Lights up dim on CYNTHIA *and* NATHAN *in their bed as* NATHAN *sits up violently from out of a sound sleep. He is panicked.* CYNTHIA, *very sleepy, half-heartedly annoyed, slapping and poking at him.)*

CYNTHIA: Nate. Nathan! Wake up!

NATHAN: Sorry! Uh, sorry...

CYNTHIA: Jeez O'Pete...I want twin beds. *(Fluffs her pillow vigorously but not very angrily)* All right. I'm awake. Tell me. Before you forget it.

NATHAN: *(Beat)* Two astronauts. Floating in the blackness of space. Attached with umbilicals to the Mother Ship.

CYNTHIA: I like that. Twins.

NATHAN: Fixing the gyros. Stabilizers malfunctioning.

CYNTHIA: Whoa. *Popular Mechanics.*

NATHAN: All this was good. This part gave me a hard-on.

(She laughs, waits for more.)

NATHAN: Then came the bad part.

CYNTHIA: Go.

NATHAN: I heard an explosion, no—I *felt* an explosion. I constricted. The tether. The tether. I was whirling. As I spun, I saw my...my...friend. My friend on fire. I thought I saw. It seemed like that. And getting smaller. Blown...farther away. But I was spinning, so I, so it was, confusing. I couldn't tell if I was still attached, and my friend was, or the other way. I couldn't tell who was falling. Who came disconnected. *(Beat)* And then his helmet was right in front of me. I couldn't tell if it was connected to the body. It was too close to my own face. *(Beat)* You. It was you in there. *(Pauses—wants to stop)*

CYNTHIA: Finish.

NATHAN: I could see my face reflected in your visor. Superimposed. Like I was looking through my own face in order to see yours. *(Pauses)* You were screaming in terror. Your face was frozen. And I didn't know if it was my face on yours I was seeing, or just yours or. Ours. Us. And it was. I looked just like you. Screaming. And then it was like I was just looking down on entire galaxies, and they were all just floatin', and floatin', like dandelion puffs like seeds.

(Silence. After a bit, she touches him. They embrace. They begin to make love. Dim to blackout. Sound in blackout: Some Bach would be nice.)

VIVIPAROUS

(Lights up on ST JOHN *at his office desk. He seems to be grading stuff and is consequently in an especially vile mood.* CYNTHIA *is hanging around, rummaging through his books. He wishes she would not. He wishes she would leave. She doesn't care.)*

CYNTHIA: How do you spell "viviparous"?

ST JOHN: Are you asking me, "Where's your dictionary?"

CYNTHIA: Excuse me, but I believe I have already accessed that source. To no damn avail. *(She pouts.)*

ST JOHN: Cynthia, don't you have some other place to be?

CYNTHIA: Nope. Free. Free all day. *(Rummaging, muttering)* Fwee as a widdle ole Tweedy Bird...

ST JOHN: Could you not...*invent* some other place to be?

CYNTHIA: Nope nope nope. Happy right here. Just me and Daisy Mae out here in Hog Waller County Middle America Bird's Nest Egg Wafer Soup—

ST JOHN: Stop that! For the love of god...! *(Beat)* I'm sorry.

(She stares impassively.)

ST JOHN: Do you have no notion whatever? What I'm attempting to do here?

CYNTHIA: Sure. You're grading. It's not like you're thinking deep thoughts.

(He holds up a sheet of paper.)

ST JOHN: Do you know what this is?

CYNTHIA: Uh, duh. A poem?

ST JOHN: It is an elegy, Cynthia. It is a cry from the heart of a lovely young girl, a bit younger than you, I think. Yes, quite a breakthrough. After three mutually agonizing years of very bad poetry, she has now magnificently processed the harrowing death of her beloved father. She has emerged clean and strong.

CYNTHIA: Can we stop talking about her now?

ST JOHN: *(Ignoring her)* And now the unseen minions who sign my checks demand that I choose one of five letters in the English alphabet and brand this poem with it.

CYNTHIA: What am I getting?

ST JOHN: Thus it falls upon me, Cynthia, like some bi-annual black rain, that I must pass judgment on exquisitely private things.

CYNTHIA: *(Growing cautious)* Uh-huh.

ST JOHN: These things have names. This one, the elegist, is called Annie van Patten, and I've grown deeply fond of her over the years. And now I must tell this suicidal twenty-year-old cocoon of quivering sensibilities, I must tell this young lady that her poem is no better than an A *minus*.

CYNTHIA: You're kidding. She doesn't get an A? Why not?

ST JOHN: Because in my class of eight, she was only the fourth best poet.

CYNTHIA: So. What am I getting?

ST JOHN: You're getting my years of accumulated wisdom.

CYNTHIA: I don't think so. I paid for one hour's worth of University credit. I get a grade.

ST JOHN: Splendid. You get a C.

CYNTHIA: A "C". *(Beat)* You're serious.

ST JOHN: Ask and ye shall receive, Miss M. *(Heading off her impending ballistics)* Do not. Anger me. At this moment. Cynthia.

CYNTHIA: You're giving me a fucking "C".

ST JOHN: In that tone, in this context into which we seem suddenly to have plunged, that particular word is now offensive. I ask you not to use it again in that manner.

(She glares at him, but when she can speak, her voice is weak and shaky.)

CYNTHIA: You told me I was getting better.

ST JOHN: And so you did. Much better. You began as an "F".

CYNTHIA: So. I suck but I don't suck as bad but I still suck.

ST JOHN: You improved hugely. It was thrilling to observe. Thank you.

CYNTHIA: That's it, then?

ST JOHN: School's out.

CYNTHIA: So. What was I to you? Sort of a...hobby?

ST JOHN: You were a student. And now you're not.

CYNTHIA: A diversion. A freak-show?

ST JOHN: Good lord, what is happening here?

CYNTHIA: This is what it feels like to be a whore. Right now. You used me. For your own rancid pleasure. You slummed with me, and now you want to go home and take a bath.

ST JOHN: Don't do this to me, Cynthia. *(Beat)* Can't you just, well, it would be lovely if, just for old times' sake, you'd flash your magnificent breasts for me?

(CYNTHIA *doesn't want to, but she smiles slightly.*)

ST JOHN: I'm a fool for symmetry.

(She's too down to play, but much calmer now.)

CYNTHIA: So. If I'm not a writer? What am I?

ST JOHN: I'm sure I don't know. And if I did, and it would be just a guess if I did, I wouldn't tell you.

(She is increasingly spiritless.)

CYNTHIA: I don't know where to go.

ST JOHN: Where do you want to go?

CYNTHIA: *(Thinks a moment)* Maui.

ST JOHN: So go.

CYNTHIA: Maui? Me? *(Shakes her head)* I'd have to rob a bank. *(She rouses herself out of her melancholy, makes her peace with* ST JOHN.*)* Thank you.

(She holds her hand out. He stands and takes it.)

CYNTHIA: You never lied to me. Never ever not even once no matter what I did to try to make you lie to me you never ever did, you bad boy.

(She leans down and kisses his cheek affectionately. He very awkwardly allows himself to hug her.)

ST JOHN: You've done more than you'll ever know to stave off the madness around me. I have great admiration for you, and yet I feel a deep fear in the room whenever you're here. I never figured out whether it's my fear *of* you? Or my fear *for* you?

(She smiles.)

ST JOHN: Will you come by and see me when you're terribly, terribly bored?

CYNTHIA: Don't count on it, Professor. I plan to be long gone real soon. *(Sexy)* I think you missed your best shot.

(ST JOHN *laughs.*)

ST JOHN: If there's ever anything I can do for you—

CYNTHIA: There is. Tell me what "viviparous" means.

ST JOHN: Why on earth, this fixation upon that word...?

CYNTHIA: I had a fight with my boyfriend, and he called me "viviparous." Ended the fight right there. A one-punch knockout.

ST JOHN: Well, I'm no zoologist, but doesn't it mean "giving birth to live young"? Yes?

CYNTHIA: Well that ain't what Nathan says. He told me, he says, it's the one thing he ever learned in school, this word viviparous, and that he knew exactly what it meant, and he said: It's animals that eat their own babies. And he said I was one. *(Beat)* Kinda hurt my feelings.

ST JOHN: Well, he's wrong. He may also be mean and emotionally destructive, your so-called boyfriend, but he is most indubitably, at the very least, *Wwrroong*.

CYNTHIA: *(Laughing)* The one thing he learned in school?

ST JOHN: Your lad is suffering from delusions of grandeur.

(She laughs again and gives him another quick hug.)

CYNTHIA: I'll see you in my dreams.

(Blackout)

TIBETAN MOUNTAIN CLIMBING WOMAN DREAM

(CYNTHIA and ST JOHN remain offstage for the duration of this scene. They are miked, and if possible, their voices are somewhat slowed and slightly lower than is natural for them.)

CYNTHIA: *(O S)* She was climbing.

(Lights hit scrim. The intent is to portray an authentically indigenous TIBETAN WOMAN in the act of scaling a very steep and rocky Tibetan path. She is carrying something heavy on her back, held in place by a connective strap around her forehead. Music on the order of Philip Glass's "Kundun" music, especially tracks 8 and 18. CYNTHIA narrates the action as the TIBETAN WOMAN, in slow motion, arduously and painstakingly climbs.)

CYNTHIA: *(O S)* She'd been climbing a long time. The cloth band on her forehead was drenched with sweat even though the air was thin and cold. The cloth band is tied into a huge, heavy-looking bundle. She's lugging it on her back.

ST JOHN: *(O S)* How old is she?

CYNTHIA: *(O S)* I can't tell. Old, I think. Maybe ancient. She climbs like she's half-dead. One step. Three, four breaths. One more step. Three, four breaths. Wherever she's going, it's a long way off. She doesn't think she's going to make it. The weather is turning ugly. *(Beat)* No. No way can she make it.

ST JOHN: *(O S)* Why doesn't she stop?

CYNTHIA: *(O S)* She's thinking about that. She knows she's probably gonna freeze to death at one point on that road or another, and she's starting to think, "Why am I killing myself? Why should I break my back to die out of breath up there when I can sit down and rest and look at the river crashing on down and just die peacefully and well-rested right here?"

(The TIBETAN WOMAN *has been miming the hesitation and reflection.)*

ST JOHN: *(O S)* A legitimate question, it would seem. Why not?

CYNTHIA: *(O S)* Her feet. Don't want to die. *(Beat)*

ST JOHN: *(O S)* Why doesn't she at least lay down the heavy bundle?

CYNTHIA: *(O S)* She can't. *(Beat)* It's full of souls. *(Beat)* One of them is mine.

(The TIBETAN WOMAN *begins to climb again. Slow fade on scrim. Fade on music until silence and blackout)*

PUKE-EATERS

*(*NATHAN *and* CYNTHIA *at their little kitchen table. It is as if she has just finished telling him the Tibetan Mountain Climbing Woman Dream. He cannot process it. Period)*

CYNTHIA: I want to go to Tibet.

(He contemplates her.)

CYNTHIA: Or Maui. *(Beat)* Or Marin County.

NATHAN: *(Beat)* Can I say something to you? Can you please not get pissed off?

CYNTHIA: Shoot.

NATHAN: You are not a sherpa. *(Beat)* Do we understand this?

(Her turn to contemplate him.)

CYNTHIA: It's very difficult to talk to you, Nathan. It's very difficult to share my dreams with you.

NATHAN: One question? O K with you?

(She nods.)

NATHAN: What good are they? Huh? These dreams of yours? They make you feel better? They improve your lot in life?

CYNTHIA: Yes. Yes they do.

NATHAN: Bullshit. You know what they do? They make you miserable. They torture you. They spoil everything good. They take you out of this life and drop you down someplace impossible. *(Beat)* I want you back.

(CYNTHIA *is listening.*)

NATHAN: I know we ain't got much. You think I'm blind? But we—we got the woods. We got our hikes, don't we? We got our secret pool.

(CYNTHIA *is feeling bad.*)

NATHAN: You see me trying.

CYNTHIA: Yes.

NATHAN: You see me trying to make it better?

CYNTHIA: Yes, Nathan, I do.

NATHAN: Maybe that ain't never gonna happen. Maybe the deck is too fuckin stacked against me, you know? That could be. *(Beat)* But you got yourself a fighter. You got yourself a man who ain't never gonna give up. You know that, don't you?

CYNTHIA: Yes, I do, Nathan.

NATHAN: Ain't that enough?

(Silence. A long one)

NATHAN: I said. "Ain't that enough?"

CYNTHIA: No, Nathan. It isn't.

NATHAN: *(Absorbs it)* What, then? What do you need? Huh?

CYNTHIA: More. Just more.

NATHAN: *(Beat)* There ain't no more, Cynthia. See, that's where you get all messed up. And I'll tell you something else: you don't need no more.

CYNTHIA: I'm messed up?

NATHAN: Let's just say you don't yet understand your place in The Big Picture.

CYNTHIA: Really? Well, help me out here, Nathan.

NATHAN: I'll explain it, but I don't want you interrupting and laughing and making fun of me.

CYNTHIA: Rave on.

NATHAN: What you have to understand is, we're Bottomfeeders. Scavengers. *(Beat)* And we were bred to be just what we are.

CYNTHIA: *(Absorbs it)* This is your Big Picture?

NATHAN: Above us are the Predators. The Sharks, the Poisonous Snakes. The Monsters of the Deep. When a Bottomfeeder gets too far out of his Mud-Hole, they eat us. *(Beat)* Above them. Above the Predators. Up closest to the light of Heaven. Are the Puke-eaters.

CYNTHIA: Oh, that's charming, Nathan.

NATHAN: There's not many of them because they eat too much. Self-controlled population that way, see?

CYNTHIA: That's it? Can I go now?

NATHAN: Wait, I'm not explaining this right, I mean you're not getting it. *(With an increasingly manic intensity)* The Puke-eaters, see, they eat *everything*. They eat all the Good Stuff and shit it out their Fat Asses. They make Bad Stuff out of Good Stuff, and they don't care because then they eat their own Bad Stuff until they puke it out—

CYNTHIA: —Nathan, for god's sake—

NATHAN: You listen to me. This is how it is. Understanding this is the key to happiness. We live off the slop that they puke up. If we're lucky, some of what they puke up filters down to us.

CYNTHIA: Then *we're* the Puke-eaters. Not them. Us.

NATHAN: You said you wouldn't make fun of me.

CYNTHIA: I'm *not*. I'm just helping you out with your metaphor, that's all. *(Beat)* You know, I'm freezing in here.

(Suddenly he grabs her.)

NATHAN: Here's where we are!

CYNTHIA: Don't!

NATHAN: Lower than Whale Shit! We *live* on Whale Shit!

(She slaps him. He makes no gesture of retaliation. He quiets. He backs off, nodding, nodding....)

NATHAN: As well you should.

(They stare at each other. Another kind of stand-off has been reached. Sound: unaccountably—for the moment, at least—a sultry woman's voice begins singing Stormy Monday *in a deep blues.)*

CYNTHIA: *Stormy Monday.*

(NATHAN *seems spent, confused, exhausted. He's not sure what she's said, nor why.*)

NATHAN: What? *(Mumbling, sort of disoriented)* Wednesday. It's Wednesday.

CYNTHIA: Not for you, Nathan. Never. It's always today.

(*She pulls him into her and kisses him. She tries to dance with him to this music. But only she seems to hear it. He stumbles. She moves off him. They stare silently at one another as* Stormy Monday *continues through blackout.*)

ST JOHN'S STORMY MONDAY

(*Lights up dim.* CYNTHIA *stretched out a bit rigidly alongside the sleeping* NATHAN. *She is lit mostly by the spill from.... Lights up on* ST JOHN *seated in his office chair as if he were in conference with her. He's in a relatively non-harassed mode, which, for him, constitutes virtual levity.*)

CYNTHIA: I believe we have had other lives. I believe there are more to come. That's why.

ST JOHN: Uh-huh..

CYNTHIA: Don't you?

ST JOHN: Well...one can dream...

CYNTHIA: What do you dream of? When you dream?

ST JOHN: *(He laughs.)* Money.

CYNTHIA: *(Disappointed)* Really?

ST JOHN: It's a joke. It's the punchline to an old joke. "When artists dream, they dream of money."

CYNTHIA: *(Respectfully)* You *are* an artist, aren't you?

ST JOHN: Oh dear. I probably wouldn't go that far.

CYNTHIA: Go that far.

(*He is embarrassed. She suddenly demands:*)

CYNTHIA: Do you believe in Fate?

ST JOHN: Uh-oh.

CYNTHIA: What?

ST JOHN: You're going to make me start thinking, aren't you? *(He smiles.)* We must be deep into the third act...

(*He picks up on whatever lyric we're up to in the on-going sound, continuing, of* Stormy Monday. *He sings along, quite beautifully, until she comments:*)

CYNTHIA: Your voice is...seductive.

ST JOHN: Of course. It's part of my package. *(He approaches her, dancing.)* My Total Package: Voila!

(She has conducted this scene from flat on her back in bed next to NATHAN, *who sleeps through it all undisturbed. But now, as* ST JOHN *moves gracefully near her bed, she laughs aloud, and* NATHAN *stirs.* ST JOHN *motions her to silence, invites her out of her bed. She consents. They dance to the rest of* Stormy Monday. *At its conclusion, in the most courtly fashion,* ST JOHN *bows to her and kisses her hand. And then he exits. A sound escapes her like a trap has been sprung. It makes* NATHAN *wake right up.)*

NATHAN: Cindy? Baby? *(Fumbling for a bedside light source)* How come you're not in bed?

(Bedside light on)

CYNTHIA: Turn it off! Turn it off!

(He does, hastily. Blackout)

THE GREAT DIVIDE

*(*CYNTHIA *and* NATHAN *in the early predawn hours. Both trying to sleep. Neither can. They lie side-by-side on their backs like children camping out under the stars.)*

CYNTHIA: I'm sorry.

NATHAN: For what?

CYNTHIA: For waking you up.

NATHAN: Forget it.

CYNTHIA: *(After a beat)* Nathan?

NATHAN: Hmm.

CYNTHIA: Do you believe in Fate?

(Silence. Then:)

NATHAN: Yes.

CYNTHIA: *(Beat)* I'm sorry.

NATHAN: Mmm...go back to sleep...

CYNTHIA: Nathan?

NATHAN: What?

CYNTHIA: You have lovely nightmares.

NATHAN: *(After a moment)* Thank you.

CYNTHIA: Nathan?

NATHAN: Jeez-o-Pete...

CYNTHIA: Am I? Uh. Like the astronauts. Am I in your nightmares a lot?

NATHAN: *(Pause)* Yes.

CYNTHIA: I'm sorry.

NATHAN: It's O K. *(Silence)*

CYNTHIA: What if they were true?

NATHAN: What?

CYNTHIA: Your worst nightmares of me. *(Beat)* What then?

NATHAN: I'd still want you.

CYNTHIA: *(Beat)* Is that a good thing? Do you think?

(Light: bedside lamp)

NATHAN: *(Staring at her)* Where is this going? *(Beat)* C'mon. I know you. You're already at the end of it. You're just going to tease me along the path with these friggin questions. I'm too tired to play.

(Silence)

CYNTHIA: I'm leaving you.

NATHAN: Yeah, Cin? Where you going? Tibet?

CYNTHIA: Sounds good to me.

NATHAN: You're fucking nuts. You know that?

CYNTHIA: Yeah. I know that.

(Now he believes it. He's getting scared, and sort of sick to his stomach.)

NATHAN: What about Noah?

CYNTHIA: Don't make me think about that.

NATHAN: Well now, that's you all over, ain't it Cindy? Problem? Complication? A little obstacle looming in the way of your weird little head-pictures? *Fuck it!* Don't exist! Just an illusion! *(Beat)* Noah ain't an illusion!

(He paces. She watches. The fight goes out of him.)

NATHAN: O K. You tell me. I ain't proud. *(Beat)* How can I change for you? What should I be?

(She just shakes her head slowly.)

NATHAN: You know why I get out of bed every morning? You know why I drag my ass into that shit job day after day?

CYNTHIA: Because you're a man. *(Beat)* Because you're *my* man.

NATHAN: I hear that alarm go off. Demons. "Time for Hell Time for Hell Time for Hell!" *(He smiles.)* And then I look over and I see your naked body in the moonlight, and I think to myself, "Not yet. Not yet. As long as I got this, I ain't in Hell yet."

(Silence. Blackout)

BLACK HOLE

(Lights up on NATHAN and CYNTHIA as above except where they had been facing, their backs are now turned. After a considerable silence:)

NATHAN: There's things that eat their young.

CYNTHIA: Would you stop sounding like some Scandinavian ice fisher?

NATHAN: *(Beat)* You're leaving me. You're abandoning your own child.

(She has become involved with packing things for the move-out and is sort of muttering absent-mindedly.)

CYNTHIA: Maybe it's for his own good. You ever think about that?

(Beat—she seems unaware of how NATHAN is staring at her.)

CYNTHIA: Some mornings, when you leave, I look around me. And I feel such rage. If he starts crying then...well, you never know.

(Like he's grabbing a dangerous snake, NATHAN suddenly is gripping her by the back of her neck. She is immobilized.)

NATHAN: No. I never know.

CYNTHIA: This really hurts. What you're doing.

NATHAN: Tell me what you do.

CYNTHIA: Let me go.

NATHAN: Tell!

CYNTHIA: I cut myself!

NATHAN: To Noah! Whadaya do to *Noah*?

CYNTHIA: Nothing!

(He releases her.)

CYNTHIA: Nothing. *(Beat)* But I think about it sometimes. I go outside and sit in my car, at those times. And I scream. And I scream.

(A silence. Things calm. NATHAN wanders the space, preoccupied. He is trying to remember something from his tenth-grade biology class. He does.)

NATHAN: "Viviparous." *(Explaining to her)* Things that eat their young. Are called: "viviparous."

(CYNTHIA *has nothing to say. As she will do at such times, she finds a piece of gum and begins to painstakingly unwrap it.*)

NATHAN: You eat your young.

(CYNTHIA *drops the stick of gum. She gropes for it on the floor. She's weeping. He tires of waiting for her to get up off the floor. He exits. She looks around, makes sure he's gone. A wailing noise comes out of her. This has to go on until* CYNTHIA *can turn it into anger. When that finally happens, she yells after him, toward offstage:*)

CYNTHIA: You wanna know what else I do? Nathan? You know what else I eat? Nathan? *(Beat)* I EAT DICK! Other men's dick! For money! And I like it, Nathan! I'd do it for free!

(*After about a five-count,* NATHAN *comes hurtling into the space. In one swooping motion he knocks her down out of sight of most of the audience. We see enough of him to know that he's on top of her and he's beating her with his fists. In just seconds he catches himself. He is appalled.*)

NATHAN: I'm sorry. I'm sorry.

(*He gently helps her to her feet. Damage has been done. They face each other. They are not touching, but they are not looking away. They seem benumbed.*)

(*Lights up in spot X-stage on the "functional, ordinary-looking dresser" highlighted in "Ruthie Babysits."* NATHAN *exits.*)

(CYNTHIA *stares at the dresser. The* JOHNS *appear, barely visible in the spill. Again, as in "Cynthia Alone," their effect is both funereal and soothing.*)

(*Sound: instrumental music or amplified found sounds reinforcing a distancing of reality.*)

(CYNTHIA *begins putting on the long-sleeved cotton shirt from "Ruthie Babysits" before crossing gracefully towards the bureau. Her elegance in these moments is dreamlike, and she moves like a princess in her palace.*)

(*Add sound:* RUTHIE's *voice, slightly reverbed*)

RUTHIE: *(Voice)* Oo got a sore toothie? Poor baby... Say "bye-bye, Mommy, bye-bye." Oo got a sore toothie? Poor baby...

(CYNTHIA *reprises her movement from "Ruthie Babysits" at this new tranquilized pace. She opens a dresser drawer, locates the shiny pistol. She raises it above her head, almost more to admire it than to make sure it's loaded, which it is.*)

(*Suddenly, spot on* RUTHIE, *who yells—*)

RUTHIE: *Cynthia!*

(CYNTHIA *snaps out of her reveries and whirls toward the sound in her shooter's posture.* RUTHIE *can't see her, so she remains unconcerned.*)

(Kill sound cues. The JOHNS *vanish. "Real" light kicks in.)*

(Note: NOAH *is not present in this moment.* RUTHIE *acts as if he is.)*

RUTHIE: Oh yeah, I can feel it. Right upper gum. Almost breaking through. Poor baby.

(Lights out on RUTHIE.*)*

*(*CYNTHIA *relaxes out of her stance. She jams the pistol into the waist of her jeans. Grabs a baseball cap off the dresser, slaps it on. She makes sure her shirt conceals the gun. She grabs* RUTHIE's *sunglasses off the bureau, puts them on.)*

*(*CYNTHIA *takes a deep breath to compose herself. Hold)*

(Lights dim to blackout.)

END OF PLAY

BROADWAY PLAY PUBLISHING INC

TWO CHARACTER PLAYS

ALFRED & VICTORIA, A LIFE
(IN PLAYS BY DONALD FREED)

BETWEEN EAST AND WEST

IS HE STILL DEAD?
(IN PLAYS BY DONALD FREED)

LET'S PLAY TWO
(IN PLAYS BY ANTHONY CLARVOE)

A SILENT THUNDER

BROADWAY PLAY PUBLISHING INC

THREE CHARACTER PLAYS

BATTERY

BEIRUT
(IN PLAYS BY ALAN BOWNE)

THE BIBLE: THE COMPLETE WORD OF GOD (ABRIDGED)

CLOUD TECTONICS

THE COMPLETE HISTORY OF AMERICA (ABRIDGED)

A DARING BRIDE
(IN PLAYS BY ALLAN HAVIS, VOLUME TWO)

FROM THE JOURNAL OF HAZARD MCCAULEY

HOUSE OF CORRECTION

JUNGLE COUP
(IN PLAYS BY RICHARD NELSON, EARLY PLAYS VOLUME ONE)

LIPS

MINK SONATA
(IN PLAYS BY ALLAN HAVIS)

PICK UP AX

SUDDEN DEVOTION
(IN PLAYS BY STUART SPENCER)

THREE FRONT
(IN PLAYS BY ROCHELLE OWENS)

TRAFFICKING IN BROKEN HEARTS
(IN PLAYS BY EDWIN SÁNCHEZ)

2 1/2 JEWS

BROADWAY PLAY PUBLISHING INC

PLAYWRIGHT'S COLLECTIONS

PLAYS BY NEAL BELL
MCTEAGUE: A TALE OF SAN FRANCISCO
RAGGED DICK
THÉRÈSE RAQUIN

PLAYS BY PHIL BOSAKOWSKI
BIERCE TAKES ON THE RAILROAD!
CHOPIN IN SPACE
NIXON APOLOGIZES TO THE NATION

PLAYS BY ALAN BOWNE
BEIRUT
FORTY-DEUCE
SHARON AND BILLY

PLAYS BY LONNIE CARTER
LEMUEL
GULLIVER
GULLIVER REDUX

PLAYS BY STEVE CARTER
DAME LORRAINE
HOUSE OF SHADOWS
MIRAGE
ONE LAST LOOK
TEA ON INAUGURATION DAY

PLAYS BY ANTHONY CLARVOE
LET'S PLAY TWO
THE LIVING
SHOW AND TELL

PLAYS BY JEREMY DOBRISH
BLINK OF AN EYE
THE HANDLESS MAIDEN
NOTIONS IN MOTION

BROADWAY PLAY PUBLISHING INC

PLAYWRIGHT'S COLLECTIONS (CONT'D)

PLAYS BY DONALD FREED
ALFRED AND VICTORIA: A LIFE
CHILD OF LUCK
IS HE STILL DEAD?

PLAYS BY ALLAN HAVIS
HOSPITALITY
MINK SONATA
MOROCCO

PLAYS BY ALLAN HAVIS VOLUME TWO
A DARING BRIDE
THE LADIES OF FISHER COVE
SAINTE SIMONE

PLAYS BY LEN JENKIN
A COUNTRY DOCTOR
LIKE I SAY
PILGRIMS OF THE NIGHT

PLAYS BY JEFFREY M JONES
CRAZY PLAYS
THE ENDLESS ADVENTURES OF M C KAT
TOMORROWLAND

PLAYS BY SHERRY KRAMER
DAVID'S REDHAIRED DEATH
THINGS THAT BREAK
THE WALL OF WATER

PLAYS BY TONY KUSHNER
A BRIGHT ROOM CALLED DAY
THE ILLUSION
SLAVS!

BROADWAY PLAY PUBLISHING INC

PLAYWRIGHT'S COLLECTIONS (CONT'D)

PLAYS BY MICHAEL MCGUIRE
THESE FLOWERS ARE FOR MY MOTHER
HOLD ME
HELEN'S PLAY

PLAYS BY JANET NEIPRIS
A SMALL DELEGATION
ALMOST IN VEGAS
THE AGREEMENT

PLAYS BY RICHARD NELSON
EARLY PLAYS VOLUME ONE
CONJURING AN EVENT
JUNGLE COUP
THE KILLING OF YABLONSKI
SCOOPING

PLAYS BY RICHARD NELSON
EARLY PLAYS VOLUME TWO
BAL
THE RETURN OF PINOCCHIO
THE VIENNA NOTES

PLAYS BY RICHARD NELSON
EARLY PLAYS VOLUME THREE
AN AMERICAN COMEDY
JITTERBUGGING: SCENES OF SEX IN A NEW SOCIETY
RIP VAN WINKLE, OR "THE WORKS"

PLAYS BY EUGENE O'NEILL
EARLY FULL-LENGTH PLAYS
BEYOND THE HORIZON
THE EMPEROR JONES
ANNA CHRISTIE

PLAYS BY ERIC OVERMYER
DARK RAPTURE
IN PERPETUITY THROUGHOUT THE UNIVERSE
ON THE VERGE

BROADWAY PLAY PUBLISHING INC

PLAYWRIGHT'S COLLECTIONS (CONT'D)

PLAYS BY ROCHELLE OWENS
CHUCKY'S HUNCH
FUTZ
KONTRAPTION
THREE FRONT

PLAYS BY LOUIS PHILLIPS
BONE THE SPEED
CARWASH
CONRAD ON THE VINE
ETHIOPIA
THE MAN WHO ATE EINSTEIN'S BRAIN
PRECISION MACHINES

PLAYS BY AISHAH RAHMAN
THE MOJO AND THE SAYSO
ONLY IN AMERICA
UNFINISHED WOMEN CRY IN NO MAN'S LAND WHILE A BIRD DIES IN A GILDED CAGE

PLAYS BY EDWIN SÁNCHEZ
CLEAN
FLOOR SHOW: DOÑA SOL AND HER TRAINED DOG
TRAFFICKING IN BROKEN HEARTS

PLAYS BY STUART SPENCER
SUDDEN DEVOTION
RESIDENT ALIEN
IN THE WESTERN GARDEN

PLAYS BY MEGAN TERRY
APPROACHING SIMONE
BABES IN THE BIG HOUSE
VIET ROCK

PLAYS BY Y YORK
GERALD'S GOOD IDEA
THE SECRET WIFE
THE SNOWFLAKE AVALANCHE

BROADWAY PLAY PUBLISHING INC

TOP TEN BEST SELLING
FULL-LENGTH PLAYS AND
FULL-LENGTH PLAY COLLECTIONS

THE COMPLETE HISTORY OF AMERICA
(ABRIDGED)

ON THE VERGE

PRELUDE TO A KISS

TO GILLIAN ON HER 37TH BIRTHDAY

TALES OF THE LOST FORMICANS

PLAYS BY TONY KUSHNER
(CONTAINING A BRIGHT ROOM CALLED DAY,
THE ILLUSION, & SLAVS!)

THE IMMIGRANT

NATIVE SPEECH

BATTERY

ONE FLEA SPARE